Cover photo taken by Lorraine, somewhere on the north coast of Scotland, Day 1, John O'Groats to Land's End cycle ride.

'End to End'

...with love. x

by Lorraine George

Published in the United Kingdom by:
Lorraine George
Createspace
Amazon.co.uk

enquiries@therobgeorgefoundation.co.uk

A CIP record of this book is available from the British Library.

First printed December 2015

Layout and design by Lorraine George

ISBN 978 - 1519712325

This book is dedicated to:

Pip, for not telling me what I should write and his painstaking correction of my grammar,

Sam, for giving me lots of ideas of how to piece my book together,

& Tom, for promising to read this book, when it's finished.

But, most especially, this book is dedicated to the loving memory of

Robert Joseph Philip George
9.5.92 - 9.12.13
"Forever Together"

Timeline October 2010 - May 2015

2010 October 2010 - Rob starts at Loughborough University

2011 June 2011- Rob diagnosed with Acute Myeloid Leukaemia

November 2011 - Fourth cycle of chemotherapy finished - remission achieved

2012

6th April 2012 - Elle's 50th Birthday

October 2012 - Rob returns to Loughborough University

2013 9th May 2013 - Rob's 21st Birthday

June 2013 - Rob's AML relapses

October 2013 - Elle's Cuba trip scheduled but subsequently postponed

End of October 2013 - Stem Cell Transplant scheduled but subsequently cancelled

November 2013 - Rob moves to St. Helena Hospice

9th December 2013 - Rob died

2014 4th January 2014 - The Rob George Foundation launch

August 2014 - Paris to Colchester Cycle Ride

October 2014 - Elle cycles Cuba

2nd - 17th May 2015 - John O'Groats to Land's End Cycle Ride

2015

Introduction...

It doesn't really matter who is writing this book, or what my name is; it could have been written by any number of grieving mothers – but, for the record, it's Lorraine (Elle). I'm married to Pip (actually we've been married for some 33 years now), and together we have created three beautiful sons, Tom, Sam and Rob. So why do I find myself gazing out to sea attempting to write a book? Well this exercise is unashamedly about me! It is an attempt to clear my head. Clear it from the memories, the gut wrenching knot that won't go away, and the fear of forgetting any of the tiny details of what happened. This book contains two stories – "How a 53 year old woman ended up cycling from John O'Groats to Land's End" and "Rob's Story".

From the outset I want it to be clear that Pip was right beside me the whole way through this... ahh, first problem, is it a "journey", a "life experience", a "crisis"? I think I'll settle for "life changing event" or possibly "tragedy". (You might think that's a little over-dramatic?). Well, it was certainly all of those things, but I won't be putting words into Pip's mouth – he can write his own book!

I've never been a particularly patient person, so I'll cut straight to the point – Rob, aged 21, our youngest son, died. He completely unfairly and, it would seem, inexplicably developed acute myeloid leukaemia when he was 19 years old, and that is the only reason why this particular 53 year old women found herself trying to cycle from John O'Groats to Land's End. So I suppose that saves you reading the rest of this book; I've got the punch line over with early. I don't think I'm a cruel person, and I wanted to save you from the shock that I experienced, when it became clear that somehow I was going to have to face the rest of my life without my youngest son. What answer am I going to give, how am I to cope with just about everyone I seem to cross paths with, who politely enquires "and how's the family?" or "do you have a family, any children?" and my throat chokes with tears and I try to work out how to phrase my response to save everyone's feelings.

Of course I want to answer, "I have three smashing boys," but I suppose that that is no longer true. So I try "Well, I had three boys, but sadly we've lost one." Well that's daft, as I know exactly where he is! So I continue in as breezy a fashion as I can muster "unfortunately our youngest son lost his battle with leukaemia just before Christmas 2013." That is unsatisfactory too, as using the word battle suggests there was a fair chance of him and us winning, but of course cancer doesn't play by any rules. Anyway, there is one of my lingering dilemmas; answers on a postcard please!!

I don't suppose this is an original question, but another thing that troubles me is "What am I now?" We have widows and widowers, and then we have the "bereaved" or even the "bereft". I want to be called something special – perhaps by the end of this writing process I'll have thought of an appropriate title.

But of course this is supposed to be an introduction. Pip and I have a dear friend, also called Rob. He is, I am delighted to report, just about the most un-vicar like vicar I can imagine. He is challenging but fabulous company, and we both love him and his beautiful family dearly. This Rob and our Rob became good friends. Our Rob's journey to death was one that the Rev. Rob chose to try to share with him and us. For me, whatever my current position might be on the existence or not of a God, that decision demonstrated the real essence, of being a Christian. Watching a handsome, virile young man die is not to be taken on by the faint hearted. Rev. Rob has continued to share our journey through grief and his wordless hugs are very special.

On a memorably muddy Sunday afternoon Pip and I walked with Rev. Rob. I tried out on him the idea of embarking upon this self-help route of writing my story down. Rob said that if I did, he would read it. So if you are bored beyond belief, – blame the vicar! Whilst we were walking, Rob got very into the idea and I began to wonder if people out there might actually be interested to read what happened. Rob actually thought there was a possibility that it might even help others. Well I sincerely doubt that, but you never know? Then he announced his idea - that the current Archbishop of Canterbury, Justin Welby, (by the way did you know he has a Facebook page? – very trendy), should be asked to write the Forward. Tragically, he too suffered the loss of a child, in terrible circumstances, and in an attempt to try to articulate the grief of a parent, he believes that you can either allow the grief to consume you, or you can attack it. Rob reckons that's what I'm doing – attacking it! If you decide to read the rest of this book you can decide if he is right or not. In any case there is no point in troubling the Archbishop as I've probably pinched his punch line now!

How the "exciting" idea of "Rob's Ride" came about I'll tell you about soon, but by way of an introduction it is safe for me to say that, of course, the very idea of *me* cycling the length of the UK is ridiculous, so please do feel free to chortle to your heart's content. The one thing to make clear is that I am no athlete. A dancing teacher yes, but a cyclist, "no!" The very idea of my slightly squidgy middle-aged body oozing out of the elastic constraints of some unsexy lycra get-up makes me squirm just thinking about it – but there is now photographic evidence – and a drawer full of kit to prove that I did it!

There is also nothing like undertaking a cycle challenge such as John O'Groats to Land's End (JOGLE) to fill your bookshelves with an assortment of dodgy books. Accounts from those folks who want to get from end to end as fast as possible, roaring their way down the high roads and A roads, dodging the lorries. Other accounts from those who do it with their worldly possessions upon their back, or possibly those who do it on a minuscule budget and only eat pot noodles. Anyway, I'm going to have a go at contributing to that pile of dodgy books. You never know, if you decide to tackle such a challenge you might be presented with this book to read as an inspiration. I suppose you might also read it if you are unlucky enough to find yourself grieving for a child – in any case, here goes!!

Chapter 1

My next challenge…
…To write a book! Well how difficult can that be?

April 2012

I have learnt that life is fragile. I've learnt that the hard way; I really didn't need to be reminded! When my eldest son Tom was only weeks old; my wonderful dad died. He was only in his early 50's and although he had been very ill for many months, the idea of him dying had never entered my head. I mean, he and Mum had just moved to be nearer to Pip and me, we had just become parents and they had just become grandparents for the first time. Everything was going to be great.

Life is precious, but however long you live, I suppose it is rarely long enough. Does a good life necessarily need to be a long life? I think I need to believe that that is not necessarily so. I have always tried to live life to the full, grab every moment I've been lucky enough to draw breath and make the most of every opportunity. Pip might even say that I can be fairly exhausting to live with. If possible, I try to take care of others, as I hope they'll take care of me if I need it. I have contributed with love and energy to the family we've raised and the family that surrounds us in the form of our friends and community. After all, when life kicks you in the teeth, it is your family and your friends who will do their best to support you. Some will do better than others, but those that try will always be treasured, and the words "thank you" will never seem enough again.

The following picture will not be an unfamiliar scenario – a fast approaching "*Big Birthday*" resulting in the inspiration to take on a challenge. 5–0 was upon the horizon and I'm no different to most; I needed to prove that there was still some life left in this "ol'bird". I felt fortified by the belief that old age seemed increasingly to be a matter of good luck rather than something to be relied upon, so I'd better get on with living. The previous couple of years had been tough, watching and supporting Rob through his initial diagnosis of acute myeloid leukaemia (AML), but the recent months of remission were beginning to help us grow in confidence. Maybe everything was going to be fine? Maybe Rob was going to make it? Everyone else seemed to think so.

Rob looked so well, he appeared to be back to full strength. He was even sporting a bit of a tan, a bristly chin, hairy armpits and a full head of hair complete with his newly much loved "high lights!" Rob, Pip and I understood too clearly the knife-edge we existed upon. But even we were getting better at burying those doubts and fears deeper and deeper inside us. The months were ticking away and still Rob's monthly blood tests were coming back clear.

A birthday party was definitely on the cards. It was all arranged a bit last minute - little confidence in the future you see - but our close friends and family gathered. A suitably "pink" cake was organised in my honour and a few teary speeches shared, but that still left the decision about a challenge – Pip groaned – what was I going to subject him to now? How relieved was he when the plan began to emerge…

A very close friend, Elizabeth, had previously cycled on a charity ride across China - Women V Cancer - raising funds for Breast Cancer Care, Jo's Cervical Cancer Trust and Ovarian Cancer Action, all charities close to most women's hearts. You may think it odd that I didn't what to immerse myself in raising money for Leukaemia Research. Well we had done a bit of that too, but at the end of the day, I really feel Cancer is Cancer – file it under whatever label you like – it's hateful and carefree. Then there are so many other awful diseases too – it's a wonder any of us are alive really! So who cares what we were going to be raising money for? I felt, they were all, equally deserving causes. Elizabeth floated the idea of doing another ride and wondered if I might be interested. "Where?" Well it's not an unreasonable question. "Cuba" came the reply, "October 2013". Oh yeeeessss! Sign me up. 400 kms on a bike on a Caribbean island – how much fun does that sound? An excuse to buy a new bike, new kit, get fit, maybe even lose some weight, raise some money for charity, what's not to like about that idea?

And so Elizabeth and I embarked upon a program of training and preparation, dieting (that's me not her) and shopping. I acquired a smashing white and pink bike – don't ask me what make it is, but it is white and pink! – that's the most important thing after all – and of course it matched my very snazzy helmet. In fact, clad in my lycra, with my middle aged protrusions squeezed into my gel-filled shorts, I probably did turn a few heads! Well I like to make people smile, and they are generally extremely polite – except, of course, my lovely husband and the two boys still living at home. Sam and Rob were fairly out-spoken on the subject of their 50-year-old mother going out in public dressed "like that!" Well, it'll take more than a few well-chosen words to put me off!!

Life is good. It's not as good as it was before leukaemia joined us - I preferred that carefree existence - but it is good enough, and improving by the day; there is optimism in the air. We are learning to laugh again, Rob is planning his return to Loughborough University to start year 2 of his degree and the diary is acquiring a few more "happy" events.

I was beginning to make some progress on the bike. Elizabeth and I had identified a Sportive Ride, the Suffolk Sunrise in May 2012. 65 miles around the villages of Suffolk on what was sure to be a sunny Sunday. The miles were beginning to accumulate on the spread sheet stuck to the bathroom wall, and rather wonderfully the pounds piled on by a massive overdose of Crunchy Bars consumed during Rob's earlier chemotherapy were also beginning to drop off.

The day of the ride arrived and off I went to cycle with Elizabeth and Nigel – two of the best friends you could ask for. So unsure was I that I would complete the course that Pip came along in the car, with his laptop for amusement, to shadow me – just in case I needed scooping up. It was a glorious day. The various Suffolk villages looked at their best, and the run up the Suffolk coastline from Aldeburgh to Thorpeness was stunning. Like lots of first experiences and first impressions, I believed that obviously every ride would be like this one - good weather, good friends, great food and not too sore a bum. I had started as I meant to go on; 65 miles under my belt, a medal around my neck. What next? Bring it on! I had obviously been hiding my light under a bushel – maybe cycling was my sport? Where had it been all my life?

We had 18 months before Cuba. By the time that trip arrived I'd be flying on that bike. I guess what I was trying to do was to begin to fill my life again. Before AML made its unwelcome appearance, I'd been living life pretty full on. My Performing Arts School kept me busy, in a profession I love. Teaching children in an environment where they actively choose you as their teacher, is a huge honour and compliment. Tom, our eldest son was already married to Julie, and had gone to Dubai to work as a lawyer; their life was full, busy and exciting. Sam was beginning to find his feet as a newly qualified music teacher and was off to London ASAP. The process of Sam qualifying had been exhausting and so we looked forward to him discovering how good he could be; we never doubted him. Which left our youngest son Rob, who simply couldn't wait to resume his studies at Loughborough University – where, as he said, he had the "best time ever!"

Pip and I had a lovely plan in our heads of regular trips to holiday in the sun of Dubai. We couldn't wait to explore a new place, and in due course to take up extensive Granny and Grandpa duties, and Pip was excited to further develop his new "portfolio" career, having recently retired from partnership in an

Essex law practice. There was the churchy stuff too, that gave our lives grounding and meaning, cricket (Pip's passion), my performing arts school, that I am so very proud of, and of course, time to enjoy our gradually emptying home, time for us. Space, quiet… So, the moral to this bit of the story is, be careful what you wish for.

The idea of an empty nest seemed appealing in so many ways. I was never sure how I was going to deal with all the boys cutting the apron strings, having loved being a busy mum, but it is after all, the natural way of things. Children grow up, and become independent. They leave home and you visit them, well that's the plan anyway – all being well. I always believed that would be the sign of a job well done; a happy, content, empty nest, with lots of weekends filled with happy family reunions.

Mid-September 2012 came and Rob returned to Loughborough. It was right, it was proper, it was wonderful, but it was also incredibly hard. Sam had already taken up residence in London. Pip and I began to breathe a little more deeply. I made various neurotic visits to see Rob, all of which he greeted with good humour and patience. Of course they all concluded with a visit to Sainsbury's to fill his cupboards, and often with a meal out, obviously all at our expense – but I loved it. Rob got back in to his fitness regime and regained his strength, working towards the forthcoming cricket season and his desire to take his place in the line up as the fast opening bowler he loved to be. Chemo had stripped his body bare; his legs had turned to twigs, and his body resembled a stick insect. His lower legs seemed to be the hardest bits of his anatomy to get to, and so cycling (though static in a gym) for him became a valuable tool. We were so proud of him. When he phoned to say that he was standing as possible Chairman of Cricket at Loughborough University, you can only imagine how we felt. What a long way we had come from those horrible days at the end of his first year, when we had watched his whole life unravel before our eyes. When we had watched the medics drip all manner of poisons under the name of chemotherapy into his precious person in an attempt to kill the blood cancer roaring around his body. Then, when the news arrived that his peers had voted for him to take on that role the next September – well quite right too!! What a fabulous chairman they had selected.

Suddenly, Rob too seemed to exude a newfound confidence in the future. He was fast approaching his 21st birthday - 9th May 2013 - and at the eleventh hour announced that he too would like a party. We explored various venues, but Rob's requirements were quite specific. Very smart, black tie, men only (although thankfully Mum was allowed) and a sit down dinner.

Rob had, whilst in remission and before returning to Loughborough, done some work experience based at The Hurlingham Club, Putney, London, working for IMG at one of the pre-Wimbledon tennis tournaments. Rob had made a good impression. Whilst a cheeky chappy, he was also a hard worker. And so our friend and Hurlingham Club Sports Director Jenny saved the day. Rob's party was welcomed into the Orangery of The Hurlingham, where we feasted upon roast beef with all the trimmings. Rob made a speech to end all speeches, surrounded by his brothers and his gorgeous friends. The banter as always was exceptional, and the champagne flowed. Pip responded to Rob's speech so eloquently, saying amongst other things how as a parent "we never knew where our children were going to take us next". How "we had been led into waters we didn't know existed and indeed to places we wished we had never seen". We can only hope that we weren't found lacking when the challenges presented themselves. On this occasion I simply couldn't speak – and that doesn't happen very often. Actually there was nothing else to be said. We were proud and happy. We were full of life, and Rob was on the cusp of his – what more could we have wanted? I felt like we'd been let off a life sentence. The door to our prison cell had been thrown wide open and life seemed possible again.

Towards the middle of May 2013 Pip's brother and sister-in-law celebrated their Ruby wedding anniversary. A great party was held in Newbury, Berkshire, and the family gathered.

Little did we know that cancer was about to play its devilish hand once more. This time our beautiful Vanessa, our eldest niece, was forced into the world of breast cancer. I don't want to even begin to try and tell her story here, and anyway it's not my story to tell. However, somehow Vanessa and Rob took some comfort in each other. The Sunday morning after our celebrations began with a voicemail from Rob. He was in Loughborough and it was clear from his message, in a total panic. He was suffering palpitations, sore throat, headaches and chronic pain in his back. This felt different from other conversations. Needless to say I jumped in the car and drove too quickly to the Midlands. Pip continued to our planned meeting with Sam, who was trying to buy his first home in London and also needed our guidance and support.

Buoyed up by the medics' words ringing in my ears, I approached Rob carefully. We had been told not to always assume the leukaemia was back. Rob's immune system had been wiped out by the previous chemo, so he was going to catch everything going. University is full of germ-filled young people, keen to share them with each other. Yes, he did feel a bit hot, but then the weather was gorgeous, and he was in a state. We had a pre-signed note informing "whomever it may concern" that Rob had a low threshold for a blood test so the challenge was on to find the nearest out of hours doctor, on a Sunday, and achieve the reassurance Rob needed. Off to deepest darkest Leicester we went, me trying my level best to remain calm and positive. The walk-in centre doctor did OK. He gave Rob a full examination but decreed the blood test unnecessary. Rob had "end-of-term-itis" and probably hoped the GP would write him a certificate to help get him out of his impending examinations. He told us how his siblings, who were all studying medicine, always felt ill when exams came around and the backache was probably as a result of poor posture whilst studying.

Well what are you supposed to do? I took Rob to the nearest park, brought us both a hot-dog, followed by an ice cream and we talked about stress management and the breathing techniques we had used when Rob had been going through his previous treatment. Rob looked better. He felt better; maybe all he had needed was some reassurance? It was only natural that his confidence in the future would be weak. I left him after our usual trip to Sainsbury's and the purchase of even more supplies of Paracetamol and Ibuprofen.

Rob had completed his second year of studies. He then completed another week's work experience with IMG at the Hurlingham Club, but was struggling. He had obviously worked hard all week, humping crates of champagne about the place and trying to fulfil the tiniest whims of tennis players such as Andy Murray, who somewhat ironically went on the following week to win Wimbledon; oh that Rob had had so much fun ahead of him! He arrived home on Sunday 23rd June 2013 in a terrible state.

The pain in Rob's back was excruciating. I will never forget the sight of him slithering down the doorframe of our spare room, the little room I use as an office. As I helped him up off the floor, the breath left me. Surely the bad back was down to all his studying, and was now made worse by having been carrying heavy boxes all week, and bunking down in Sam's London digs? Surely the Leicester doctor was right; we couldn't simply jump to the conclusion that the AML was back? If wishing or praying were to do any good... oh well let's just say it didn't – again.

The following morning - first thing on Monday 24th June - I slightly irrationally presented Rob and myself at the Haematology Day Unit of Colchester Hospital. Despite the fact that immediately after Rob's initial diagnosis he had been transferred to Addenbrooke's, Cambridge, he had had many appointments in Colchester and was well known to the staff. He was renowned for hiding the remote control for the day unit TV, so that he could choose the programmes he wanted to watch during his hours and hours of blood and platelet transfusions. He hated being surrounded by so many "old" people as he put it. So many of them moaning their heads off, but from Rob's perspective – at least they were old! Anyway, despite the fact that we had effectively wandered in off the streets, they took bloods. The Sister said later that the look on my face said it all.

She took my fears very seriously – she believed that a parent knows his or her own child best of all – well, bless that woman! Her professionalism and experience inspired her to request full blood cultures and so whilst the initial blood counts came back fine, there would be results to be phoned through to us later, once the slides had been examined under a microscope. Still there was nothing to worry about, surely? The counts had been clear; this was just a formality – Rob's blood counts looked OK.

The hours ticked by, Rob rolled around in agony, he finally fell asleep in the lazy boy chair in the lounge – the one I had ordered for him the first time around, but it had taken so long to be delivered that he was in full remission by the time it arrived. The phone rang, and it was the news I dreaded the most. The leukaemia was rife, fully visible by microscope, though not yet evident in Rob's blood counts. Addenbrooke's had been notified, and we were expected there at 8.00am the next morning. And so on 24th June 2013 our worst fears were realized. Two years to the day since his first diagnosis, it was back. Oh my God – here we go again. This time I knew exactly what lay ahead. I knew it would be too horrible for words. I knew exactly how hard a fight we had on our hands. I knew I had no choice but to watch it all again. Unlike the first time around, ignorance was not bliss – this was not going to be pretty.

Pip and I sat and held each other watching Rob sleep. How on earth were we to find the words? Rob seemed to sense the tension, and stirred. One look at our faces said it all. As we gathered him up in our arms again he shook. Maybe with fear, maybe with anger, who can say? The feelings of despair and confusion, terror and fury all needed to be set aside. Again our energies were needed to support Rob. Our promise made two years earlier stood firm.

"We will remain by your side every step of the way – until you tell us otherwise"

Rob never asked us to leave him, and we never did.

Chapter 2

JOGLE minus 2 days

30th April 2015

As I stood and looked into our garage, the reality suddenly dawned. So this was really going to happen; I was really going to attempt to cycle from John O'Groats to Land's End, (JOGLE), and by the looks of our garage I wasn't going alone! Packing for a trip like this takes some planning. I think all 16 of us had been writing copious lists for weeks. It wasn't as if we were going up the Amazon - after all there would be shops en route - but who wants to be shopping when there are miles to be covered on a bike each day? The plan was 16 consecutive days of cycling, mileage varying between 60 and 85 miles per day, making a total route of 1114 miles. Ha! Piece of cake!!

Of course you need all the normal stuff you would take on holiday, but add to that all your favourite snacks and food supplements. It's important to try to look after your energy levels and help your poor aching muscles into speedy recovery, so canisters of protein shakes need to be squeezed in too. Then there is the technology: Garmin for navigation, iPhone for photographs and online tracking, Go Pro for videos (taken from the top of my helmet), back up power packs in case we are cycling so late everything goes flat, adaptors so all these things can be charged up simultaneously at the overnight stops, memory cards so I can take loads of photos, laptop so I can download from memory cards as we go along – goodness, who knew I could work all these things? Clothes for the evening and cycle kit for the days, including our precious especially designed cycle tops. Diary to write into each night so I didn't forget a moment and a book to read before I went to sleep, just in case I was too excited or hyper active to nod off. Wet weather gear, though obviously it wasn't going to rain on our ride! Copious quantities of Sudocrem were required to lather onto our nether regions and that was about it. Shimples!!

Of course the reality was that most of that stuff never even saw the light of day. Clothes for the evening – well they were so short, due to how long it took me to cover the mileage, that I only wore one set of soft trousers and my Rob George Foundation t-shirt, and that lasted me for 17 days. I didn't open the book, as I was so exhausted that I passed out as soon as my head hit the pillow each night. Ditto for the diary, which I am really disappointed about; I'd really wanted to make sure I didn't forget anything. Go Pro – gave up on that early on as others had mastered the art much better than me, and on Day 1 I managed to take 144 photos of the tarmac 2 feet in front of my bike! The wet weather gear was useless – in other words fine until it actually rained, or indeed poured as we experienced on some days, in which case I was wet to my skin very quickly, which I decided was better than an ever increasing dampness. Well, you have to try to put a positive spin on everything – after all, you can only get thoroughly wet once a day; might as well get it over with! Most of the protein shakes returned home unopened as I had been instructed that you have to consume them within a 30 minute window of finishing your ride, and we were so late arriving at most of the hotels that we needed to go straight to dinner, so there was no time. So actually all the list-making and packing could have been happily replaced by a carrier bag with a spare pair of shorts and my toothbrush. As cyclists tend to go commando - it's the chaffing you understand - there wasn't even any real need for clean knickers!!

It felt strange, though, to watch our garage fill up as one by one the JOGLE'ists delivered their bikes and luggage. We'd developed a bond over the preceding months. At Christmas time, we'd shared our first "training session" - champers around our Christmas tree. The group of 16 cyclists was complete and the company fun. Of course, you'll always get some folks that are higher maintenance than others, but hey, we are all grown ups and everyone would fend for themselves.

Pip & Elle

Whilst I had organized this trip to within an inch of its life, whilst I had agonized over every junction, whilst I had designed the top trying to accommodate everyone's likes and dislikes, whilst I had nearly driven Pip mad on the subject, eating, sleeping and dreaming about it, ultimately you'll never please all the people all the time! Once we departed Colchester in the morning I really felt everyone could sort themselves out. Most of us had shared some or all of the training rides organized over the winter months, one of them even taking place in the snow – good training as it turned out. We were in for the trip of a lifetime.

I knew I would have my work cut out with the cycling. My final month of training had been disastrous, which was a shame. With a combination of a bad back, a tooth abscess, a trip to Dubai and then finally a chest infection – who would have thought you could fit all that into just one month? - I wasn't exactly departing the honed athlete my husband was claiming to be. Pip, the reluctant cyclist – I knew he did love it really, but he had never really wanted actually to cycle. He'd promised Rob he'd look after me – but then he is such a gentleman that he felt compelled to join in. So the mileage would need to be tackled one mile at a time for me. This wasn't a school trip after all; I didn't need to fulfill the role of responsible adult. I had confidence in the plan, and we had ample back up with our professional Carl, and our friend Terry. So all I needed to do was concentrate on myself, and all the other better prepared, fitter folks would probably head off and leave me in their wake – which is exactly what just about everyone did. All would be well; after all, there was going to be two of us on my bike, although I have to say Rob could have done a bit more pedalling!

Everything was ready; time to put the kettle on and reflect, look at my finger and toenails that had been especially painted for the trip. Each fingernail was painted blue (Scotland), red (Wales), green (Ireland) or white (England), complete with our little RGF logo on each thumbnail. The effect was mirrored on my toes. It was a ridiculous thing to have had done, but it made me smile – and that was going to be important. How on earth had I got myself into this situation?

Well that was easy – Rob! After his relapse was confirmed, the plan was clear, three further cycles of chemotherapy, the third one leading into a Stem Cell Transplant. It's hard to write down everything what goes through your head, but for Rob it must have been like facing the North Face of the Eiger, in a pair of flip-flops, and that's a massively stupid over-simplification. He had already somehow or another managed to get his body back into shape for his beloved sport after his initial treatment of four cycles of chemotherapy, and now he knew all that training would be lost again. We needed a plan; something to think about, something to talk about, something to look forward to, something to help get him fit after all this was over.

We talked through various hair-brained schemes - many of these conversations taking place in the middle of the night when sleep was impossible - but we quickly realized that we would need to stay in the UK. Rob admitted that it would be a long time before he felt confident enough to leave his trusted doctors too far behind. We both loved our cycling, and we quickly hit upon the classic cycle challenge, John O'Groats to Land's End. Rob immediately started looking the ride up online, and discovered that starting in Scotland was the hard way around. Apparently you didn't get the benefit of the prevailing winds. So that would be the way we would go. No easy options for us. And in any case, I felt that as I had hardly seen any of Scotland, and knew how lovely Devon and Cornwall was, at least in this direction, if I didn't make it, I'd hopefully get to see something of "Up North" first. On the day we were admitted into the Transplant Room, three more cycles of chemo under his belt, (that's 7 in total) we went armed with maps, a laptop, an iPad, and an old fashioned notebook and pencil too – we were ready to spend those six weeks in isolation, planning our trip. I didn't really think too long about how I was going to keep up with him - that was a detail!

Tragically, the transplant never happened. Just hours before it was due to commence, the remission achieved by those last cycles of chemo was confirmed to have relapsed for a second time, the leukaemia had returned even more aggressively than before. The sound that came out of Rob when his consultant broke the news was heart breaking, like a howl. Everyone was in tears, Rob had been so brave and upbeat, everyone had worked so hard, and the cancer had uttered the last word. Soon after that terrible day, Rob made me promise him I'd do our ride, for both of us!

So, back to JOGLE! The kettle had boiled, as I waited for Carl, our trusty support man, to arrive with his van, I placed one hand on my bubbling nervous tummy, and the other on my treasured Pandora bracelet, the two charms Rob gave me before he died, between my fingers. One is a silver heart; the other is inscribed "Forever, Together". Well Rob, I hope you're going to help cycle this bike, even if it's only on the uphill bits!

So, a few hours later I watched as Carl departed with all the bikes and luggage, Scotland bound. I posted on Facebook, "If you want your bikes back, you'd better come to John O'Groats – see you all tomorrow". It was the last night in my own bed for best part of 3 weeks – failure could not be contemplated – if I didn't succeed I would simply have to look at my diary and work out when I was going to try again, after all, I had promised Rob I'd do this – you can't break a promise.

****

25th June 2011

Of course all this planning and organization was nothing compared to the time when Rob was first taken ill. We'd brought Rob home at the end of his first year at Loughborough. He'd been ill for a few weeks, and had been to the University doctor multiple times. The events of that day resulted in us abandoning Colchester in a flurry of panic. No lists, no planning, no packing. That night I sent the following email out to friends and family. Revisiting this time now I can still feel that sense of disbelief as I composed my message. How could life swing on a sixpence in this way? One moment Rob had his summer holidays ahead of him, now...

From: Lorraine George
Sent: 26 June 2011 02:25
To: Special friends
Subject: Rob

Dearest Friends,

Pip had been due to drive to Loughborough today (Sunday) to collect Rob for the summer, but Rob felt so unwell that he asked us late on Friday evening to go and bring him home. We drove through the night, and to be honest I believed that a few early nights and some wholesome home cooking would sort him out.

After a busy day on Saturday I got home about 6.00pm to find Rob burning up, we went to the walk in centre, and by midnight our world had been turned upside down. Rob has

Acute Myeloid Leukaemia - blood cancer. He is having platelets and blood transfusions alongside intravenous antibiotics through the night and today, with the hope that he will be well enough to transfer to Addenbrooke's on Monday to start aggressive Chemo.

I don't know how this could happen to a beautiful handsome 19 year old, but it has, and some how we'll get through it, hopefully with Rob by our sides at the end of it all.

Lorraine. X

Of course telling our friends and family was one thing, telling Rob's two brothers would be completely different. One was upstairs asleep and the other across the globe in Dubai. I sat at home through that night, having left Pip at the hospital with Rob, hoping that we would make it to Addenbrooke's the next day. I reflected on Rob's year away. He had absolutely loved life at university. The first year of his Geography and Management degree had gone well, but if the photos had been anything to go by Rob had had a lot of fun. There seemed to be no photos of him in anything other than sports kit or fancy dress – my favourite being the Noah's Ark night, with everyone going two by two. Rob and his mate had gone dressed as bumblebees, simply hilarious.

Rob, second bumblebee on the right

Over the last few weeks of term Rob began to feel unwell. His girlfriend at the time took great care of him, and insisted upon sending him to the University doctors – twice. On both occasions he was put on antibiotics for tonsillitis, offered a sexual health check and told they wouldn't sign him off his end of year exams, as "that's what everyone wants at this time of year!"

****

I'm going to take a pause here to explain a bit about Rob. You will quickly glean that he was not and had never been a slacker – so the doctor's assumption was especially hurtful. For the record he was always the easiest going of our three lads; I don't think anyone would mind me saying that. He was what I have often described as a round peg in a round hole. He would be the one who came in from school and would shout, "I'm putting the kettle on, anyone else want a tea?" He was always comfortable in his own skin. He rattled through the Boys High School in Colchester, and then Colchester Royal Grammar School, with flying colours. He played the violin reluctantly and the saxophone beautifully.

Rob was a fabulous skier, stylish and fun, and happy to ski with me. Although he obviously did prefer his mates, I came with the added attraction of my plastic flexible friend! On the slopes I am going to miss him so much, his chirpy suggestions on how to improve my technique, with yells of "if you insist on skiing like that, I'll leave you here", meaning I needed to stand up and stop sticking my bum out. Or the occasions when he patiently talked me down a slope, and the wonderful selfies of us he would take on the lifts. I can still hear his voice on those quiet chair lifts.

He played Cricket for Colchester & East Essex 1st XI, was elected a member of the MCC just before he died, played Hockey for Colchester & Loughborough Town, played Golf off a handicap of 4 at his best and had been Junior Captain of Colchester Golf Club, and was about to be Chairman of Loughborough University Cricket Club. He was a 100% merchant. A sick note to get out of exams was simply not his style – ever!

He was the life and soul of any party - and please believe me - he went to many. Every one loved him. He approached everything he did with energy and enthusiasm, kindness and positivity. But one of his all time favourite pastimes was shopping. We often ribbed him that he should have been a girl. The clothes, the deliberations over every purchase, and the hair – the gel, hairspray, blond highlights - shopping trips were never a quick outing, but always fun, not to mention expensive. Anyway, he always had a smile for me, and a hug – and those I will never stop missing, and I'd give the world for one more.

****

And so as we approached the end of Rob's first year at University we had no idea what lay ahead for us all. Rob had been unwell, he had been to the doctors, and he was surviving on a diet of Paracetamol and antibiotics and somehow sitting his end of year exams. Then a rash appeared on his legs, some hefty unexplained bruises and his gums started to bleed. His girlfriend was brilliant, and did the "glass test" – you know the one, if you press a glass against a rash and it disappears then it's not meningitis and everything is OK. But, Rob felt so lousy he rang home. He often rang home to have a chat, which usually ended in asking for some money – and his Dad was excellent at dealing with that - but never to complain or ask to come home.

This time he wanted to talk to me. It was a Friday morning, "Mum I really feel ill! I know Dad is coming to collect me for the summer on Sunday but is there any chance of you coming earlier?"

If there was ever a conversation I'd like to have again it is that one. You see, and I hope you'll understand – I was busy, it was, as usual, the busiest period of my year, the end of the summer term. I run a performing arts school and every summer we put on our big show at the local theatre. That Sunday was the planned big run through, hundreds of children for the whole day at our school, running the show from start to finish. I was rushing around like a blue-arsed fly trying to sort out all the last minute bits and pieces needed to make sure it all worked. Pip was busy as usual working, and weekends in the summer usually feature cricket umpiring, too. "Sorry, Rob, but you'll have to cope, wrap yourself up, take some more pills, drink lots of water, and Dad will see you bright and early Sunday. Please try and pack your stuff up ready, so Dad can get a quick turn about!" Anyone who has ever cleared a University room at the end of a year can imagine the quantity of "stuff" we anticipated.

Anyway that Friday trundled by, Rob never far from our minds. By the evening both Pip and I were uneasy. I decided to phone him again just before we turned in for the night. As I spoke to Rob, Pip listened in and as the conversation progressed Pip just mouthed to me, "Tell him, we are on our way." That sense you have of something being wrong is difficult to explain, but, anyway, let's call it a parent's intuition, or a sixth sense...

We drove through the night, which for added dramatic effect, happened to be a lousy one. Colchester to Loughborough is about 3 hours, and the rain lashed down all the way. We arrived to find Rob looking terrible. He was bravely trying to bundle his possessions into black bin liners, and rather than moan at him that he "really could have tried harder with the packing", we just stuffed all his things, and him into the car as quickly as possible, and got him home.

He slept the whole way, and we whispered about what might be wrong. I absolutely believed what he needed was a bit of TLC. Some early nights wouldn't go amiss and a bit of home cooking. A good dose of my enthusiastic motherly attention and he'd be as right as rain in no time. After all, he had been told twice by his Uni' doctor that he had bad tonsillitis and he had obviously been burning the candle at both ends like all youngsters, and we all know that bad tonsillitis is awful.

The next morning I got up to the hallway stacked with bin liners so high, you couldn't get out of the front door. But Pip went off to cricket umpire, and I went off to finish all the last minute stuff for the next day's rehearsal and do my Samaritan's shift. We decided to leave our lovely lad asleep – confident that it would help. My SAM's shift was a hectic one - they usually were - and I was delayed leaving. I happened to be on duty with one of Rob's old primary school teachers and I told her that I needed to get home; I was really worried about Rob.

I came through the front door and was immediately disappointed by the unchanged sight of the bin liners. My first words were to moan at Rob for making no effort to even start to sort the mess out. He was laid out on the sofa. He stood up; he looked so poorly, and immediately threw himself into my arms in tears. He was so hot – it was like being wrapped in an electric blanket.

Now my style of mothering had always been that if anyone thought they were ill, and possibly fancied a day off school, I'd take their temperature. No faking that. So, "Rob, you're pretty hot chum, let's just find the thermometer and see what's going on."

From that point on things moved pretty swiftly. Rob was so hot that I was actually scared he was in danger of having a fit. His 5'10" vs. my 5' nothing, was not an equal match so he agreed to "pop his flip flops on" and we drove over to the local walk-in centre attached to Colchester General Hospital.

People can be quick to criticise such services, but on this occasion they were spot on. I, for the first time in my life, tried to jump the queue. I was frightened. I told the very young, and, if I'm honest, slightly surly receptionist, that my son was "VERY" hot, and I felt he was in danger of fitting. If he did, she should be aware that he was sporting a very high fever. Anyway the waiting area was heaving and we settled down for a long wait.

We didn't go in next, but nearly next. A foreign doctor, whom I found quite difficult to understand, and wasn't what you might describe as particularly "cuddly," greeted us. His first words to Rob were "Your mother says you have a temperature." With that he stuck a thermometer in Rob's ear and looked him in the eye, "Your mother is right". I hate to say it, but at that point I felt pretty smug – well we all like to be proved right. I then proceeded to tell the doctor that Rob had tonsillitis, "I don't think so," he said.

Now, looking back, I think that doctor quickly had a fair idea what was wrong with Rob. He didn't say much, but did a complete head to toe examination, then looked Rob in the eye again. Well, that was the beginning of it; Rob was 19 years old, legally an adult, and nobody wanted to speak to me again; he was supposed to deal with whatever life threw at him, on his own. At that point, and for what turned out to be the rest of his life, I think he'd rather have still been classed as a minor. Sometimes being an adult is too hard. It's lonely and in any case, who truly ever wanted to be a grown up? I know I, for one, have spent a lifetime fighting it off. Suddenly I felt very old.

We were dispatched to the Emergency Assessment Unit, - a short walk across the car park. It's never a good sign when, by the time you arrive, there is a doctor (very young, from New Zealand and in need of a shave) and a nurse waiting for you. We were shown into a side bay, and the curtains were drawn around us. Anyway, I rabbited on about being in the right place, how they'd soon sort him out, and how we knew it wasn't meningitis because he'd already done the glass test. Even by my own high standards, I spoke a load of rubbish.

He was examined from head to foot, and then a nurse came to take bloods. It was so weird; she struggled to get the sample. Rob's blood was a really silvery colour and thick, we looked on amazed, horrified and fascinated all at the same time. This turned out to be his dangerously high white cell count, actually visible in his blood. I did ask something along the lines "Is that normal?" But she expertly fobbed me off, with the usual "Don't worry – the doctors will come and see you soon" sort of answer. Rob, having found himself in a hospital bed, seemed to deteriorate in front of my eyes. I decided that I needed to make the call no wife ever wants to.

Rob was exhausted and dozing, so I dashed outside to phone Pip. It went something like, "I'm really sorry because I know you'll be near the end of your umpiring and you know I would never phone you unless I thought it was urgent, but Rob's been admitted into hospital, and I think we might be in trouble here. Please come home as soon as you get this message. Oh, and please drive carefully and get here safely. Oh, and please try not to worry, I'm sure by the time you get here everything will be fine!"

Well Rob wasn't getting any better, in fact he started getting short of breath. We were sent for a chest X-ray, during which time I phoned Bonny who I work with, to say I thought I'd be struggling to make the following day's rehearsal, I wasn't sure what was wrong with Rob, but I thought it was shaping up to be serious. She was simply brilliant – "Forget work, do what you need to do, and I'll sort out everything, for as long as I'm needed to." Neither of us knew at that stage, quite what she had said, and just how long that would end up being.

Anyway, back in our little isolation bay, and Pip arrives. The dishy young New Zealander pops in looking knackered. "Have you any idea what might be wrong?" he asks us. I prattled on about how it wasn't meningitis, so that was all right. But with hindsight, I now realise he was desperately trying to encourage us to try and work out the diagnosis – to prepare ourselves. Well bless him for trying, but he failed miserably. Even if I had heard of blood cancers, I probably wouldn't have known leukaemia was one. I was about to enter an extremely steep learning curve - one very reluctant student. Rob had managed just 15 hours at home of his summer holidays. How could this have happened?

Apologies now if this is all too much detail, but I did warn you at the beginning of this book that it was all about making sure I didn't forget anything, it is important to me that every detail gets written down; then I may just sleep again – just skip a few pages if you're bored. I promise not to ask questions at the end.

Chapter 3

Journeys I'll never forget...
...approaching John O'Groats

1st May 2015
JOGLE, minus 1 day

Most of our group of intrepid cyclists departed by coach in the early hours of the 1st May 2015 from Colchester, bound for Stansted Airport and a flight to Inverness. A few made their own way; Terry and Nicola by car, as Terry was going to be on support duty and shadow the ride in his car, and Adi, because he's afraid of flying. Yup, that's right, if you met Adi you would never believe it was true. He is a wonderful example of mankind. Honest, funny, loving and humble, he spent the whole ride like a puppy dog, dashing about from right to left, taking hundreds of photos whilst also trying to run his business from wherever he could find a suitable signal to catch up on his phone calls; he must have paused in nearly every bus stop on the 1114 miles route. He just loved every moment. He is a stage rigger and runner by profession and apparently prefers trains to planes. Nigel C. was also missing; he joined us at the end of Day 3 having attended a family wedding. Poor Nigel C (as distinct from Nigel H) - he took merciless amounts of ribbing on the fact he missed the first three days. Day 2 was an especially good miss in my opinion – I think lots of us thought we'd like to have missed Day 2 – anyway I'll tell you all about that in due course.

Those of us who were flying sat around at Stansted airport waiting for Easyjet to oblige by turning up with our plane. Paul and Hazel were often hopping back and forth from Northern Island and had endured some disappointing trips of late – they had nicknamed the airline "Sleepyjet"! I bet the marketing department hope that doesn't catch on!! Anyway, it gave Fossie an opportunity to start his journal, Elizabeth to read the instruction manual for her Garmin, and the rest of us to drink a few bubbles to toast us on our way. After all, Rob had promised me he'd "be in every bubble" – so cheers Rob!

As we flew into Inverness and looked down at the snow-covered mountains, I remember gulping – blummin' heck this was all getting a bit real now. Almost exactly a year previously I'd watched a Sunday evening episode of Country File on TV with Pip. We'd laughed that in a year's time we'd be flying into Inverness ourselves. "Fancy there being snow on the mountains, how unlucky for early May. Surely it wasn't usually that cold in May?" That very day, as we arrived, the road we were due to cycle on the next morning was closed due to snow, with a severe weather warning; surely we weren't going to be thwarted on Day 1? How would we feel if we didn't even make it to John O'Groats to get started? Fingers crossed that by the next morning Scotland would have cheered up, weather-wise. On the bright side, having now become a devoted follower of the weather forecasts, if you looked at the West Country's weather, you had to feel just a little smug. They were in the grips of a monsoon-like storm. From the weather reports that followed, I think it is likely, that if we had been attempting our route in the other direction, we would never have got out of Land's End! For now, though, we were all checked into our first (of many) Premier Inns and enjoying a gorgeous sunny evening in Inverness. A stroll along the banks of the River Ness, with the beautiful daffodils waving merrily, and we seemed to have got off to a good start.

As I cast my eyes down the long trestle table in the restaurant, the emotion welled up, my eyes filled with tears and my throat tied itself into a knot. All these friends had given up 18 days of their precious holiday to attempt this ride. They were all hoping to spend the next 16 days on their saddles. They had all trained hard, much harder than me. They had all made huge efforts to raise much appreciated and needed funds for The Rob George Foundation. They had all invested so much, not just of their money to pay for their trip, but their time and energy, two incredibly precious commodities. Many of them were sporting their RGF t-shirts, polo shirts, or hoodies. With the exception of the highly focused and disciplined Fossie and Kevin, they were all getting stuck into the wine. This should and would be, a once in a lifetime trip.

As we pretty much had the restaurant to ourselves it seemed the right moment to kick off the speech making – I love a good speech! I got to my feet and looked beyond Pip at the furthest most point of the table, out of the large picture window across the River Ness to the snow capped mountains beyond. It was a poignant moment. I explained all the details for tomorrow's trip and probably said a whole load of other unnecessary stuff too. But most importantly I launched the presentation of the tour "Moustache".

So this was how it was going to work. There were 16 of us cycling, and 16 days of the Ride. Each night the "Moustache" would be presented to someone, who would then be required to fix the 18" beast, using the Velcro straps thoughtfully provided, to the front of his or her bike for the entirety of the next day's ride. It would then be presented to someone else the next night. No one was allowed to receive the "Moustache" more than once. I kicked off the fun by presenting it to Pip. I felt he deserved some kind of recognition for the months and months of pain and suffering he had gone through living with me, and my preparations. His patience had been astounding, although if you know Pip, you probably aren't particularly surprised. He's actually not always perfectly patient, (just to keep things in perspective, not to mention the size of his head!)

Abi and I sat together for our first dinner. Abi had been Rob's special girl. It's difficult for me to talk about their relationship. Apart from anything else it's not up to me to tell. However, I do know without doubt how special Abi was to Rob – he told me so himself.

Abi had remained alongside Rob throughout everything. Despite the fact that Rob had been seeing another young lady at the end of his first year at University, the childhood sweetheart of Abi had never been far away. Their young relationship had developed into a deep friendship, which had latterly returned, I believe, back into something potentially more serious. When Rob had first been diagnosed, Abi had been about to go off on a VSO placement, digging toilets in Fiji or some such exercise. Distraught that she would not be able to visit Rob, she delivered him a plastic box containing letters, each sealed in an individual envelope, one for every day of the five weeks she was going to be away. Rob was to open a letter each day, each one full of Abi's individual sense of fun and flare, often with a wildly useless fact, (for which Abi became infamous on our JOGLE trip) or a terrible joke. For example:-

Q. What did one saggy boob say to the other?
A. If we don't get some support, people will think we're nuts!!

She also sweetly gave him his Pandora bracelet, with its four-leaf clover and lucky dice charms on. Rob put that bracelet next to his hospital band, and it only came off in extreme situations – Rob loved it. (Sam now wears the bracelet, and I have the charms – two treasured possessions).

This was going to be a bit of an ordeal for Abi too. Of all the JOGLE'ists, it was only Abi and I whom Rob had made promise that we'd do the challenge. We felt we were very much in this together. Abi had been a total rock to Rob, Pip and me throughout this whole ordeal. We know that we now have to let her go – it's only natural and the right thing to do; she needs and deserves to find a new happy future, full of fun. We can't tie her to our sadness – that's just not fair. Nevertheless we are still working on how we will achieve this. I think maybe completing this challenge together will help Abi sort of "close the book" on Rob. She, I know, will never forget him, but you can't forge a future with a ghost looking over your shoulder.

Abi's Dad, Nigel C, would be joining us at the end of Day 3. It would be good for Abi to have his support too. I wasn't sure if I could be strong enough for both of us – I was feeling a bit needy myself - so it would be great for her to have her own Dad there too. Nigel C knew that of course; he's a great bloke. It was going to be lovely to watch the pair of them over the coming weeks, their banter and leg pulling was incredibly entertaining.

I have to laugh at young Abi, who had been so loyal to Rob, and so amazingly supportive of The Rob George Foundation, the charity set up in his memory. Abi had been there from the launch. She had supported every event, had set herself amazing fundraising challenges, and raised enormous amounts of money. Her "Four Challenges" (with a twist) created quite a stir.

Challenge 1: Colchester Half Marathon. Abi is a fit, sporty young lady, a bundle of energy. As a youngster she had been a talented tennis player and had trained on the full-time circuit until she was 16 years old, she had then decided it wasn't the life for her. Now aged 21, she dusted off her running shoes and began pounding the streets, all for Rob. Abi is never far from my mind, and as I sit here and try to write, I can feel the energy of her grief as real as I do my own. If I could have run, I might have tried, although maybe in a straight line!

There were times when I wanted to leave. I naively hoped that I could leave the pain I was feeling behind. I am blessed to be surrounded by good friends, and loving family, but when you look into the eyes of the people you love the most and see nothing but a reflection of your own pain, well, let's just say it's not easy. The idea of removing myself to somewhere where this pain didn't exist seemed like an option – I don't mean suicide, I mean to become anonymous. Fortunately sanity or good sense prevailed, and as my Mum pointed out, "Hasn't leukaemia robbed you of enough?" In my heart I knew the grief, the pain, the tears, the memories would just travel with me; they always will.

People, whose experience of grief is more within the boundaries of "normal", sometimes talk about grief as if it is some airy-fairy emotion. It's not - well, it's not in my experience. People die all the time, of course they do – it is, after all one of the remaining certainties of life. But I do not believe that all deaths are sad or indeed tragic. There is a natural cycle to life, and when a life has been well lived, and reaches its natural conclusion, of course friends and family will feel sad, will feel a sense of deep grief and loss. But this is not, I believe, like you might feel when the loss suffered is of a young person. This grief, for me, as a mother, feels like a physical pain, a knife in the side, a shard of ice lodged deep inside, and it is debilitating. I can sit at my desk for hours, and achieve nothing. I can stand at the kettle and become lost in memories, and forget to make the tea. Day after day of my life seem to fritter away, with nothing ticked off my ever expanding "to do" list. Even sitting down now, to try and write, about the things I think of all the time, is a painfully slow exercise. The rhythm of my life is lost. I don't expect to find it again, I do however, hope to find a new one. As Rob the Vicar said, "You can attack grief, or let it consume you." Somewhere, from deep inside me, I can hear Rob shouting at me, "Attack! Attack!"

So, back to Abi and her challenges... She ran the Colchester Half Marathon - I mean really ran it, what a girl!! As I stood at the finishing line, proudly poised with my camera ready to capture her moment of glory, you could hear her before you saw her, "I hate running, I am never running again!" "Ha, Ha, here she comes!"

Challenge 2: Tough Mudder. This is not my idea of how to spend a Sunday morning, but Abi was up for the challenge. Nearly another half marathon, but this time a 12½-mile undulating route with a version of an Army assault course thrown into the mix. Twenty-six huge obstacles, a selection of freezing muddy pools to negotiate, and tunnels of electrically charged wire, all to be scrambled under and over. Have I convinced anyone to sign up for next year? Yet more of Abi's wonderful friends joined her, and challenge 2 was successfully ticked off the bucket list she and Rob had written together.

Challenge 3: The 3 Peaks Challenge. This one is easy to understand; you simply have to climb the highest mountains in Scotland, England and Wales – all in 24 hours. Of course, as soon as you start to think about it thoroughly, you realize that it's not quite as straightforward as it sounds.

Armed and supported by family and friends, a campervan and total determination, Abi set off. The intrepid group began their climb of Ben Nevis (1344m) at around 6.00am, on a chilly, but bright, Saturday morning. All went to plan, although three huge areas covered in snow near the summit did take them by surprise and slowed them down. Six hours later, and they were ready to head off to climb no. 2

Scafell Pike (978m) was of course, their destination, but they got a bit lost, and climbed an adjacent peak by mistake. A group of cyclists, carrying their bikes, directed them to the path they were looking for, and after traversing a section, which included a river that Abi managed to fall in, they accessed the climb to the summit. Then the fog came down, and finding the way down proved a problem, too.

The team had chosen to climb Scafell Pike second, so as not to have to do it in the dark. It was notoriously the trickiest of the three. But by this time it was 10.30pm, and all the head torches were well and truly coming into their own. Finally at the bottom, they discovered that they were not at the agreed meeting spot; the vehicles were 47 miles away - an hour and a half's drive. I can't imàgine how Nicky, Abi's mum, felt, as she sat in a car park, somewhere in the depths of the Peak District, in the dead of night, waiting for her daughter to come off a mountain. Exhausted, Abi wrapped herself in her foil blanket and curled up on the pavement to sleep, whilst Nicky raced to them by road. The gentleman accompanying her had to fight off the police, who stopped, convinced that she was suffering from a surfeit of alcohol at the very least. He was able to convince them that she was simply a participant on a mad challenge and they left her to sleep.

It was gone 2.00am by the time everyone was reunited, and the journey to Wales and Mount Snowdon could begin.

The time lost convinced the team that the challenge was also lost and so they pulled in for a lusty helping of bacon rolls before setting off up Snowdon (1085m). This climb went well, but they didn't push it believing that the 24-hour deadline was well beyond them. They made a few friends along the way, and even helped a dog. They finished the challenge in twenty-six hours, and when they saw the time, they were understandably frustrated that they hadn't pushed themselves on the final ascent. Even with their disastrous routing on the English peak, if they hadn't loitered over the bacon rolls, and with a bit of a push, it all might have been possible.

Abi, despite our reassurances, was devastated. I'm not having a word of it though; she did it, and who cares about a couple of hours? Abi scaled the 3 highest peaks and we all salute her and her intrepid support team! She refuses to say that she completed the challenge; I fear there may be some unfinished business there! Poor Nicky!!

Challenge 4: Cycle from the Eiffel Tower to Colchester & East Essex Cricket Club. Now this deserves a whole chapter to itself, so more about that little bike ride later.

Which just leaves "the Twist". Abi decided to go vegan for a week. This was arguably the most painful week of all, especially for the rest of us! Abi loves her food, but she is also the most honest young lady you will ever meet. She was determined that there would be absolutely no cheating or inadvertent mistakes. Abi would painstakingly examine every food label, most memorably phoning me from the Albert Hall, to tell me that you can't even eat Extra Strong Mints or drink wine – they both contain gelatine!! Poor Abi; she basically existed for a whole week on rice and baked beans!

Abi was named the top fundraiser on the My Donate website for the last week of August 2014. She had amassed a total in excess of £25,000 in aid of the Rob George Foundation.

She had also managed to cross a few things off their joint bucket list, things they had planned to do together – when Rob was better. The support of Abi's family, friends, and any person that happened to cross her path, or the paths of her wonderful family, was simply amazing. We could all see the pain in her love and grief; we wanted the running and the climbing and the cycling to help, we're not sure if being a vegan helped, but fingers crossed for that too!

But to get back to JOGLE, of all of those challenges, the one thing Abi especially hated was cycling! I laughed when I read her www.MyDonate.com fundraising page:

"What do you do when you don't really like cycling? You sign up to another cycling challenge...well I seem to have done anyway! Cycling John O'Groats to Lands End is the one challenge I promised Rob that I would do, so unfortunately, there is no getting out of it for me!! I will be tackling over 1000 miles over the course of 16 days with 15 fellow cyclists...if we can call ourselves that!? The charity means a huge amount to me, so if me cycling will help raise some funds for RGF then cycling I will do! Thank you to everyone for your support and generosity over the last year with my previous challenges and now with this one, it really does mean a great deal to me.

Anyway, on the evening of the 1st May 2015, in a lovely restaurant in Inverness, Abi and I ordered Rob's favourite drink - gin (Bombay Sapphire, of course) and tonic, with lots of ice and a slice of lime (it has to be lime). In the evening sunshine we raised our glasses and shared a nervous smile. We were going to do this – Rob's Ride – we were as ready as we'd ever be!

****

Saturday, 2nd May 2015 – Early on JOGLE day 1

It's actually three hours by mini bus from Inverness to John O'Groats - not actually the best warm-up in the world for a long cycle ride but, not to worry, we were excited. It was a surprisingly long way. In fact, one thing that became clear early on, was that none of us had really appreciated just how big Scotland is. There are a few big cities and towns, and lots of little villages, and then quite a lot of odd houses dotted about the place. But mostly, there is mile after mile of mountains, highlands, sheep and lochs. Oh, they are all, of course, beautiful. In the end though, it did get a little difficult to tell one from the other. That is, of course, assuming that you can see anything at all – the weather was rich and varied, but more of that as we go along.

Early on that Saturday morning the roads were clear, the sun was shining and the sky was blue. The severe weather warnings of the previous day were long forgotten and we were all desperate to get pedalling. I sat up the front of the mini bus with my cycling buddy Elizabeth. I get disgustingly travel sick in the back of anything, but especially a bus, so it's best to put me up the front, as a general rule. The conversations were varied, and often amusing. None more so than one instigated by Kevin.

I'm not sure what sparked it off, but we got onto the subject of otters. I think there may have been a poster or sign warning folks to beware or perhaps "Look out for the Otters!" Kevin waxed lyrical about how otters could be found in Lower Castle Park, the big park in Colchester, where some of us live. It seemed ridiculous; a total wind-up. Kevin took a fair amount of stick on the subject; that continued for days. We found posters about otters, photographs in shop windows of otters… never a real one though.

We nattered away to the mini bus driver as we followed Carl driving our support vehicle, loaded high with our bikes and luggage. Our driver regularly did this run, and had obviously seen a fair few selections of cyclists off to start this classic challenge. I think it is fair to say though, that he had never met a group quite like us.

So here is the unlikely line up:

1. Me – Lorraine (Elle), Rob's mum, Pip's wife, dance teacher, enthusiastic cyclist, though only a recent convert, disappointing fitness level, totally determined, allergic to traffic!

2. Philip – (Pip), Rob's dad, husband of Elle, reluctant cyclist, surprisingly good fitness level, scared stiff, totally committed to looking after his wife – 100% star material!!

3. Abi – Rob's special girl, natural sportswoman, allergic to bikes, terrible grasp of geography, extraordinary ability to stop and then start part way up a hill with little or no notice, fabulous knowledge of useless facts, sings terribly out of tune, eats for England, loves for the world.

4. Elizabeth – one of my best friends, cycle and ski buddy, close family friend and good friend to Rob too. I'm ashamed to say I never really asked Elizabeth if she would like to do JOGLE – I rather assumed that she wouldn't let me go alone. I do feel a tiny bit guilty about that!! Excellent cyclist, one of the most focused and dependable people I have ever met.

5. Nigel H – partner of Elizabeth and "ditto" for above. Total cycle nut already, and up there at the front of the queue to join the JOGLE crew. Nigel was the best-dressed Jogleist, with a different cycle t-shirt for every evening – top effort! Nigel and Elizabeth were there close by us, every step of the way. Before ever leukaemia entered the scene we shared the very best of times, but now we've shared everything, the best and the worst of times. A dear friend who I wouldn't want to face the future without.

6. Nigel C – Abi's dad, a new recruit to the world of cycling - in fact so new he had to buy a bike for this ride. He runs a Firework Display company. Even after 1114 miles he hadn't completely mastered his cleats and held the record for the most falls. Guilty as charged of the taking hostage, maiming and photographic ransom notes of Adi's jelly babies. Nigel C would be a few day's late due to family wedding; we'd see him in Fort Augustus.

7. Adi – Nigel C's best mate. At an age and stage where he was up for a challenge and when he heard about this ride, jumped at the chance. Adi was new to cycling too. He actually cycled twice as far as everyone else as he kept darting off course to "see the sights" and take photos. Adi, along with Emma his wife, and his wonderful young family will retain a special place in our hearts forever. He signed up to do a "Wing Walk" after Jogle! I hope our lives continue to mingle.

8. Liz – my oldest childhood dancing friend. We learned to dance together and grew up together. Liz now lives a long way away but our friendship remains strong. Cycle fitness level akin with mine, so that was lucky as we could chat away together at the rear of the pack. A wonderful excuse to share some quality time and re-kindle a dear friendship.

9. Hazel – newly married to Paul – all the way from Northern Ireland – we made friends via Nigel H and Elizabeth. She started cycling because of JOGLE and also had to buy a new bike for the trip – now officially a convert!

10. Paul – newly married to Hazel – very old friend of Nigel H. Also purchased a new bike for this ride, also now a big convert to cycling. A big heart and big laugh to match – you can hear him before you see him!

11. Max – mad Max she calls herself. The wife of one of Pip's former business partners. Already a cycling enthusiast, used to cycling with a club. Recruited during a very nice party, where I can confidently report that there must have been a few drinks floating around, enough to encourage Max that this ride was a good idea.

12. Claire – married to Antonius. Family friend for many years, their son was at school with our eldest boys Tom and Sam; we had also worked together as volunteers in the charitable sector for a few years. Claire is a tri-athlete and a very strong lady. God, I wish I could cycle like her! Indeed I probably wish I could swim and run like her too. Anyway, although I didn't actually cycle all that many miles alongside Claire, she and Antonius, came out nearly every night, however late we arrived, and helped us with our bikes, and steered us to our room – thank you both. You both appeared to have a complete blast!

13. Antonius – married to Claire. What this man can't do on a bike is not worth trying! He loves his bike, he can take his cycle top off, put it on, re-program his various navigational tools whilst in motion – when asked if he could juggle whilst going along, he proceeded to do that too! Claire and Antonius did cover a few extra miles as they arrived everywhere first and Antonius loved to search out some real ale. They also won the prize for attending (well technically gate crashing) the only funeral of the trip. It was a good job Antonius and Claire came together, so at least they could keep each other company going at hyper speed up the front.

14. Colin – (Fossie), was the first person to whisper in my ear at Rob's funeral that he would cycle this trip with me, and actually the last person to sign up, as a last minute

fill in for our one and only drop out. Colin has cycled his whole life, being a non-driver. A retired schoolteacher and marathon runner his dedication to the challenge was without competition. Every training ride would encompass a trip past Colchester & East Essex Cricket Club, so that he could remind himself of Rob, and the reason behind the ride. Colin was the only cyclist on a mountain type bike and he wore shorts for the whole trip – top bloke.

15. Kevin – room-mate with Colin, retired head teacher and cycle enthusiast. Can talk the hind legs off a donkey, but cycles so fast it didn't really affect me. Very knowledgeable on birds and otters! Heart of gold.

16. Nicola – wife of Terry – very close family friend for 34 years. A fantastically enthusiastic supporter of the RGF and totally committed to the work we are trying to do. Nicola is a very fit lady and although a new cyclist, a very talented one. She loves gadgets, so was probably the best-equipped Jogleist, although the worst at actually using any of them. The fun was each day waiting to hear what she had left behind, as despite a limited opportunity Nicola seemed to manage to spread her luggage far and wide. The technique in the end was each morning, for Terry to remain behind for a more leisurely breakfast and await the message from Nicola as to what he was to go searching for. Actually lots of us left stuff behind each day too, so we were very grateful for Terry's collection service. Generously, for which I shall always be grateful, Nicola spent much of the ride at the back with me, a real Rob's Rider!

(17.) Terry – husband of Nicola, and Pip's friend since aged 11. As with Nicola, we've seen a lot of life together. Terry is the most loyal of friends and totally into fitness but also completely risk adverse – so never wanted to actually cycle with us, but always wanted to be full member of the challenge. He spent day after day driving backwards and forwards along the route. Nothing was ever too much trouble for him and he is the kindest man you'll ever meet – although his team motivational talks need a bit of work! Whilst fairly impractical himself, he was totally brilliant at finding a way of fixing all problems – a star.

(18.) Carl – our professional support crew. A truly smashing bloke; he is a fixer and a solution finder. I never heard him moan, complain or even appear to mutter under his breath. I never saw him in a flap, not even when it was pouring with rain and he was planning to camp for the night, not even when he woke to find he had a flat tyre on the van and nowhere was open.

And so the common denominator of our team, with the exception of Abi – we were all old enough to know better, but absolutely determined to succeed.

Liz
Elle & Abi
Carl & Terry
Nicola
Pip
Elizabeth
LANDS END 2015
NEW YORK 3147
JOHN OGROATS 874
ISLES OF SCILLY
THE ROB GEORGE
FOUNDATION 17TH MAY
Claire & Antonius
Colin aka. Fossie

I would say to anyone who would listen - never underestimate the power of determination. Terry will agree with that. He, for one, questioned the likelihood of us all crossing the finishing line. I think anyone could have been forgiven for looking at us lot and having a hearty chuckle. 1114 miles on a bike is a long way by anyone's standards, and there was a lot of climbing to be tackled en route. Land's End looked a mighty long way down the road. But, do you know, despite everything that was thrown at us, nobody even once muttered anything about giving up. We started together and we fully intended to finish together. The success would be getting all 16 of us over the finishing line – we couldn't lose anyone along the way. Of course we would need a little luck too. I don't think many gamblers would have put their money on us!

... and so, back to the minibus, on the morning of 2nd May 2015. You know what it's like up the front, when you are not used to anything other than an ordinary motorcar. You feel very high up, and also it's all a bit steady. It feels like you can see everything and we all marvelled at the amazing coastal views as we bumped along up the A9. We weren't going to be coming back down this road for a number of good reasons. The first was that my extensive research had shown that it was a dangerous road for cyclists. The mortality rate was alarmingly high and so the recommendation was it was best avoided. It was also reckoned to be very busy – but I have to say that on that Saturday morning it was pretty deserted. Except, that is, for the various groups of cyclists we saw. We couldn't resist cheering like a bunch of school kids out of the windows and tooting encouragement. They seemed to fit into a pattern of colour co-ordinated, lycra-clad, heads down, tight peloton formation and going at one hell of a pelt, sort of cyclists. They all appeared to be bound for Land's End, but certainly not in our style. There would be no stopping for photos for them, no admiring the view. They were all in such a rush – my worst nightmare. I wondered if some of our group quietly wished they were in one of those pelotons. Anyway good luck to them all – vive la difference! I should mention, though, the chap we overtook approaching John O'Groats on a Penny Farthing – now that is quite some achievement and quite a sight – well done that man!!

Perhaps you'll recognise that feeling, as you drive towards the coast, as the scenery seems to disappear and is replaced by the sight of the sea. As you approach John O'Groats it really does feel like the end of the country – well I suppose it would really! It was incredibly exciting. No sign of the possible sea mists we had heard about, or the gale force winds, or the rain, or even the snow from the previous day. The sun was out sparkling on the sea, and the sky was a stunning sight, with a few peeps of blue. Our bikes were laid out in the car park for us by Carl as he did a last minute check of our brakes and chains, and fitted Garmins to those bikes not already equipped. Then we lined up for the obligatory photo, Land's End 845 miles it said – well not the way we were going – we were going to milk this trip, no short cuts for us. I'd never really been to Scotland before and couldn't wait to get started and explore as much as possible.

****

26th June 2011

Rob had spent the night being pumped full of IV antibiotics and a trickle of chemo to attempt to slow the leukaemia down, with the aim to give him a blood transfusion – this would hopefully dilute his blood a bit, adding more red cells, the ones that carry oxygen, and help him breath more easily. Basically acute myeloid leukaemia occurs when the white blood cells go mad, and start splitting and multiplying at an out of control rate. Rob's blood was massively overcrowded with white cells, sort of suffocating the red cells; his poor body was being suffocated from the inside out. He couldn't simply be given a huge bag of nice red blood, as it would have been too much of a shock for his system, so the doctors were trying to control the white cell count first. Anyway, by the morning things weren't going well, and the decision was made that Rob should be transferred to Addenbrooke's, Cambridge, immediately. It was a risky strategy, but the only option.

So once again, I was sat up the front, but this time in an ambulance. Rob was stretchered into the back with one ambulance attendant, and another drove. Sam managed to make it to the hospital in time to give Rob a hug in the ambulance bay, and to wave us off. It was one of the most heart-breaking sights I've ever seen, one brother waving the other off – to they both knew not what. I was clearly told that this ambulance was not going to stop – for anything. Pip would drive our car, but was firmly advised not to try and keep up with the ambulance; we'd see him in Cambridge. Rob's only chance was to get to Addenbrooke's. If he arrested en route...well we'd just try and get there as quickly as possible. The blue lights went on, the sirens went on, and off we went. I still can't hear the sound of an ambulance siren without filling with tears, one of the many flashbacks that continue to take me by surprise.

Our two ambulance men were on weekend cover from Leeds, so had no idea where they were heading. The Sat. Nav. was programmed with Colchester to Cambridge and proceeded to scream directions, but at the speed we were travelling the poor woman commentator could barely keep up. If the situation hadn't been so dire, you might have had a good old laugh. I've never been in a blue light ambulance before, or since, thankfully. It is pretty scary. The siren is wailing and you seem to accelerate into every situation. Of course, what is supposed to happen is that drivers hear the sirens and see the flashing lights in their rear view mirrors, and move out of the way! Mostly that does happen, but there are a disturbing number of morons out there, who pootle along without a care in the world, oblivious to what's going on around them. This ends up with the ambulance up the rear end of their vehicles, hoping against hope that they'll be spotted. It's all pretty stressful; thank goodness Rob slept through the whole experience.

As I'd been strapped into the front seat, a small cool-box had been handed to me – it looked like a sandwich box. As we swung into Addenbrooke's, heading around to the bays for expected ambulance arrivals, we were again met by a doctor and a nurse; they were actually standing waiting under the arrivals canopy – for us. The sandwich box turned out to be all of Rob's blood cultures from Colchester. Microscope slides of samples taken and other samples. I wish I'd known how important it was, I'd have held on a little tighter!

We were whisked up onto the ward. C10 - It's right at the top of Addenbrooke's, (great views), right at the end of the corridor. You don't stumble upon it by mistake; it's very quiet up there. To ensure infection control, there are many intercoms and buzzers to get past before you gain admission. Visitors are not really encouraged. Everyone is too poorly. Here Rob's new consultant met us. She sat on the end of his bed, took a good look at the file, at Rob and declared, "There is no need to panic; we have 24 hours before we lose him." If ever you wonder what it feels like to have the rug pulled from under you; that was one of those moments.

From: Lorraine George
To: Friends
Sent: Sunday, June 26, 2011 11:35 PM
Subject: Re: Rob
We are now at Addenbrooke's having been blue lighted here this morning. 110mph (well that's what it looked like from my viewing angle) up the M11 is not something I recommend. They are throwing everything they've got at him but can't get his White cell count down so that he can have the transfusion he desperately needs. They've started a trickle of chemo even though they still aren't sure exactly which strain of leukaemia it is. Bone marrow test tomorrow. This feels like it is happening to someone else!

As I look back at that journey, I have lost count of how many times we did it. Colchester to Cambridge is about a 120 mile round trip; sometimes we were making the journey 3 or 4 times a week. Whilst Rob was an inpatient, we were often lucky enough to be able to make use of hospital accommodation, like the Karen Morris Trust flat. This is for leukaemia patients and their families, and was a total godsend. It is free to families and of course is in great demand, but when it was already booked, or right at the beginning of Rob's treatment, we stayed in hospital nurses' accommodation, which was very expensive and the bills soon mounted up.

Often I camped out on the ward with Rob; he hated being left alone. I regularly had a run in with various nurses, sisters, doctors, Teenage Cancer Trust counsellors and Consultants on the subject. As far as I was concerned I was doing what Rob wanted. We regularly revisited the promise Pip and I had made to be with him every step of the way; he promised us in return that he would say if he wanted us to leave.

You have to laugh - on one such run in, I was doing my "I will not be moved" routine, mostly quietly but firmly (sometimes maybe not so quietly), whilst Rob appeared to be fiddling with his phone. When all the commotion had died down my phone pinged, and there was a message from Abi. I can't find the original text, mores the pity, but it read something like:
"Hey, hey! Thought you'd like to see what Robbie has just texted me – "Heaven help the nurse that tries to come between my Mum and me" – keep fighting Lorraine, it's what Rob wants."
What a bugger though, he didn't help me with the fight, simply enjoyed the spectacle. There were others along the way for his amusement too!

****

The Rob George Foundation:

Our family set up The Rob George Foundation in Rob's memory. It was launched on the 4th January 2014, a month after Rob's death. Following his express wishes, we aim to try and:

"Make a difference, one individual at a time."

Aim 1: To offer financial and/or practical support to young people with life threatening illnesses.

In our first two years of existence we have already supported many families facing the same sort of expenses that we did. We were fortunate; we could afford all the accommodation, the petrol, the food, the loss of earnings, the... well the list goes on. Just take a second to think; it's not difficult to imagine how crippling the expenses of the travelling alone might be.

Can you imagine not even being able to afford to visit your own child in hospital? Can you imagine being unable to afford the petrol to even attend your own appointments?

These days, if you are unlucky enough to be diagnosed with a serious illness, you are likely to be referred to a specialist unit. This is unlikely to be in your hometown. Our choices had been London or Cambridge – we had opted for Cambridge. We know there are young adults that may potentially die because they simply cannot afford to attend their appointments. The medics themselves describe them as the "Forgotten Tribe".

Then, try and imagine for a moment that your young person has been admitted for treatment; imagine not being able to afford the fare to visit them.

The RGF has already helped, and will continue for as long as it is able to help, many such young people and their families. Hospital is terrifying enough; no one should be deprived of their family too.

I'll tell you about aim 2 later on – so you'll need to keep reading...

Saturday 2nd May, 2015 – 11.45am,
JOGLE Day 1
John O'Groats to Tongue (65.6 miles +4378ft)

As I stood next to that famous signpost I gazed out to sea. There were so many emotions coursing through me, and a tinge of sadness too, but it really did feel like Rob was screaming at me, "Go Mum! Go!" I didn't feel confident, far from it; I did feel a bit under-prepared, but I also felt incredibly determined. I wasn't sure what might stop me reaching Land's End, but it was going to need to be something fairly significant.

Apart from the cold, it was a perfect day for a bike ride. The sun was shining, the sky was cloudy but blue too, the wind was gentle, but crikey it was freezing. Looking down into the little harbour side there were piles of fishing baskets, and painted on the quayside was a version of our signpost. The only difference was that is was down a steep slope. No, we'd stick with this one; it was at the highest point – much better place to start!

We were lined up for the first official photo of Rob's Ride, just one of us missing, Nigel C – all we needed now was the matching photo, 1114 miles further on. We were all bundled up with two pairs of cycling gloves, beanies under our helmets, and our thermal vests tucked in. Fossie of course had his legs out – now there's a real man for you! We hailed a passing dog walker, and the order "Tops Off" was decreed. Everyone flashed their special JOGLE cycling top, complete with their names between their shoulder blades, and the classic photo was taken, approximately 15 times, as of course everyone needed it on their own camera or phone. Carl later referred to this as the usual faffing that goes on with large groups of cyclists at the start of a challenge – we did cut the faffing time down as the trip progressed, but this moment needed to be thoroughly recorded. I couldn't wait to get going. The Go Pros were turned on, and with the only "tour rule" of "No Moaning Allowed!" ringing in my ears, we were off.

Well, cycling is delightfully simple like that. You clip your helmet securely on your head, point your bike in the general direction you have chosen, carefully adjust your bum on that instrument of torture called a saddle and pedal. Then you simply need to keep pedalling, for a long time!!

We launched ourselves down a short gravel path onto the road, Abi and I leading the way, the better cyclists allowing us to lead the ride off. We giggled that it wouldn't last for long – we were right! A few random folks visiting John O'Groats kindly waved us off and wished us luck – it was all very low key. But hey, who needs a crowd – there were enough of us, all in this together; we were a party on our own!

My first mistake was to natter from the start. The pull up out of John O'Groats took me by surprise and left me panting by the first junction, turn right for Thurso – 20 miles – hurray – this had not been a very encouraging start.

The A836 runs along the north coast of Scotland. It is renowned for being either spectacular or invisible. Sea fog is a real danger, or as on the previous day, snow, at almost any time of year can close the road completely. On Saturday 2nd May it was simply stunning. The clouds rolled away and the sun really did glint on the ocean. I was really excited about seeing Scotland. It was an area of the British Isles I'd never before had the chance to explore. I'd had a lovely weekend in Edinburgh once, and a week at St. Andrew's supporting Rob at a golf competition, but that was about it. There was the alternative A9 route south, but I took the view it might be a long time before I came this way again, I didn't want to miss a thing.

Almost immediately you feel pretty remote. There are a few houses dotted along the road, but that's it. The fields to our left were flat as far as we could see, and boggy – the rain was obviously not too far away. On our right was the coastline, and we could already see the first little bay coming in ahead of us. The daffodils were still nodding their heads in the verges, a couple of weeks behind their southern relations, waving us on our way. Our mood was sky high, what a buzz! Everyone was beaming from ear to ear. Not far along the road came my first surprise for everyone. Yup, the road ahead looked great; travelling in the right direction, flat, quiet – so we were going to take a left fork. Actually we were sticking to National Cycle Route 1 – a theme that was to be developed as the trip progressed.

This single carriageway road was perfect. Abi and I could continue to cycle side by side, keep the nattering going and enjoy the view. Pretty much everyone else had already steamed ahead – that was fine. It wasn't a race; but I wanted everyone to ride it the way they wanted to. Antonius had declared 14 minutes into the 1114 miles that he simply couldn't cycle as slowly as me – well, what can I say – it's a skill!!

The few of us at the back took our first pause at the Canisbay Parish War Memorial. A beautiful marble plinth surrounded by daffodils. It was covered in names and as you lifted your eye line the backdrop was the sea. Names of highlanders lost in the 1st and 2nd WW's were remembered here and yes I remembered Rob too.

On we went, past vibrant yellow flowering gorse, and the odd lush pine forest. There was nothing much in the way of traffic, but a fair smattering of cows and lots of sheep. We followed signs down into Castletown, re-joining the main A836. For those not totally concentrating, the slightly surprising right hand turn off the main road was to take us the long way around Castletown, but more importantly along by the beach and old quayside. This little lane took us within 5 meters of the sea, which was looking its best, gently lapping on the rocky beach. As we looked into the distance the beach turned into a golden strip of sand – I have absolutely promised myself that I will return here, with a pack of sandwiches and a flask of tea – it is a view that deserves more time.

As we stood there eating jelly babies and swigging our energy drinks, a car pulled up, and Pip got chatting. Anyway, one thing led to another, our story struck close to home for this lovely family on their holidays and a £10 note changed hands – what lovely people – we met a lot of lovely people along the way – I hope they had a good holiday too.

We wiggled along beside the sea and through some derelict stone buildings. A couple of wrecked fishing boats nestled in the wild flowers and a few small vessels bobbed around in the tiny quay. It felt like a film set – all that was missing was Captain Ross Poldark with his ponytail and floppy shirt. I could so be Demelza – oh, hang on a minute, wrong country/county – that'll be near the end of the ride in Cornwall! Elizabeth and I discussed a couple of potential building projects along the way. It's all about location, location, location, don't you know? Except these places were beyond renovation – I think knocking them down and starting again was the kindest option. If I win the lottery I'm off to try my hand in Castletown. A gorgeous B & B overlooking the sea, you are all invited!

Castletown itself didn't seem to have too much to commend it. A fine collection of typically Scottish grey/white painted houses, and a Spar. I'm not sure if it actually has a Castle; if it did, we never saw it. Signs for National Cycle Route 1 were spotted and off we went. Well, that was the warm-up over; here was our first proper hill – that shut me up! Mount Pleasant Road takes you into Thurso; I suppose the clue was in the name.

Thurso sits on the River Thurso, which flows into Thurso Bay. With a population of about 9000, it's not huge, but it's the biggest town we were going to see all day. As we approached the centre of town, the Church of St. Andrew's and St. Peter's acts as a giant roundabout. We heard the piper before we saw him, but as we drew up at the traffic lights, conveniently red, out walked the bride and groom. Wow, I know it's a stupid/obvious thing to say, but with the strains of the bag-pipes and the groom in his tartan kilt, it really felt like we were in Scotland!

We continued on the main road, nearly deserted of traffic. We had been warned of the huge logging lorries that can terrify unsuspecting cyclists; we had been warned of the impatient locals who get heartily fed up of parties like us – but no, we didn't meet any of them. Spotting a signpost for Tongue, not to mention a smart little white bike on a blue background attached to a lamp-post, we headed back into open countryside with something new to talk about.

I'd counted on the GPS profiles that there were 13 hills between Thurso and Tongue. The numbers didn't sound too bad if you said them quickly – but in truth I had no idea what to expect. I'd never managed to find any hills locally, when I'd been out training by cycling in circles around Colchester, which might have helped me make any sense of those profile maps. What exactly did a steep hill look like on the map? It would all just need to be a surprise. As I lifted my eyes I could see what looked like a small mountain range ahead of us. I could only assume Tongue was beyond it. Excellent! This was my first sight, from the bike, of the fingertips of the North West Highlands. They were stunning shades of pink and purple, but there was no going around them.

By the time we passed the sign announcing we had arrived in the county of Sutherland, the scenery was breath taking. It was barren, the earth was water logged, full of peaty bogs, but most memorably it was silent. It was easier to cycle if I didn't chat, and in any case my thoughts were being pretty noisy. Sometimes you are more acutely aware than at other times, just how good it is to be alive. I felt very alive at that moment. It was cold but bright. The sky was clear, and off to our right you could still see the coastline. There are no trees, just tufty grass and gorse bushes. I don't remember any sheep here, which seems unusual, as I would have said that Scotland was full of sheep. The road surface was excellent and you could see forever. Abi and I did have fun trying to pronounce some of the road signs, printed here in Scottish Gaelic and English. We thought we should try and learn a bit of the local lingo whilst visiting – that didn't last long!

After about 38 miles we reached Portskerra. This was to be the scene of my first slight disappointment. You see, when I had started planning our route, I had obviously started at Day 1. I had this picture of us all cycling together shoulder to shoulder, lycra to lycra. Portskerra is a tiny village hanging onto the northern edge of Scotland. It has a pretty little sandy bay, and I had calculated that this would be a perfect spot for us to sit, enjoy our first picnic stop, and possibly even have a quick paddle. Of course I hadn't bargained on those hills being quite so hilly. Carl was parked up on the main road, next to the very nice public toilets – very timely - and picnicking by the sea required a 2-mile deviation from the main route. Not everyone ahead of us had agreed that this was a good idea apparently, and in any case, had now set off way ahead of us up the main road. A few looks were shared and Pip said to me, "Well, what do you want to do, time is ticking on, shall we give it a miss?" My heart sank, we were still right at the top of my wish list and we were considering "cutting a corner" already. I replied, "We might never come this way again, I'll always regret not going down to the beach." "Right then," said my wonderful rear guard. Elizabeth, Pip, Liz, Abi and I set off, to explore Portskerra. It was a pretty spot, unfortunately down a steep hill. Whether it was worth it I'm not actually sure. Well actually I am sure, and it was worth it – it was part of the challenge that I had set, and we had not faltered. Portskerra was beautiful.

Back onto the A836, and I'm looking out for the Marie Curie Cancer Care Field of Hope. The information had warned that it was badly signposted and so easily missed – and I did miss it! Another reason to return. This is apparently a beautiful area, over-looking the sea and planted with all manner of colourful flora – a contrast to the moorland and heather. It is a place to take a moment to stop and reflect; perhaps to remember those touched by cancer. Perhaps it's as well I did miss it – I'd probably have wept – it was a bit early to start that.

We drag Pip past the Strathy Inn, his tongue hanging out for a pint, but we need to press on. These hills are taking much longer than anticipated. At this rate, we'll miss dinner!! We still have 20 miles to go, and now they've started adding cattle grids to the assault course! We are not getting any quicker. The debate begins: get off and push, take them steady, or, go like the clappers and keep your fingers crossed. The camp is divided. Elizabeth and Liz decide caution is the best approach. Abi, Pip and I decide fairly quickly that we can't be bothered to keep getting on and off the bike, so what the heck, pedal like mad and keep that front wheel straight at all costs.

The road ahead of us can be seen for miles, winding its way through this beautiful but baron landscape. Distance seems to have taken on a different perspective. I wish I had one of my photos to show you here, but on that first day I had my Go Pro

Nicola – up the front

camera mounted on my helmet, set to take a picture at regular intervals automatically. You can only imagine my disappointment, as I've mentioned previously, later that evening when I downloaded my photos onto the laptop to find I had taken 144 pictures of the tarmac 2 feet in front of my bike – ahh! This stunning shot is one taken by Antonius – and is probably better than mine would have been anyway!

As that first day's cycling went on, the undulations became, well, more undulating. Nobody moaned, well not in our group they didn't. I carried in my head the instructions given me by my lovely neighbour Gavin. Gavin's in the Army and used to motivating groups of squaddies. He had looked me in the eye the night before we left and said, "Just smile your way from top to bottom, if you let your chin go down, you'll be done for." Great advice – smiling got me through many weary moments; not all, but many.

As we approached Betty's Hill, we didn't just smile, we had a good old laugh. Dear Abi was busy telling us some of her "interesting facts".

"Did you know that if a female ferret doesn't have sex for a year it dies?"

Apparently this is true. Abi spots a waterfall off to our left. Suddenly she starts waving her arms about to make sure we don't miss it, and of course takes our first fall of the trip. The waterfall was immediately renamed "Abi Falls" and will forever be referred to as this, please.

As you drop over the top after Betty's Hill the estuary cuts in. It's the River Naver, and with the tide out, the golden sandy riverbed shone magnificently in the evening sun. Yes, you are right, we are going to be making an entrance for dinner this evening. As we follow the river, we finally change direction. After cycling in a westerly direction all day, at last we are beginning to progress in the right direction – south towards Land's End.

As we neared the end of our first day we went through a little place called Colbackie. It was gorgeous. The sea was lapping gently on the sandy beach, and I wanted to stop – sadly not on this visit – where the hell had Tongue disappeared to? It became a theme of the trip, that no matter what the total mileage for the day was, the last 10 miles seemed to go on forever and ever. Finally however, we hit a smashing downhill section. Tongue was in sight, and we knew from Terry, who had been shadowing us at the tail for the last hour or so, just in case we needed scooping up, that our hotel for the night was just at the bottom of this hill. Of course, silly me, this was not all-good news. Tomorrow would start with a good old-fashioned uphill warm-up – well how many of you didn't see that one coming?

It was quite an emotional sight as we freewheeled into the Tongue Hotel. Parked out the front was Carl with the van and the rest of our group, all showered, changed, sporting a variety of gin and tonics or beer, or in the case of our temporarily abstemious Fossie, a Sprite, all cheering us in. Fossie had sworn not to take any alcohol since his New Year's training regime had kicked off - he was saving himself for our middle weekend – but I'll tell you about that later on, too.

The Tongue Hotel is a former hunting lodge. It was perfect; rich tartan carpets and stunning views across the Kyle of Tongue. Our room was welcoming, our luggage already stowed, our bikes were whisked away by Carl for the night, and so we got stuck into a well-deserved shower before dinner. The dining room was a sumptuous oak panelled affair, with far reaching views across the water. The homemade soup slipped down a treat and the air was thick with contentment. It was Pip's turn to pass the "Moustache" on, and Kevin was the willing recipient. It was presented on the strength of his interest in otters!

Talk turned to how everyone was planning to "look after themselves" on the trip. Talk of nuts, nutrients and magnesium – it's such a pity that last one didn't start with the letter "n"! Pip and I listened, in awe. Anyway, that is how, Pip found himself with Claire crouched behind him in the middle of the dining room of the Tongue Hotel, whilst his trousers were rolled up over his knees. She happily shared her magnesium spray with us, which each evening was to be rubbed into the back of our legs to aid our recovery. We'd take all the help that was on offer!

Hugs were exchanged; Day 1 was complete, so that just left 15 to go! Off to bed, phew!

Abi & Elle

Chapter 4

Sunday 3rd May, 2015 – 9.00am, JOGLE Day 2 Tongue to Tain (63.6 miles +2933ft)

There is a lovely photo of us all gathered outside the Tongue Hotel on this Sunday morning. I think we were all fairly nervous but keen to be on our way. The weather was dank to say the least. The sky hung a heavy grey, with a fine mizzle in the air. Still we all donned our high viz waterproof gear, stuck our rain hats under our helmets and pointed our bikes up the hill – never a good way to start!!

Today's ride took us in a southerly direction, with a bit of a veer to the east coast towards the end of the day; basically the A836 all the way continuing on our trusty National Cycle Route 1. We were doing a giant zigzag across Scotland, essentially following the water. Yesterday we had zigged; today we would zag. I'd studied the GPS profile for the day's ride and concluded we had four big hills to climb. I was looking at the first, and then there was to be a down and flat section to mile 10. Uphill for a couple of miles, downhill or flattish until mile 24, a big uphill at mile 24 then downhill nearly until the end with a bit of a slog up into the hotel for the last couple of miles. Didn't sound too bad; I could manage that. So off I went. First problem: I'd left my bike in a downhill gear at the end of the previous day so nearly fell off before I'd even begun – school boy error!

We quickly veered off the main road, and headed up a single-track lane with a good road surface, which immediately got steeper. I was already feeling pretty warm. With all the waterproof gear on, you soon get a bit steamy inside – you are then left with the dilemma of removing layers and potentially getting wet on the outside, or keeping them on and drowning in your own perspiration on the inside. Anyway for now I just kept pedalling.

As the team ploughed its way up this never-ending hill, I had to work pretty hard to keep chirpy; after all it was still so early in the day! Liz and I stopped at one point to take a photo of the two of us. We were at the back of the pack and I was busy waxing lyrical about how wonderful it was to share this amazing experience with such a treasured friend. We talked about the value of friendship, and, well, it all got a bit emotional. There was a "viewing" point signposted off to the right, so we stopped to share the view. Oh my, what a view! It looked back towards our hotel of the previous night. There was the river flowing out to the sea beyond, the wonderful sky full of scudding stormy clouds and sunshine piercing in beams highlighting the scenery, like a stage set. It's a gorgeous photo. Anyway, no time to linger, there was a full day ahead of us – let's get this first hill over with and find that flat bit!

As we turned back up the hill, we laughed that the weather looked better behind us than up front; perhaps we were going in the wrong direction, but we were certain it wouldn't be too bad. By this time we were in open countryside. The lane was lined with dry stonewalls, and the sheep hardly even raised their eyes as we passed – obviously mad cyclists were nothing unusual. The single-track road had regular passing places, and we politely stopped and let cars pass when needed – which wasn't very often.

Eventually we came to the crest of that first hill, and oh boy, that's when it all began to kick off! The view was incredible. The open Scottish Highlands were stretching before us with the road gently undulating into the distance, framed by mountains, covered in snow. The sky was dark and menacing, and the wet stuff described earlier was beginning to change from that fine mizzle into proper rain. Nothing too bad, but it didn't look like it was going to stop any time soon. The worst thing though, was the wind.

I've cycled on windy days before but I was reminded of the words of wisdom spoken by the young men in the cycle shop at home. "The heat's OK, the rain's OK, but if you get a bad headwind – it can spoil a good day out!" Well there was nothing to be done about it; this road before us was the only one on offer, so head down and get on with it girl!

We battled our way forward, even pedalling on the slightly downhill sections, every mile had to be worked for. So hard were we working that we didn't really notice that the rain was now pouring down. You couldn't stop pushing those pedals for fear of being driven back the way you'd come. I quickly lost patience with anyone in a motorcar, the passing places became where they waited for me to get past them – after all they had an engine!

The edges of the road were lined with tall poles. I tried to raise a laugh by saying it was like skiing down a piste with the markers each side. Then we realized they were indeed to mark the road – when it snowed. Abi and I cast our eyes upwards and at that moment we weren't totally sure what the sky was full of. We desperately needed a wee, and you know what it's like, once you've had that thought, you really need to go. But what do you do? No bushes, no trees, ditches full to the brim with freezing water, no sheds or shelters to duck behind... it was miserable. As Abi commented, "There is no signal, our satellite's stopped picking up on the tracker, there are no people or animals, no-one even knows where we are! If we gave up – no-one would even know!" Anyway, we didn't give up – that was not an option.

The road began to drop down, (although you'd never have believed we were going downhill) and ran along the banks of Loch Loyal. We looked out for the 1000 strong population of grey-lag geese and the rare black-throated divers supposed to be in evidence. Perhaps I was blinded, by the rain running down my face? I didn't see a single bird, of any description, for most of the day. At the end of the loch, though, was a small stone boathouse – Hallelujah! – Pip held the bikes, Abi and I picked our way through the muddy verge and tried to work out where the wind was coming from. It's very important if you are going to have to pee in the wilderness, that you consider the wind direction!! Having totally circumnavigated the boathouse we realized the wind was coming from all directions. So needs must, we just had to get on with it. If a car came, well they were in for a surprise – by this point, I couldn't have cared less.

So onto the second hill of the day – well it was just more of the same really except that instead of pushing those pedals downhill or on the flat, we were now pedalling uphill again too. The funny banter had stopped; this was going to be along day. We realised we were all soaked to the skin, although we'd only completed 10 miles. It had taken us ages, and we had another 52 miles to go. Abi asked me if my lights actually worked – cheeky madam!

In defence of my route, I feel it has huge unrealized potential. Here too I shall return one day, although probably in a car. I have never felt so isolated. If I hadn't been so totally uncomfortable, I'd have loved it. Here the world has the potential to be a silent place, close to nature, just at one with your thoughts, whilst travelling at a steady pace on two wheels. Of course, today the silence was drowned out by the howling wind. None of us moaned, though; we just had to keep going.

Retracing my steps with the aid of Google Earth I smile at one shot that contains a lone cyclist on this baron stretch of road, being tailed by a small white transit van. There is a rain-smeared homemade banner across the back of the van advertising that the cyclist was raising money for a hospice, with the Just Giving link. Well done that fella – I wondered what the odds might be of us bumping into one of those vans with the camera on the top on our journey. We too could then be posted onto the Internet for folks to stumble across.

The rain continued to come at us from all directions but we pushed on. Despite the repeated signs warning us to beware of the deer, we didn't see any; just us cyclists out today. Those snow-covered mountains were getting a bit closer though – excellent.

We arrived at the hamlet of Altnaharra where we had been promised a refreshment break. We all lifted our eye lines and tried to locate Carl, and our trusty white support van; his company was wanted as much as a cup of tea and a chocolate biscuit. I really needed someone who knew, to tell me this was all going to be OK, that everything was going to end happily. On our left hand side we spotted the Altnaharra Hotel, and there parked up by the front door was Carl.

If I'm honest I was a little shocked. It looked a bit posh, especially as you can imagine the state of us. Carl and Terry appeared and waved us in. Carl declared that despite the fact that he had supported multiple trips like ours, he'd never seen weather like it and told us that the rest of the crew had only just left. The owners were totally welcoming. Having just mopped up one trail of puddles, they were happy for us to come in and make a new mess. We all sunk into huge sofas in front of the roaring fire, leaving untold dampness on the said sofas for someone to sort out later. We sat in silence, shock really I think. Terry chatted excitedly away. He'd been on his own all morning and was thrilled and relieved by equal measures that we had all made it this far. He'd also found a piano so had managed to have a fix of his scales and arpeggios; playing the pianoforte being a hobby he is dedicated to. Whilst we sipped our steaming tea Terry even sang us his latest composition – entitled "A Happy Song", on a guitar he'd found lying around. I'm still not sure if he was serious or joking – we were no longer capable of laughing, and my sense of humour was long gone. That bloody song got in my head though, and annoyed me all the way to Tain!

Well there was nothing for it, the longer I sat there, the worse it was going to feel. No one mentioned giving up, so we pushed our bikes up the gravel drive and pushed on. We were heading for Lairg; we had covered a grand total of 16 miles, another 20 to Lairg where we would have lunch.

The road was unchanging, windswept, deserted, wet and uphill. That headwind simply didn't know when to stop. I now had earache, as hailstones seemed to find their way into my left ear – nice! The cold and damp seemed to settle into my chest, and my signature cough began to feel troublesome. The road stretched out before us, straight and seemingly endless. Progress was painfully slow.

On another day, the little humped stone bridges would be picturesque, but not on this trip. Next time maybe I'll pause, put my sunglasses on the top of my head and have one of those windswept photos taken – you know the kind, where you look a right poser! We didn't take any photos to speak of on this run, although Abi did try and make a recording of the sound of the wind – it really was like some kind of monster.

Eventually the road dropped down to the banks of Loch Shin. We had arrived in Lairg. Carl and Terry were spotted and we were ushered into a little teashop. I remember feeling a bit confused, not really sure what to do. I was beyond wet; I peeled my gloves off and wrung them out onto the floor. The young lad in attendance didn't bat an eye, he just twiddled his mop between my feet – I think he had seen it all before.

As I began to thaw out a bit, the cough started with a vengeance. Terry told us of the various states of those cycling ahead of us, and the discussions about how sensible continuing was under such vile conditions. Apparently Elizabeth was half frozen and Nigel H's teeth wouldn't stop chattering. Whilst Antonius and Claire had sensibly stuffed themselves with cake, others had been too cold to think what was needed and failed to stock up adequately on the calories. I could relate to that feeling. When you are exhausted, frozen, wet to your core and under pressure, it's hard to do the right thing. Paul was worried about everyone's core temperatures dropping dangerously low; I wasn't really thinking at all, except that there was a sort of panic setting in. I looked up between my coughing episodes to see Abi on her phone through in the little craft salesroom, crying. I knew she'd be on the phone to her mum Nicky; goodness knows what she would find to say. Terry reminded us that he was there with the car if we needed him. He looked at me with concern and in total bewilderment as I coughed my guts up. "How sensible is it to continue in this?" he asked. "Maybe in order to salvage the rest of the ride, it would make sense to cut our losses today and head indoors?"

I texted Sam in London; thankfully he was in. Well it was a filthy day in London too, and he was in watching the sport with a beer – sensible lad. I said something like, "Sam this is awful. I don't know if I can go on today. Abi is crying, I am crying, everyone that's just left was crying." His reply pinged straight back. He had been charting the weather from the safely of his armchair, and knew we'd been battling the elements for hours. "Mum, we always knew this wouldn't be easy. I'm so proud of you, and you know Rob would be, too. Don't sit in that teashop for too long, get out there, and get the job you've started finished. You can only get on that bus once!"

You might think that was harsh, but Sam knew what this ride meant to me. I absolutely would not have asked anyone else to ride with me, they could and would make their own choices, but onwards I was going. Pip got us all upright. We struggled with our sodden gloves to get them back on. The teashop even gave us plastic bags to line our gloves and shoes with. Then off up the road we set, making a weird crackling sound due to all our new attempts to keep the rain out. 25 miles to the hotel, we actually set off with renewed vigour – it was just weather after all. Everyone, for his or her own reasons had made the same choice. The final 25 miles was scattered with bedraggled cyclists, all determined not to give up, all focused on Tain – our destination for Day 2.

We returned to the single-track road, but the landscape was now littered with copses of pine trees, and the odd little house. I felt like there were actually people in the vicinity, though not many were in view – the rain was still lashing down, no change there.

We turned off onto the A864, the idea having been that those with the energy could take a small hike off the road to visit the beautiful Falls of Shin. Needless to say that is a treat that remains for a future visit too! Southerly we went towards Invershin, where those paying attention picked up the cycle route that required bikes to be carried up and over an old footbridge next to the railway, onto the cycle path that runs alongside the river feeding into the Kyle of Sutherland. I gather there was a little "taking of my name in vain" at this point – understandable really; I wouldn't have found it particularly amusing, either, on that day. Anyway, in all honesty, we missed it. Yes my Garmin beeped and buzzed that we were off course, but they do that a lot – I knew from my hours spent pouring over the GPS maps that Bonar Bridge was a good place to head for, so we continued down the main road. The traffic was a bit of a shock, and the spray horrible. We had unintentionally veered off the route; we were no longer on our trusty National Cycle Route 1, and we didn't like it.

The only good thing to say about Bonar Bridge was that the public loos are exceptional – well, that was all we experienced on that day. Liz and Abi set off like a rocket at this point; we didn't see them again until Tain, which left Pip and me at the back. I know he was worried about my cough, but I didn't want to talk about it – we needed to polish these last miles off somehow, and retreat into the dry.

Our hotel was about 15 miles from Bonar Bridge, and those last 15 miles seemed never ending. As Pip and I pushed ourselves to a place of fatigue and discomfort we had never previously imagined, I thought back to what we had laughingly referred to as the JOGLE's first training session – the Christmas Party held at our home. We'd raised a glass or two of fizz and toasted our epic challenge. I had tried to give my version of a rousing speech based upon the idea of "Team Spirit". I wanted everyone to buy into the idea that whilst of course, each one of us ultimately had to pedal our own bike, how much of the personal sense of achievement would be lost if any one of us didn't last the course. At this moment it all came back to me.

We've all, I'm sure, heard the team talk that goes along the lines, "We're only as good as our weakest link", "there's no 'I' in team" etc. I'd delivered that self-same speech many a time to my girls and boys at the dancing school. Those sportsmen and women amongst you may not consider dance a team sport – well you'd be wrong. I'm a competitor too; I just don't feel any motivation to compete over a ball, no matter what size, shape or colour it might be. In other situations though, I want to win, just like everyone else.

Pip and I had decided from the off that we would be at the back of the ride. We felt cast in the roles of "hosts" and as such we did carry a sense of responsibility towards everyone else. After all the harsh truth was, that they were only all there because our Rob had died. The pride-damaging difference was, though, that we thought our position at the rear was going to be a matter of choice. It's one thing to choose to be sweeper - after all, it was my event. I needed to ensure that no-one failed because they felt dejected at the back, or that something happened or they got lost and nobody realized. However, it was quickly becoming clear that we weren't making the decision to be at the back, the decision was being made for us. It was lonely. It was tough. We had each other, and again we stuck together, we were good at that, we'd done it a lot, particularly over the past couple of years. I didn't blame anyone for not wanting to spend a second longer than was necessary out on a day like this, but we looked forward to the company of some friends over the days to come, and seeing that 'team spirit" in action.

As I got colder I hoped those who I had shared many conversations with over the months, folks who had doubted their own cycle ability, who I had reassured would never be alone at the back, were safely in the hotel. I began to question what a mug I had been for believing them. Anyway, by the nature of things someone had to be last, I could live with that.

Sometimes in life you just need to get your head down and pedal. That's what we did. Pip silently supported me and if I'd have had the energy, I'd have done the same for him. On a different day it would have been a gorgeous run home. As I said before, this route didn't really live up to its full potential on this particular day.

I was still sporting my fluorescent yellow waterproof (or not so waterproof) jacket. Pip had begged an extra layer from Abi's stock of borrowed kit, and had added a black jacket on top of all of his other sodden stuff; it did at least serve to keep the wind out. The light was beginning to fail, so I turned my lights on. It was then that we realized that we had forgotten to charge Pip's lights up before setting off – bugger!

We were back on National Cycle Route 1 at this point, and the run hugs the banks of Dornoch Firth – it really is stunning. Tain was on the signposts now and we managed to locate a small reserve of energy for the final few miles. As we passed the Glenmorangie Distillery, I looked to my left, waiting to see the promised "Million Dollar View" the guidebooks had highlighted. Yes, well, I'm sure it was there somewhere, but we'd need to wait for the morning to see it. Tonight, the rain was beating down and the low clouds had shrouded the view from sight. We were on the final countdown and as we rounded that last roundabout at the 61 mile mark, what do we see, but a horrible dual carriageway stretching up the hill ahead of us. It's not what you want at the end of a long day!

Carl's van surprised us by emerging out of the spray coming in the opposite direction. He pulled up, giving us a big smile. "Well done you two," he says, "I thought you would be further back than this, I wondered if you'd like some hot soup to keep you going?" No talk of giving up. No talk of how late it was. Carl absolutely "got it"; I guess he had seen variations of the look in our eyes before. He has supported many similar rides. I for one needed to finish this ride; it was a promise I'd made to my dying child. He did suggest though that I should follow Pip rather that the other way around. Pip naturally wanted to follow me, to try and protect me and make sure I was OK, but he was in black, with no lights; we hadn't realized it was almost pitch dark.

As we finally arrived at The Carnegie Lodge Hotel, Tain, everyone came out to greet us. I've never felt anything like that moment before in my life, and actually once was enough! A smiling stranger greeted us, who could only possibly be the sister of my next-door neighbour from home; she looked more like Louise than Louise did herself! I wasn't very gracious I'm afraid; actually possibly more on the delirious side if anything. I remember Antonius taking my bike, and Claire sort of steadying me as my knees began to wobble. Elizabeth looked me in the eye and guided Pip and me indoors. We had made it, and our hostess Heather was already rather fabulously collecting everyone's soaking wet kit and tumbling it dry for the morning. Carl had already boiled the kettle in our room; we were totally battered, but not beaten, nearly but not quite, after 10 hours of cycling – Day 2 was over.

We would talk about it for the rest of the ride. We talked about that teashop in Lairg. We talked about Elizabeth getting lost, cycling extra miles around Tain alone, trying to find the hotel, and refusing to get into a kind stranger's van who offered to help her to the hotel. Not because she was worried about her personal safety, but because she was "on a cycle challenge" – she wasn't getting in the van for love nor money. We would talk about how Nigel C had missed out on this memorable day – we even have a plan afoot to accompany him on a repeat of those first three days! Of course, I'll be sitting in the back of the support van chucking buckets of iced water over him along the route!

As I think back now, from my dry and warm office chair, I remember Day 2 as beautiful. Many of us learnt lessons about ourselves. Exactly what it is that it is possible as a comfortable middle-aged adult to endure. Yes, I'll tell anyone who wants to listen that it was hideous, the weather biblical, but it was beautiful too. The highlands of Scotland are wild and unforgiving, but also very special. It was a place where I remembered what it was like to feel really alive, wet, freezing cold and miserably uncomfortable, but alive.

Of course I'd lived through other storms, one memorable one with Rob...

Late June / Early July 2011

It was all such a shock; in fact as I look back, it all still feels like a surprise. One minute Rob's summer holidays loomed ahead of him - actually the rest of his life loomed ahead of him - and the next moment we were pacing around a hospital bed worried sick. The speed at which Rob deteriorated was incredible, and of course I can't help but ask myself how things might have panned out if Rob hadn't asked to come home two days early. The "what if" game is to be avoided at all costs – there indeed lies madness!

Our great strapping lad became like a fragile butterfly. You couldn't touch him without a huge bruise appearing. His gums and lips were constantly bleeding, and I spent days repeatedly washing his mouth, or gently melting an ice cube onto his lips, as every time he managed to doze he would awake with his lips tightly sealed together with dried blood. Dental hygiene became paramount, as this was an obvious entry point for infection. We also became obsessed with bowels – or rather the movement thereof! Constipation would cause straining, and this might lead to Rob bleeding out - just imagine having leukaemia and dying whilst trying to use the loo. The irony was not lost on him.

The plan became clear. There would be four cycles of chemotherapy, the aim being to achieve full remission after the first cycle. The remaining three cycles were to try to consolidate the position hopefully achieved. Each cycle would take four weeks. Week 1: as an inpatient whilst the chemo was administered over 5-7 days. Weeks 2 and 3: spent trying to keep Rob clear of infections whilst we waited for his blood counts to drop, and he went through a stage of neutropenia. (This is when your immune system has been totally wiped out and you have no natural defences. All your white blood cells have been destroyed and your bone marrow stops producing new ones, so Rob would be susceptible to infections, and if this happened we'd have to hold onto our hats, as things could turn very nasty very quickly.) Then week 4: blood counts recover to "normal", his bone marrow would start working again, (hopefully minus the white cells that had gone mad in the first place and caused his AML,) and so the whole thing could be repeated. For the first cycle we would stay in hospital for the whole thing, so we prepared ourselves for a 5-week stay allowing for week 1 of cycle 2. That was it, the summer disappeared, and we started counting the days until the end of October, when this would all be over.

Just when you think things are grim enough, a young doctor appears to talk to Rob. Rob wanted us to stay, too, and so we heard that he needed to understand that the chemo was 99.999% likely to render him sterile. How did he feel about starting a family in the future? The answer to that question was silence – he was 19 years old at the time. There remained a small window of opportunity to harvest Rob's sperm. He was currently on a "trickle" chemo whilst they tried to get his counts vaguely under control, but they needed to start chemo "proper" ASAP. The recommendation was that we take Rob to a clinic in the Cambridgeshire countryside to attempt this procedure.

You need to try and visualize how ill Rob was. He had a temperature off the scale. He was bleeding from his mouth constantly; he was exhausted, covered in bruises and attached to a drip stand containing a constant low dose of chemotherapy. Coping with the most mundane of bodily functions was a major event, driving off to anywhere seem a totally stupid and ridiculous idea. Still the theory was that Rob needed to focus on the future, his future, when the leukaemia would be gone, and he embarked upon the rest of his life. Rob had to believe that he had a future to aim for. Eventually we all bought into this idea too.

And so off we went. Pip driving, me in the front seat navigating, and Rob laid out on the back seat wrapped in a duvet. We had directions from the hospital – how hard could this be? We circled around this beautiful little village, deep in the Cambridgeshire countryside, a few times, and in the end had to ask for directions. Of course we were looking at the place; it was just so huge we hadn't believed our own eyes. Bourne Hall is actually predominately a private fertility clinic. It is a huge Elizabethan manor house set in the most stunningly sculptured gardens. Ducks swim in the moat and the interior is filled with over-stuffed silk covered sofas with multiple cushions, and the walls are lined with photos of babies, presumably successful IVF stories.

Anyway, we led Rob in, wearing his hospital gown and flip flops – no dressing gown or PJ's as he didn't at that time own any; and in any case we'd left Colchester in a bit of a panic. We sat in a waiting room surrounded by anxious looking couples, who of course couldn't take their eyes off us – we must have looked a curious sight, I suppose. We were eventually called through to see the "Man in Charge" who waded in with "Well young man, and what brings you here?" It was the first of many occasions when I wanted to grab someone by the scruff of the neck and say "Why have you not read the file, you are making this even more painful than it needs to be!"

We endured an incredibly insensitive interview about the process of storing any successfully harvested sperm; how they (the sperm that is) would need to be of a suitable quality to make freezing viable; and how in the future it would be best if Rob fell in love with a young, nubile, potential mother for his children, as this awful bloke would find it easier to fertilize young healthy eggs rather than if Rob found himself an older "wanna be mother" for his potential off-spring. It was unbelievable!

And then we watched his bum encased in his trendy Superdry boxers, clearly visible through the back of his hospital gown, (you know the sort with half the ribbons missing,) drag his flip flopped feet up the lushly carpeted corridor to a sterile room to "do the business" into a plastic cup. We were shown to a small room. I have no idea what the use of this room was intended for. It just had two chairs in it, and an amazing view of the grounds, and the moat – please don't forget the moat! I think the idea was that we would be more comfortable here away from all the other patients and their quizzical gazes – I guess that was a kind thought.

We waited… We waited… and we waited. We watched the most incredible storm approach and then the thunder and lightning started. We had no idea where Rob had been led, or what was happening. We didn't even know whom to ask. The storm broke, the forked lightning circled around us, and the rain lashed down. The ducks ran for cover – all very dramatic; well we don't like to do things by halves. Still no Rob! After too long, he re-appeared – wet to the skin!

Rob had been taken to a "sterile room" adjacent to the main house. This room was apparently attached to the laboratory, joined by a hatch, so transfer of harvested sperm was efficient and safe. Rob was distraught. He could hardly stand let alone "perform". He had tried and tried. I suspect he had cried and cried too. But unsurprisingly he just couldn't manage anything. Having finally been too exhausted to continue he decided to come and find us, only to discover the storm raging and himself the wrong side of a door needing a security code to regain entry to the main house. Enough – we were leaving; Rob needed to be back in hospital. Apparently we could try again tomorrow…

The next day came and we were persuaded to return to Bourne Hall. Well at least this time we knew where we were going. Rob stuck some shorts on and off we went. Pip and I had no idea what to do or say for the best. We were torn between saying we didn't care about the potential for babies in the future - he was our baby and we just wanted to save him - and following the lead of the doctors who made it clear they felt very strongly that Rob needed to do this, for his future. So off we went again. This time, I assumed our visit would be, let's call it, smoother. An enormous bosomed, aged, experienced Sister showed Rob back into "the" room again, and presented him with a pile of "magazines". She had that "I've seen it all before" look on her face, and Rob was left to get on with it, this time with the magic number to get back in when the business was over.

We waited…. We waited… and we waited. Rob returned, still no good. Were we surprised? No, not really, you just had to look at him. He looked like the living dead. His skin looked like wax, he was clammy, wild eyed, with a blood stained mouth. "Let's get back to Addenbrooke's," he said – so that's what we did, as quickly as we could manage.

Everyone on the ward was waiting with baited breath for Rob's return. The doctors, the nurses, the lady who prepared the food, I suppose they had all seen this before. We though, were new to it all. Everyone was willing him on. The doctor approached us later and said she wanted him to try one last time. We had one day left, proper chemo would start the following evening, and then the window of opportunity would be closed, probably forever. Rob said he would think about it, Pip and I looked at each other - there were no words.

Looking back, I have no idea how on earth Rob found the strength, or indeed the enthusiasm, for a third, and final visit to Bourne Hall, but he did. It took an heroic effort on his part.

It is possible that you might be reading this book and may not actually know our family personally. You'll probably have gathered that I tend to speak first and think much later, Pip is not from the same mould. He thinks a lot. He is a proper gentleman – I'm a very lucky lady. The whole idea of pornographic magazines, wanking into plastic pots and the like is not a subject we had ever talked about. I had a "Mum to Son" chat. Rob for this final trip was resting his head upon my shoulder in the back of the car. He was so gravely ill, this really was a ridiculous expectation. "Just give it a bloody great yank," I whispered – he looked at me and gave his cheeky grin. "If I pull much harder Mum, it'll come off in my hand! It's not helped by the pile of sticky magazines they leave you with, they are full of middle aged, overweight women – how's that supposed to help a virile young bloke?" And that is how my demure, straight up, straight down husband, ended up telling the enormous bosomed Sister, that she should try and help our wonderful young man by upgrading her supply of magazines appropriately. I think both Rob and I wanted to cheer – very loudly, and of course we did, silently.

Off Rob went, he didn't need directions, and I gather he phoned Sam. A discussion followed and YouTube was utilized.

The deed was done; not spectacularly, but anyway a plastic cup was passed through the hatch. We returned to Addenbrooke's and a phone call would follow later to find out if the "little wigglers" were worth troubling the great man's deep freeze for. Rob was greeted like a Gold Medal Winner on the ward, the chemo was hooked up and that was that. Fortunately we were later told that there was enough sperm now frozen to attempt fertilization of 5 cycles of IVF – bloody hell Rob, go you!!

The next few days went by in a blur. Day and night blend into one. You go past being exhausted and anyway sleep is not welcome. If you do manage to nod off, you simply have to face the truth once more when you wake up. I received this most lovely email from a friend. She got it. She had previously nursed her own daughter. I hope she realizes how much her words meant to me then and now?

From: A dear friend
To: Lorraine George
Sent: Wednesday, June 29, 2011 11.40 AM

Words are so inadequate now. All the "I'm so sorry's" and "How awful" are not any help at all. But I hope it helps to know that you have a whole other family out here, and we are with you every inch of the way.

I, personally, am with you every time you put a smile on and pretend your heart is just fine when in fact it has splintered and all the old safe, familiar things are no longer; every time you rush to the loo because you need to howl and can't bear to let anyone hear you, every time you can't sleep and think of the little boy who is now grown up but in pain and so very ill. I promise I am there every time a doctor gives you news, good or bad, and every time you have to fix your face so that no one knows that you are honestly not sure if you can take another step without breaking down, every time you hold his hand and wish that it was you instead of him in that hospital bed. And every single time you ask yourself "Why us?" I will be there to give you a hug.

Rob is in the very best place. He has all the best specialists doing what they do best. And you have the love and good wishes of absolutely everyone who knows you and your family to get you through this.

I know how much it helps to know that everyone is thinking of you. And believe me, everyone is. So take care of yourself otherwise you will have a whole load of us coming to Addenbrooke's to do that for you.

And give Rob a great big hug from me when you are next able to.

Please, and I know that everyone says this, if there's anything at all that I can do, just let me know. Day or night, doesn't matter. The 24-hour clock doesn't mean much when your child is ill. What does matter is that you and Pip know that you are well supported.

With love,

Rob had the original diagnosis of Acute Myeloid Leukaemia confirmed. There is no real understanding or idea where it comes from, or why. Well they know if you stand next to a nuclear reactor and a Tsunami hits said reactor you'll probably end up with it, but that didn't explain Rob. And so Rob was immediately bombarded with requests to join current drug trials. So few people of Rob's age get AML that progress with any trial is painfully slow. We were told they didn't really know how to treat patients like Rob. They were fit, they were in the prime of their life, they metabolised everything quicker than other age groups and so the best plan they had was to fire as much of everything they could think of into their bodies as they could.

Hopefully something would work, and when they can tolerate no more, they stop. There was no better plan on offer.

Rob was signed up to possibly trial a new drug. This wasn't going to help cure the leukaemia, but it was hoped it would work by effectively giving a high viz. jacket to the cancer cells. The idea being, that in the future chemo could be developed to only kill the cancer cells, the ones glowing brightly, and not have to kill all the good cells too. He also authorised extra tests on his bone marrow samples; they would be used to try to find out what caused his AML – sounded like a good idea to me, crack on with that then, chaps!

Rob's name would be entered into the new drug trial, and then randomly selected to either receive the trial drug proper, or the placebo. If he got the real deal, he would be told, as the side effects could be fairly unpleasant. Of course Rob got the drug. So we sat tight, the curtains were drawn around his bed, and this light sensitive, fluorescent green drug, Mylotarg, was gently plunged into him. The nurse talked calmly and I probably nattered inanely as per usual. We had a window of 6 hours before Rob was out of danger of an allergic reaction. So Pip and I sat, we watched sport on TV, Rob dozed fitfully.

Pip needed to pop home. We were effectively camping in Cambridge at that time, in vacant nurses accommodation. I had a carrier bag of stuff with me; I needed some clean clothes and Pip needed to sort out our home, our life, the post and his work, all of which we had abandoned. We agreed a dash home for him was in order. Rob was five hours into the 6 and all seemed fine. Pip left uneasily, but with our blessing.

From: Lorraine

To: Friends

Sent: Sunday, July 3rd, 2011, 10.30PM

My Mum always taught me it was rude to eaves drop; however, I have just queued at the cash point machine in Addenbrooke's reception and - well I just couldn't help it.

These two young chaps, I can only gather, had been to visit their mate on another oncology ward. "My God that was hard work! I know he probably isn't feeling that good, and I suppose it's not much fun losing your hair, but he was so b****y miserable, not sure I can stomach that again." You would have been proud of me, both young men still have all their front teeth, and I said not a word.

How can people be like that?

Anyway, Rob is brighter today. His white count is down to 1, which from a starting point of 127 last Saturday is good. Chemo is vile, and that's if you are supporting, I can't begin to imagine what it's like if you're the one watching various quantities of different coloured stuff, some of which is light sensitive being plunged or dripped into you. Having thrown up from the start, they seem for now to be helping with the sickness. His haemoglobin is still low, 5, so he is having regular blood, and his clotting is "off" as the doctors put it, so platelets too. His gums are better today; perhaps that was the lolly at bedtime? His nose is bleeding every now and again, and he has blood in his urine which they are trying to sort. His chest infection is better but not quite gone, so still on stuff for that too. Huge bruises keep appearing in random places, we're terrified to touch him.

Rob signed himself up for a drug trial, and got the drug not the placebo. They have to tell you which side of the trial you fall if you are getting the drug so that you can opt out at any time. So he has had an extra bag of stuff called Mylotarg. We were warned that most people have a reaction to it, and so it would be hourly obs. for 6 hours. I had just allowed myself the luxury of thinking he had got away with it when 5 mins before the 6 hours were up, the shakes set in. I've always been a fan of Casualty and Holby City on TV, but I don't think I will ever consider them to be entertainment again. When everyone appears around you and you find yourself standing helpless in the corner of the room terrified you will get in someone's way or that whatever they are doing won't work its truly shocking. Anyway, jabs of this that and something else and calm was restored. He was due his next dose of chemo after that and they had to sedate him in order to do it - he was terrified, so was I.

Anyway, we are now day 5 of 10, cycle 1 of 4. We have been warned that we are likely to be here for around 5 weeks this time, and then back and forth for some months. We have settled into this strange world, and I think it is best not to fight it, just "keep calm, and carry on" as one of Robs cards says. I think I prefer the one with a picture of rather sweet meerkat sitting up in bed with a bandage around his head and thermometer.

Pip is doing brilliantly, having now mastered the art of pouring water from the jug into the glass without flooding the bed and the table, now we just need to brush up on his skills with the TV remote! Rob is patience personified - I am not.

I know you are thinking of us, and perhaps praying. That is a real comfort. My relationship with God is a little strained just now; in fact we're not speaking! I know we should be waiting to share in God's healing powers, but right now I haven't moved on from how he could possibly have allowed this to happen in the first place. I'm sorry that was a bit over dramatic, but I'm not going to delete it!

If you get the chance please email. It would be great to hear what's going on out there! I apologize if I have already said some of this, I lose track of who knows what.
Take care,
L. x

The following day dawned; I had spent the night in the chair next to Rob's bed. He had held my hand most of the night. Pip returned from his quick flit to Colchester, shaky to say the least. We were pleased he was back. We were in a two-bedded bay, sharing with a young lad called Sam. On top of Sam's leukaemia, he had Down's syndrome. Sam loved Morris Dancing, and listened to the music on his dad's laptop constantly. On this particular day Sam was fed up with listening through earphones, and felt, with a lot of enthusiasm, that we should all listen too. Rob managed a good few hours, but it had been a particularly testing time. The nurses took pity on Rob, and us, and Sam and Sam's parents too. As we had a good month ahead of us, when a single room became available later that day, Rob was wheeled in. Our first piece of privacy for a week, we were all immensely grateful.

From: Lorraine
To: Friends
Sent: Wednesday, July 6th, 2011

The consultant says Rob is where she would hope he would be; we take that as good news. His White count is now pretty much zero and they keep working on the red one. Yesterday was a day of nosebleeds and as Rob moaned what's the point of pumping it in one end only for it to come out my nose! Anyway more blood and platelets over night seem to have helped.

Rob has been a bit sad; the reality of unraveling Uni. has been a big blow. I have also started to try and talk to him about losing his hair. I suggested we might beat the chemo to it and clip his hair short - I got such a look I left it. I know what he is thinking - it will be the outward sign that he has cancer. I'll take my next cue from him.

Chemo is given morning and night now. Each bag takes hours to run through the drip. There were extra doses days

1 to 5 but now that his system is almost wiped out they just try to stop his bone marrow working completely for a bit. After day 10 the waiting begins and they monitor to see if/how/when the bone marrow regenerates. Healthy and free of Leukaemia would be good! L. x

****

The Rob George Foundation:

I mentioned that first single room we were put into. In that little room was a small fridge. The father of a previous young patient had donated it. What a wonderful gift. We could keep small pots of fresh fruit, yoghurts and fruit juices ready for Rob if he fancied them. Pip and I even put our sandwiches in it.

In the first 18 months of the RGF I have lost count of the white goods Pip has purchased on behalf of some of our grantees. His skill of purchasing online knows no bounds; he will also expound the virtues of www.easyfundraising.com at every opportunity.

At the Rob George Foundation, families who can't take their young person home from hospital, because they don't have a working cooker, fridge or freezer, often apply to us for help. Neutropenic patients need a clean diet, so all food must be prepared freshly, how can you achieve that with no fridge or cooker? Or maybe their washing machine has broken due to the mountains of laundry that chemo produces. A tumble dryer is almost essential, as chemo patients are really susceptible to damp environments, so a home with wet washing strewn all over the radiators to dry is not a suitable environment for them. Thank goodness for the wonderful supporters of the RGF who make these gifts possible.

We pride ourselves on helping with the unsexy needs of families facing these difficult times. We don't offer to make a young person a princess for a day, or send them on the holiday of a lifetime; we concentrate on the knitty gritty – we don't seem to have any competition for this kind of help. Applications arrive daily!

Chapter 5

Monday 4th May, 2015 – 9.00am, JOGLE Day 3 Tain to Fort Augustus (77.4 miles +3975ft)

Well, what a difference a night can make! As we gathered in the dining room for breakfast, the most magnificent view across Dornoch Firth and out to sea greeted us, closely followed by an equally stunning full Scottish cooked breakfast, served merrily by the wonderful Heather.

Day 3 was going to be spectacular – I just knew it. Of all the bits of the route I was most looking forward to, this was going to be a real highlight. I was so looking forward to seeing Loch Ness, and possibly even a monster, and the route only appeared to have one hill to mention, although we won't linger too long over the fact that it was a climb of over 1¼ kms – hah! Bring it on!!

My dear Mum had not shared my excitement over my Loch Ness experience. She'd travelled to Scotland years ago with my Dad and queried whether it even actually existed! Apparently they'd driven past Carlisle, towing the family caravan, and the rain had started falling. It continued to beat down, day and night, for the full 7 days of their holiday. On their day out to

Loch Ness, they'd boarded a boat, so as to get right up close and personal with Nessie. The combination of rain and mist meant that you couldn't see your hand in front of your face. Apparently Mum had insisted upon sitting up on the top deck, obviously wearing her holiday pack-a-mac, with the hood tightly tied under her chin, so as not to miss anything. As she said, she remains unconvinced that Loch Ness even exists! Well Monday 4th May 2015 was going to be different, and I was going to tell her all about it.

Loaded up and ready for action, we gathered outside the Carnegie Hotel. The tour moustache had spent the night on a radiator drying out and was duly presented to Antonius. From what I can remember it was Kevin's selection made on the basis of Antonius's impressive and various skills, whilst on a bike. A very worthy recipient, we all agreed. The staff came to wave us off, which was a lovely gesture and totally in keeping with one of the friendliest hotels I've ever stayed in. Immediately I knew I had a small problem with the trusty steed. Something was rubbing, the noise was pretty alarming, but more importantly it was really difficult to move forwards. Oh well, I'd get going and see what happened. Our bikes had taken a real hammering the previous day, out in all that wretched weather; they were bound to groan a bit today. Carl had oiled us all up, so fingers crossed everything would settle down.

If you look at a map of the area, and you want to cycle from Tain to Fort Augustus, you are not exactly spoilt for choice of roads. That's actually true for the whole of Scotland – I guess it's due to all that spectacular scenery – it gets in the way of too many highways. I really wanted to avoid the A9 at all costs – I'm allergic to traffic, you see - so a selection of minor roads was selected. We trundled out onto Scotsburn Road and back out into open countryside. It was glorious – apart from my bike.

It was a lovely day to be out on two wheels. It was still cold, but so bright and sunny. I even had my sunnies on. No distance at all up the road, I had to stop. It was no good – this really was too much like hard work. Pip, Abi, Elizabeth, Liz and I all pulled up and started poking and prodding various bits of the offending beast. It became clear that my problem was simply a mudguard issue. Everything was totally choked up with mud and debris from the previous day. We hunted for suitable twigs to try and free up my wheels and were fairly successful with the front wheel. The back one was not so good.

We'd been advised before we left home that if you are doing a long ride with a group of cyclists, and you want anyone to still be speaking to you by the end, you need mudguards – even on snazzy road bikes. When it's wet all the muck sprays up behind you and the cyclist following your back wheel gets a face full. It also makes an enormous difference to the state you end up in yourself, protecting your back from everything coming up off the road. Anyway, it became clear that my rear mudguard was beyond repair - but how to get it off? It was secured with cable ties; what we needed was a true boy scout.

Right on cue, Adi arrives. He developed a habit of arriving just in the nick of time. Out came his multi tool, and off came the offending rear mudguard – just like that, problem solved. And what do you do with a black plastic mudguard when you are in the middle of nowhere? Oh dear - and I'm not proud of this - you chuck it into the nearest ditch, and hope nobody sees you! I hate myself for having done this, I loathe litterbugs, and there is no excuse. If I had that moment of my life again I'd think of a different solution to that problem. When I repeat this trip, with the help of an engine, I promise to find that mudguard and deal with it appropriately. Anyway, our little group was rolling again, onwards and upwards.

National Cycle Route 1 is really pretty along this stretch. There are lots of wooded areas and on this day, even the sun had his hat on! The road ahead was dappled and enticing. The day felt full of promise. I think Abi might even have been singing – which is a bit of a mixed blessing! Sadly my cough was being a pain, and my chest felt really tight and wheezy; keep sucking the cough sweets!

With the wonderful benefit of hindsight I would realize that I had a pathetically slim grasp of how to read the map profiles on the GPS. Relatively late in the day I realized that the scale on the left hand side of the graph alters. The ride might be displayed and measured on a scale of 1cm = 100ft, or 1cm = 200ft, or as in the case of today, 1cm = 500ft. So you see, yesterday's hills looked the same as today's to the uninformed eye - sometimes technology makes you feel very old – and today's hills took us a bit by surprise. It turned out that at around 13 miles the road started to go upwards, and on and on it went – upwards. Liz was struggling to get her legs moving this morning. She'd gone like the clappers at the end of yesterday, and was perhaps now regretting it. Pip alerted me to the fact that she'd stopped a little way behind us, and as I turned to look, her head was resting on her handlebars.

I knew it could have been any one of us. So I suggested Pip, Elizabeth and Abi cycled on slowly, and I'd go back and have a chat; we'd catch them up. At that moment Liz was just so tired. I offered her a jelly baby and a smile and a hug. "I'll be fine," she said, "I just need a moment." We didn't mention the possibility of giving up, we talked about being a team – about us all finishing what we had started, together. I told her what Sam had said to me yesterday about "only being able to get into the van once."

It meant the world to me that Liz was there; we'd known each other for most of our lives. We'd met at dancing lessons, aged 5, and our friendship had endured from then. I vividly remember going around to Liz's for Saturday lunch after dancing as a child. Her dad was a glorious Yorkshire man; he liked to bake the week's bread on a Saturday morning. We'd arrive to the sight of him hammering three bells out of the week's dough, through a cloud of flour – her mum must have spent the rest of the week clearing up. When I had occasionally retreated to the parent's accommodation at Addenbrooke's Hospital, Liz was one of the people I had rung and cried/howled down the phone to – and she was still here for me, and Rob's memory.

Who knows whether it was my wonderfully inspiring pep talk, or the jelly babies hitting her stomach, but her tears dried, her smile returned and off we went. Neither of us ever spoke of possibly giving up again. We did however progress with a renewed respect for the challenge we had undertaken. When exhaustion hits, the decision to stop, would be totally understandable. It would help, though, if we could crack this blummin' hill. We finally reached the crest at mile 21, Mount Gerald – that was a 7 mile pull up – nice photo at the top though looking down over the Cromarty Firth and towards the Cromarty Bridge.

As we wiggled our way through Dingwall the Google Earth mapping vehicle, with the huge 360° camera mounted on the roof - I mentioned it earlier - overtook us. We laughed that we hoped they'd caught us on camera. I asked Abi if she thought my bum would look too big in their photo? Our ride would be captured for the World Wide Web and GPS maps of the future. Well, as I retraced our ride on my computer at home, there we are, Station Road, Dingwall. The four back markers of our team, pedalling for all we were worth towards Land's End. What a fine sight!!

Pip, Liz, Abi & Elle (google earth photo)

The main road after Dingwall gets a bit hairy, but our lovely National Cycle Route 1 diverts to run away from the road on a parallel path. Down we went, cycling over the River Conon and then upward towards Leanaig. We pause to catch our breath and as we looked behind us, the most stunning view of the mountains covered in snow, shining in the sun against the blue sky, filled our eyes. Scotland had its crown on that day. I'd take some persuading to repeat this trip as JOGLE - I think it was a once in a lifetime thing - but looking behind us, I did tinker with the idea that a LEJOG (Land's End to John O'Groats) might be worth a go. Perhaps I won't mention that to Pip for while? With that, the rest of the team appeared – I'm not sure from where as we thought we'd been at the back of the pack - I think probably from a local coffee shop, lucky them. We never managed to cycle fast enough to manage a coffee shop stop.

It was fun all being together, and we enjoyed the extra company as we pushed on towards Beauly, beyond which we were looking out for Carl and lunch.

34 miles under our belts, and there he was, with the picnic table set, and the kettle boiled. Fossie was excited as he had a friend locally who had been in contact; it was always very special when a message of support came in. As we stuffed our faces with pork pies and cheese rolls, Nicola started getting really excited. She'd just found an Internet signal and discovered that she'd received a really fantastic donation on her "My Donate" page. We were having a top day - well after yesterday, anything would have been an improvement - but this news really brought us up short. After all, this was all about Rob, and all about the Rob George Foundation too, for whom we were all busy trying to raise funds. But yes, we were having a blast along the way.

A couple of us were a bit disappointed. A dear friend from Colchester, Linda, who is Scottish and was up on her holidays, had said she would try and catch us on the bridge over the River Beauly. We must have missed her. Of course it was always going to be a long shot meeting up with anyone, but we still felt sad. Anyway, energy levels restored, we set off alongside the Beauly Firth, bound for Inverness.

We quickly spread out along the road. Even if it were desirable, it is dangerous to cycle in a large group, so small parties were the best way to proceed. We all shared the same laugh, though, as we cycled up the towpath of the Caledonian Canal and actually passed right alongside the Premier Inn from our first night in Scotland – we really were back where we'd started!

We wound our way through Canal Park, in search of the cycle path that would take us over the Islands in the River Ness. The way across was spotted, a small iron suspension bridge. The islands were full of people seeking a peaceful spot to walk, sit and read, look at the River, generally minding their own business. It's a proper cycle route so we weren't offending anyone, but as Linda leapt out of a bush with her camera clicking, the cheering undoubtedly shattered the peace.

It's really emotional when someone makes a huge effort to be part of your challenge. We were all so incredibly happy to see her. I spoke to Nigel H later that day; he had been in advance of us. He said the same – it really made the spirits soar. Linda recorded the moment and promised to be at the restaurant at the end of the day's ride. We had 31 miles left to conquer. I was looking forward to my dinner already, but we had the best bit of the day to come....

Loch Ness was our next landmark. Abi had been chattering all day about whether or not there was really a monster; well, we all wanted to believe there was! The final roundabout as we left Inverness was home to an entertaining sculpture of Nessie herself, surrounded by beautiful spring flowers. My normally sensible husband and Abi insisted upon throwing their bikes onto the grass verge, dodging the traffic to mount the roundabout for their photo to be taken – confirming that we are all children at heart. Mission accomplished – Nessie had graced our trip.

There had been a fair amount of debate about which approach to Loch Ness was the preferred option on a bike. Kevin had been given some fairly forthright advice – avoid the A82 at all costs. So that was pretty easy, the old Military Road on the south bank was our choice. Despite the promise of a big climb at the end of the day, I still don't regret that decision. The B862 rolls along, with the promise of the big reveal and the tantalising warnings that we might even see some red squirrels. On that day in early May 2015, we didn't see any red squirrels but the rest of the ride didn't disappoint.

The moment really should have been accompanied by music; something along the lines of the theme tune from "The Blue Planet" would have done nicely. We stopped, propped our bikes up against a farm gate and stared in wonder. Pip burst into tears; well it was "that" good! Loch Ness spread before us, reaching out into the distance. It was simply breath-taking. Surrounded by purple tinged mountains tipped with snow and lit by bright sunlight, it was a truly beautiful sight. And yes mum, it really exists!

Loch Ness is the second largest loch in Scotland, the largest being Loch Lomond. It is 23 miles long, and we were going to cycle the whole length. Our reward would be dinner at Fort Augustus in the recommended Boathouse Restaurant, and a good night's sleep, hopefully. The loch is full of fresh water, a volume that apparently exceeds the total of all the lakes in England and Wales combined. Its murkiness is caused by the high peat content, but we weren't planning on a swim, so we didn't worry about that. Our teary photos taken, Pip and I filing our hugs away, our memories of Rob and his promise to "be in every beautiful place" remembered, we set off once more.

Once you reach Dores the road clings to the water's edge. Off to your right hand side you can see, and indeed hear, the water lapping on the little stone beaches. Trees line the route, with the wooded hillsides becoming mountains pulling up to our left. We even passed a road leading towards the ski slopes of Aviemore on the landside, and across the loch to our right the mountains pulled away too. It was a magical and very special vista. The road is single track with passing places, but lots of parking spots too. Carl had been concerned that he'd struggle to park up the van for our afternoon tea break, but he needn't have worried – he could pick his spot, each one more stunning than the last.

People on road bikes, in my experience, can become a little neurotic about tarmac. I don't tend to share this preciousness. If you keep your tyres well inflated they cope with most things. I get more concerned about hitting a pothole on a main road, or getting sucked under the rear axle of a lorry as it overtakes me. Obviously you need to go steady on the loose stuff, but I'll have a go at most things. I think that, as a rule, almost by definition, road bikers are out to go fast. Bearing that in mind, perhaps I'm actually on the wrong kind of bike? Anyway, pootling along dear old General Wade's Military Road, I hardly blinked; it felt like my senses were on high alert. My research on this particular road had been unnecessarily alarmist, with warnings about shingle and damaged surfaces. I'm not sure which bits they were talking about, as a better track you couldn't have asked for. My chest was becoming increasingly concerning though, and even I could hear my wheezing.

As we progressed along the loch, I never did see the "un-missable" view of Urquhart Castle on the opposite bank. As I'd asked everyone at dinner the previous evening in my "notes for the following day" to keep an eye out for it, I felt particularly daft. It would appear though from our next debrief, that no one had seen it. I did however love the never-ending swathe of smiling lemon primroses.

My friend and cycle/ski buddy Elizabeth, who rather conveniently also happens to be a GP, was cycling with us, I think she knew I might potentially be in a bit of trouble – what a fab' friend. As we found Carl, parked up, admiring the view, Elizabeth chucked me her inhaler – "Have a quick puff, it'll help" – what a star!! I think Elizabeth had a much better grasp than me of the "hill" that lay ahead. If my chest closed up on me now, I'd never make it. She and I had talked so much whilst out training, about how much this ride meant to us both, I just know she wanted more than anything to try and make sure I made it.

We enjoyed mile after mile of this gently undulating road - well a truly flat road seems only to exist in my dreams! - and then the climbing began. You could say that we had enjoyed the lull before the storm.

The "big" hill starts at about 61 miles. It "only" lasts for 10 miles, and in that time we had to propel ourselves 1¼ km upwards. When we reached the summit, we had an amazing 6 mile equally steep downhill run into Fort Augustus – now that sounded like fun. Firstly, it should be called a mountain; it's not a hill. Secondly, whatever it looks like on the GPS profile, it's horrendous. Even if you can breath easily, it's a challenge to top all challenges.

Across the group we had all kinds of game plans. Claire and Antonius had been and gone hours ago, I assume having sailed up. Probably even they though would have the decency to break into a slight sweat, and then I can imagine them flying down the other side. Paul and Hazel were tackling it in their usual tandem formation. I did hear, though, that at Whitebridge, which is about a quarter of the way up this particular mountain, Hazel had had a bit of a lean on a local's fence. An old boy out stretching his legs asked her what she was doing. She explained our challenge and he simply agreed that it was a long way, and that "she shouldn't have started something she couldn't finish." Well that's sympathy for you! He continued a few steps, then swung around and came back towards the now much recovered figure stood glaring at her bicycle. He handed her a £1 coin and said, "You can either buy yourself an ice-cream or give it to the charity." Nigel H had set his heart on cycling to the top, steady but sure, but definitely non-stop. Go Nigel! Go!!

As we reached Whitebridge, the old boy dishing out ice-cream money was nowhere to be seen, but we did bump into a stunning young lady doing the LEJOG challenge. She, though, was totally independent. All her daily needs were contained in her pannier bags, along with her tent and cooking implements – we were truly impressed, and felt just a little bit inadequate by comparison. She was raising money for Leukaemia and Lymphoma Research – we shared a deeply meaningful hug.

Well these were all good efforts. Our rear group - that's Pip, Abi, Liz, Elizabeth and me - took a steadier approach. Elizabeth was now GP on duty, but she still insisted upon cycling every inch. However she did have to patiently wait here and there whilst Liz and I walked sections. Progress was steady – actually progress was pretty slow.

The road wiggles up the mountain, and you travel through dense forests, which in the early spring were still leafless. The trees were tall and spindly, and the forest floor deep in moss. It was like some sort of enchanted land. As the sun began to drop down, and glinted through the trees, I stopped to take one of my favourite photos of the trip. As I mentioned earlier, it has been known for Pip and I to enjoy Country-File on a Sunday evening on TV – that makes us sound so old – and every year they drone on and on about their calendar competition; well this photo is going to be my winning entry! It's very spooky!!

Eventually we'd climbed so high that we were, like yesterday, above the tree line. The road stretched ahead of us, reaching out for the summit. Nigel H later told me how his legs had been screaming at him, but he had just remembered Rob, and thought of how he would have loved to be doing this ride. He didn't stop until the top.

By the time the five of us reached the summit, it was getting a bit gloomy. You could indeed, see for miles in every direction, it was an awesome view; but it was now pretty cold, and we were exhausted. We dug very deep and found our enthusiasm for the spot. Terry was waiting for us, worried that we were going to miss our restaurant booking. Surely they wouldn't turn us away? Terry was dispatched to plead our case, and ask everyone else to go ahead to the venue, and order slowly! We stopped and looked round us. Suidhe viewpoint truly

Nigel H at the top – Suidhe

Rob
"on top of the world"
in the mountains of the Wadi, UAE, taken whilst he was in remission, 2012.

felt like the top of the world - well the top of Scotland anyway.

Now, you know how things that you have greatly looked forward to, so often fail to live up to your expectations? Well, a 6 mile steep down hill is a bit like that! As we departed Suidhe, the road literally fell away before us. It was a bit like launching yourself off the top of a giant rollercoaster. It was fun, for a bit, but then it got really fast. I gather Abi and Antonius recorded speeds in excess of 40mph! (Perhaps I've remembered that incorrectly and it should be kms?) I hung onto my brakes, but then my hands started to cramp and it wasn't quite so much fun. Having waited for hours to reach this section, it too seemed to go on forever. The reality is that I felt much more likely to injure myself falling whilst going too fast downhill, than at any point pushing my bike uphill. The rollercoaster continued until we just had to take a stop, and give our hands a shake and a rub. The other problem with going downhill is that you get really cold and stiff. Well, there is simply no pleasing some folks!

As we paused, the silence was eerie. Then Pip suddenly whispered and pointed up to the skyline to our right. It was jaw-dropping, a magnificent herd of deer, with a couple of handsome hugely antlered fella's as well, perfectly silhouetted against the evening sky. We all kind of eyeballed each other, and then they started to gallop down towards the road. I did manage to snap a couple of shots on my phone, but this was a moment I didn't want to miss fumbling around with a camera, I needed this memory clearly in my head. The stags led the way, simply leaping from one side of the road, clearing the fence, the road and the other fence, into the field on the other side – it was incredible. Now you see, if we had been cycling as fast as everyone else, we'd have missed that!

We let the brakes off, lifted our feet off the tarmac and allowed ourselves to pick up a bit more speed. It was quite exhilarating, but I did feel just a teensy bit out of control. We wound our way down to the banks of Loch Tarff and found ourselves somewhat bizarrely on a brand new stretch of road – it was like cycling on a smooth airport runway. Suddenly coming towards us was a car, headlights blazing, and horn tooting.

Don't panic, it was Linda, she'd come to find us – I think she was hungry. Linda was able to confirm that we were indeed nearly there – thank heavens for that!

As we entered the little village of Fort Augustus, there tucked into the side of the road were John and Jean, frantically waving their homemade banner. They too, were in Scotland on holiday, and had come to cheer us on. It meant the world. We were exhausted, and cold, starving hungry, but now we felt supported and loved too. Well, we felt all of those things anyway, but it was good to feel even more loved and supported!

Terry guided us into our B & B for the night, and there, patiently waiting on the pavement for us to arrive, or more especially Abi to arrive, was Nigel C – Abi's dad. Fresh from his family wedding and keen to get started, the full line up of 16 cyclists was now complete and the banter, especially between Nigel C and Abi, and Nigel C and Adi, rose to a new level.

Our party was split between two establishments. One side of the road was the converted Royal Bank of Scotland building, where some were staying, whilst we were staying at Caledonian House on the other side, and on the banks of the Caledonian Canal itself. The welcome was warm, and our arrival timely, if massively overdue, but I have to say, it was the smallest hotel room you can imagine. There was everything you would expect to find in a B & B room with en-suite facilities, but having achieved all of that, the result was that there was actually no floor left. We were so tired, but we enjoyed a good laugh. Having got ourselves and our two bags into the room, there was no-where to actually put them to open them up, apart from on the bed, but then I had flung myself diagonally across that! Pip got himself sorted quickly for a shower, which proceeded with a great amount of banging and crashing. In the event he had to shower with the door left open, he is tallish, with long limbs, and it simply wasn't possible to get all of himself into the shower and close the door! It was hilarious! I had no such difficulties!

We quickly turned ourselves around and strolled down to the Boathouse Restaurant. It is adjacent to the canal lock-gate, connecting Loch Ness to the Caledonian Canal at its most southerly point and it literally hangs out over the water. The position and the view on that night were awesome. The food was pretty good too! The Boathouse was bustling and bursting at the seams with customers. Our friends John, Jean and Linda joined us; it was such a special evening. All briefings and speeches would need to wait for the morning, as we all concentrated on food and conversation. Nigel H and I found ourselves standing on the beach, just looking and thinking. The evening light was finally fading. The water glowed a deep rose colour, and was calm, shining like glass. "In every beautiful place" Rob had promised. I definitely felt his arms around me that evening.

****

I am certain that I will repeat this feeling over and over again during the course of writing this book, but at the risk of annoying anyone kindly reading this, I'm going to make my point again here. Of course, our ride was all about reaching Land's End, but it, for me, was also very seriously about enjoying the journey.

My typical bedtime reading is usually of the "totally trashy" category, but I am currently rather surprisingly reading a book by Danny Scheinmann, a double love story (no surprise there then!) with one of the main characters being a soldier who escapes from a Prisoner of War Camp and walks thousands of miles across Siberia to return to his young love. The following struck a cord with me:

"He has travelled the globe but when his friends ask him to describe the wonders of the world he is unable to reply, for his eyes have been blinded by the sun. Now what I am suggesting is that you remember your journey and forget the arrival. Otherwise you too will be blinded, and you will grow old like me and wonder where your life has gone, and you will realize that you spent all your life planning for a future that never happened.

Find your happiness now, and if you happen to find your love you will double it."

Danny Scheinmann, (Random Acts of Heroic Love) - I think we're on the same page!

****

July 2011, Chemo Cycle 1 of 4

Pip had nipped home and brought back all the post. Various parcels were distributed, mostly cards and gifts for Rob, brown envelopes for Pip and me. One of these was a squidgy padded envelope obviously containing something interesting. Rob opened this envelope first, unwrapped the item carefully encased in kitchen towel and then replaced the item back into the envelope. He stretched out his arm to give the item back to Pip, and calmly said "You'll need to return this for me please Dad."

The envelope had contained his key for his new student house in Loughborough. The sky came crashing down, at that moment, all his plans totally unravelled. He had to admit that he wouldn't be going back to Loughborough that October. A year out was going to be the only sensible course of action.

From: Lorraine
To: Friends
Sent: Friday July 8th, 2011

I am tired today and short tempered. I am fed up of losing things even though I only have a handful of stuff here but everything is in a muddle. I always knew I was a bit of a control freak but now that is confirmed - and this is all so out of my control. I think the thing of the moment for me is the total lack of personal space. It's our 29th wedding anniversary on Sunday, Rob will receive his final dose of chemo for this cycle that morning, and we have always enjoyed being together, but I had not realized how much I also enjoy being alone. I like my own space and silence. You wouldn't believe that of someone so noisy would you? When we are not with Rob we are together, it's kind of suffocating. That is so selfish and of course it doesn't matter in the grand scheme of things, but it's today's emotion. I'll get over it - quickly.

I just said to Wendy who was nattering whilst standing tin rattling for SAM's at the time, we seem to be entering the lull before the storm stage here. Rob is sad/tired/bored by rotation but is currently having to face the unraveling of his plans for Uni' next year, not helped by the key for his planned house share arriving in the post the other day. Anyway we'll just have to get on with all that. I am tired and I think sort of numb? We have settled into this strange world surrounded in part by people even worse than Rob and then the moaning masses who think they are extremely ill and actually (the way I feel right now) have much to be grateful for and very little to moan about!!

Sorry, I don't mean to be cranky but I'm slightly stuck in the "it's not fair" groove but I suppose it is finally time for me to grow up, and acknowledge that sometimes life just isn't fair! Apologies for my mood! We all intend to bounce back from all this, but probably not any time soon.

Lorraine. X

Somewhere around this time the decision was made to give Rob a Hickman Line. This central line (not to be confused with the London Underground line with the same name!) is a long thin tube that is inserted into a vein on the chest, in this case going straight into the vein leading to Rob's heart. This would allow drugs to be given and blood samples to be taken without the constant need to use needles. Rob agreed willingly to this – he hated needles. The Hickman Line could stay in for months so long as it stayed infection free and didn't get blocked. This was to be our next experience of being "off the ward". After our experience at the Fertility Clinic I should have been prepared, but it still took me by surprise – it wouldn't be the last time.

We accompanied Rob, as his bed was wheeled through the hospital labyrinth, to be greeted by a young man who was simply way too chirpy! Over the years we would get to know this chirpy chap better than we would have liked! He would greet Rob like a long lost friend, or maybe just a regular customer. Obviously there were other patients in the department waiting, too, all in varying degrees of perkiness, but mostly aged, and to Rob's amusement mostly lacking their teeth. Pip and I were busy wearing our brave faces. The stress of the past days was catching up with us, and the idea of watching him be wheeled away, for any procedure without us, certainly had me on edge.

Again, the first mistake of the day was a lack of preparation. Because Rob was young, the assumption by almost everyone we came across who were not directly connected to the leukaemia ward was that he had "done something silly" or was here as a result of something that "was his own fault". Rob's old cricket master, Roger, was very fond of motivational quotes, which he would plaster all over Colchester Royal Grammar School's changing rooms: "Fail to prepare, Prepare to fail!" was one of his favourites. Well that seemed fairly apt on this occasion. To be greeted by the question "Well what have you been up to?" was an insensitive start, and Rob looked daggers at the chap and suggested he read his notes. He was totally exhausted and the simple act of breathing was a major effort for him; that this bloke could in the name of chitchat be so insensitive was insulting. Then this bloke starts flapping about the place. It appears that when the notes had been read, due to all the chemo and other drugs roaring around in Rob's system he is what is classified as "hot". The irony of "being hot" was not lost on Rob either, but what it meant was that he had to be kept away from everyone else. So more hasty shuffling of beds, and being made to feel like some kind of leper, and we are tucked into a corner, out of harm's way.

Rob is eventually wheeled away, into the operating room, and it felt like my arm had been ripped off. Without Rob there to see me, I cried. I couldn't stop, and Pip tried his best to comfort me. Everyone had a good old stare, and I couldn't have cared a less.

Rob was sedated for the procedure, and a local anesthetic used, but he was not totally anesthetized. Once the line was in Rob was wheeled back out into the recovery area. By this time the exhaustion/relief/sedation had kicked in and he was fast asleep. Actually snoring his head off – quite an impressive amount of noise was emanating from his handsome self! – and sorry, but no, I wasn't going to disturb him to shut him up – it was the first time he had been properly asleep for days and days – everyone could simply put up with it! When Rob stirred, he looked around him and said, "Just get me back to the ward please." "That chap", for all his chirpiness, had failed Rob. Rob had been made to feel uncomfortable, and felt mis-understood. What a horrible way to be left feeling when you are too sick to fight your own corner!

From: Lorraine
To: Friends
Sent: Monday July 18th 2011

Life right now has taken a turn for the bizarre. Pip and I were staying in perfectly good parents accommodation on the hospital site. Yesterday amidst a fanfare of trumpets we were moved to a brand new flat, complete with cedar cladding, solar panels, and landscaped gardens, every possible facility but no toilet brush, loo rolls or t-towels!

These flats have been provided by the Karen Morris Memorial Trust; for patients, and families of relatives suffering from leukaemia. I'm not sure what the weirdest bit is, but the luxury/kid glove treatment, beside this young woman's death is an uncomfortable mix, and one you can't articulate because you might look ungrateful. It's beautiful but I wish I weren't here, or at least we are here because Rob is struggling over the road, anyway...

Rob is now neutropenic, and has a chest infection which the doctors are struggling to get under control. We are waiting for the respiratory specialist to come and see him with the view to putting a tube into his lungs later to try and take a sample and pinpoint the infection. Rob is terrified and exhausted. Chemo finished on Sunday morning and although it was a landmark, strangely, it has left Rob feeling a bit depressed. He says he feels as if they have stopped doing anything now - I can see what he means. Of course that is not really true. He is on two anti biotics and an anti fungal drug to try and keep him infection clear - it's just that they are not working at the moment.

He is as white as the hospital sheets due to the anaemia and is being given regular transfusions and platelets (nose bleeds are less frequent but still happen.)........

From the moment of diagnosis, it seems no matter what concoction of jollop was dripped into Rob, his chest wouldn't clear. The Consultant settles into a chair alongside Rob's bed, which is never a good sign, and opens talks on the subject of trying to establish, once and for all, whether the infection is viral or fungal. In order to do this a bronchoscopy is suggested.

Rob had no idea what that is, and so the gaps are filled. He will visit another department of Addenbrooke's, will be given heavy sedation and a tube will be passed into his lungs to take a sample for the labs. He won't remember a thing!

Reluctant doesn't come close to Rob's reaction; pass a tube into his lungs via his throat – not on your nelly! What is the answer for a parent in this situation, especially one when you are leap frogging from on the one hand being the parent of officially an adult, and then on the other where that particular adult would rather be a child and asks you to be the parent? So, we set to, trying to persuade him that, this particular test, which is done as a matter of routine, will be fine.

He demanded to meet the Consultant that would actually perform the procedure. She came to his room and made all the expected assurances. In fact she absolutely promised him that he wouldn't even know what was going on. Speed was of the essence, and she could fit him in later that morning. Rob signed on the dotted line. Before we knew what was going on, a porter had arrived and we were off to pastures new.

The Endoscopy suite at Addenbrooke's in July 2011 was shiny and new, and huge. It is like half a football pitch, with a capacity of at least 50 beds. I shudder to think what it is like when it's in full swing. On this day, at this time, Rob made the third patient. Despite all the available space, despite his susceptibility to infection, despite how ill he was, despite his age, he was placed right next to the only two another patients. A young nurse auxiliary was assigned to "keep an eye" on Rob, who immediately filled us with no confidence at all, by despite the "nil by mouth" sign attached to his bed, offering him a glass of water! Well I soon put her straight! Then the nurse "in charge" came over to make sure they'd got the right patient!

It was like an action replay of our last jaunt off the ward. This nurse immediately launches into jolly chitchat, asking Rob, "Well, what on earth have you been up to young man? I hope you had a good time landing yourself here." Rob turned his face away from her, unable even to speak. I was furious and told her I thought she should go away and read Rob's notes. She did, and in fairness did return with a completely different demeanour, but of course the damage had already been done.

We watch and hear the aged lady in the next bed receive her pre-procedure chat, and pre-med and drift off to sleep. Not before, though, we have heard her shout at her Consultant "As long as you don't stick that camera down my throat like last time, I thought I was going to die!" By the volume required to communicate with her we could only assume that she was a little hard of hearing. She is wheeled off and her procedure is completed. All the while we could hear everything that was being said to her, even as she was wheeled into the treatment room. I guess on a busy day, this wouldn't have been a problem. Rob looked more and more stressed. The old dear was returned, and still we waited. A little time later the Consultant of our neighbour reappears, and draws the curtains around them. "Have you done it?" "What did you find?" the old lady asks. The Consultant shouts, "It's fine Mrs. X. I've had a good look around your stomach and you definitely don't have cancer!" "Well lucky old her!" Rob muttered. Are these people so completely insensitive, so utterly crass that they think we couldn't hear them? The whole thing beggared belief.

Rob's pre-med is administered, and we sit and wait. Apparently any minute Rob will begin to feel dozy and with any luck will nod off. Well, he was wide-awake, not surprising really! Surprise is expressed at his perkiness and a top up dose given. In the end the decision is made to get on with it. They will sedate him in the theatre and Rob doesn't need to worry about a thing.

As Rob was wheeled away, with a look of sheer terror on his face, we had to let him go. We needed the doctors to be able to treat him, and they needed the information that this test would give them. The clock ticked and we waited. In the depths of my soul I knew things were taking too long.

Eventually Rob reappeared. It's hard even now replaying the look on his face, as he was wheeled back out into the huge, now completely empty cavern of the treatment suite. His eyes were on cocktail sticks; he began talking almost hysterically as soon as he saw us. Essentially the sedation had not worked. His stress levels and so his metabolism were running so high and fast that however much sedation was given, all it did was raise his heart rate, it didn't have the desired effect in sending him to sleep, or even making him relax. They had proceeded with the bronchoscopy with him wide-awake. "I thought I was going to drown! I couldn't breath," he sobbed. I can't imagine what it must have felt like to be fully aware of the wash being pumped into his lung, before it was flushed out, to be analysed in the laboratory. The whole thing was hideous. How could the procedure have been so far from the one he was promised? We couldn't wait to get back to our familiar ward. What a pitiful mis-management of the whole thing though? You won't be surprised to hear that I did fill in and submit a "Patient feedback card" to the hospital. Not about the procedure, but about our experience whilst waiting. I believe that if Rob had been offered a better level of care whilst waiting, his stress levels would have been better managed, and then (maybe) the sedation might have worked. Caring in hospital is not just about the obvious medical needs; it can be totally wrecked if the rest of the care isn't joined up too.

The final twist in that particular little saga was, that the sample taken didn't give any clear diagnosis, when looked at under a microscope. So Rob considered the whole process to have been for nothing. However, the chest infection did then begin to ease, the view being that the wash had actually done some good in its own right.

........previous email continues

He has agreed to let me take my scissors back with me later and take something off his hair. It will start to fall out any day now and I think it may be less of a shock if we take it slightly by degrees - it is pretty long right now (apparently he didn't bother about a hair cut whilst at Uni, in order to save money!)

I think nursing your sick child is horrendous. People think they know how you feel, and thank goodness mostly you have not got a clue. Pip is dealing with all this in his own way - so we don't actually say the words then it will all be fine, but one of us has to be brave enough to try and let Rob talk, so that is me. Pip leaps around pouring squash and ringing the bell for the nurses and when Pip can be persuaded to leave the room for a bit I stroke Rob's head and we talk about what is frightening him.

Writing this email feels totally selfish as if I am trying somehow to suck the life out of all of you, to try and bolster our own strange existence here. It also flies in the face of that "stiff upper lip" we all so bravely hide behind - I'm not feeling particularly brave today I suppose. I hope you don't all feel as if you have to walk around with long faces all day just because the George's are struggling right now, please don't do that. I know we are leaning on you all heavily just now and thank you for being there for us, it's just so much easier when you are sharing good news isn't it? Please share your good news with us now, life is rumbling on, I know.

Rob's hair was going to start falling out – soon. He had managed to grow a fairly impressive mop during his first year at Loughborough, arguing that he hadn't had a haircut as he was economizing! He was very fond of this "floppy" look, although it had irritated me with it in his eyes all the time, but now, of course, I loved it! I decided to head off into Cambridge City Centre on the bus, my first trip away from the ward. My destination was a shop call Hollister – Rob's favourite – but certainly a new experience for me. I was in search of a hat, preferably one of a trendy trilby variety, that I hoped would help.

Firstly you don't find a Hollister shop by looking. I now know you find it by breathing deeply, perhaps that's in preparation for the massive hit your credit card is about to take? I had walked up and down the area of the precinct I thought it was to be found on, but with no luck. I hailed a random trendy looking young person to be told that the shop was the one that looked a bit like a Chinese restaurant from the front, but that if I sniffed deeply I'd be able to smell it before I saw it! Well, actually, he was right!

Once inside I suddenly felt very old. It's dark. There is a large screen upon which the sea is being projected relentlessly crashing onto a sun-drenched beach and all the clothes appear to be in heaps. (Just as an aside, how do folks work with all that water sloshing around them all day? I'd never get out of the lo) I suppose I didn't really have the patience that day so ended up flagging down a bright young thing that looked very like Rob and was a similar build to him too, although he didn't have tubes in his chest, and, if someone had turned the lights on, probably looked a picture of health. Anyway, about to lose it big time, I briefly explained the situation. I told this delightful, if somewhat surprised young man that if he could please go and select me some joggers, a sweatshirt, a t-shirt and a hat that he might like himself, I'd be sitting on this couch by the till. He probably thought I was mad – even Rob laughed and rolled his eyes when I recounted the story. It's a total reflection of his delicious sense of humour that he sent me there in the first place!

Anyway, whilst Rob loved the clothes, he hated the hat. It sat on his hospital locker, and was regularly glared at. Then one morning the inevitable happened, the first handful of hair came away. Why doesn't anyone warn you? I think we had kind of imagined that when Rob's hair started to fall out, it would do it gradually. Perhaps becoming thinner and thinner – but no, suddenly a damn great handful comes away, and you are left with a shiny patch of scalp. Then another one falls away, somewhere else on your head. Your pillow is quickly matted with loose hair. It's itchy, it's horrible, and it won't stop. And so, Rob agreed that I should take the clippers to his head, and shave the remaining clumps off. I spread a newspaper on his hospital room floor, he sat on a chair with his head forward and eyes closed, and I did the business. It was no fun. I'd regularly clipped Sam's head, he liked a No. 2, but this was different. Of course it doesn't stop there. His armpits and privates became bald. His eyebrows thinned, and even the stubble on his chin fell away. At that moment there are few words to be shared.

The look completed, Rob walked into his bathroom and stared into the mirror. He looked totally heart-broken. "It's like a badge," he said. "Now everyone will know I have cancer." Pip offered to shave his head too, in support. Rob retorted, "What's the point, no-one will notice the difference!"

I know you'll maybe be thinking, he's a boy, so why does that matter? But it mattered to Rob. You might choose to shave your hair off, that's one thing, but being forced to endure it all falling out, is quite another. His cancer would no longer be private, everyone would see. He lay down on his bed, and turned his head away from us, towards the wall – he didn't and wouldn't speak to us.

At that point I remember wishing so badly that it could have been me rather than my precious Rob. Failing that I would even have rather it had been Pip. I know that sounds terrible, but before you judge me too harshly, you need to stand in my shoes. People talk about how much a parent loves its child; in this situation I felt it like a real wound, a wound so deep inside me that nothing could help. Not a dull ache that will fade with time, but like a knife, that threatened to take my life, my life as I knew it.

From: a special friend
To: Lorraine
Sent: in response to July 18th 2011

Oh Lorraine, it was so nice to hear from you, and yes it did make me cry reading your email because I get what you're going through. I think about you all every day. I think back to my son and his meningitis and I couldn't even think about what might happen to him and if he did recover if his brain had been affected but his recovery was quite quick, poor Rob has such a long road to walk before he improves and that is so exhausting and depressing. I remember "X" just crying in my arms as he felt so weak, couldn't even walk to the toilet, using commodes, not nice for an 18 yr. old. He cried and I hugged him and smoothed his forehead too, always our babies aren't they!!!! Rob must be feeling awful, with the chest infection on top of all the chemo and anemia; it's more than we could even imagine. He is a very brave boy/man and as all of your boys will fight with all of his being to combat this. It's so hard for you and Pip too to

hide your fear from Rob, I never know what the answer is to be open or hide your emotions? Pip obviously likes to do the practical stuff, that's me a bit, if I keep getting drinks may be things will go away!!! But then I also want to just shut the world out and hold him and say everything will be ok.
I'm so glad that accommodation is provided, these places are a god send for people like you, it amazes me how good people are to raise the funds to make one part of this horrendous illness a bit easier. Take care. x

Pip and Elle, with Ben Nevis?

Chapter 6

Tuesday 5th May, 2015 – 10.00am, JOGLE Day 4 Fort Augustus to Taynuilt (79.1 miles +3743ft)

Day 4 was probably the day I was looking forward to the least. The route sort of chose itself – and it was going to be predominantly main roads. I awoke feeling pretty rough, but there was nothing for it but to get myself moving and put on a brave face. Nobody was going to cycle my bike for me, and you often feel better once you get going, so off I went.

Breakfast was delicious, but took ages to serve. Our B & B ran a slightly later timetable first thing to the converted Royal Bank of Scotland opposite, so our breakfast room became cosy with those that were already full of sausages from over the road. It did however offer us the opportunity to do the day's briefings and present our "Moustache Award". Nigel C had no idea what was going on, although he learnt fast as Antonius awarded it to him, for "turning up 3 days late, and missing Day 2!" Spirits were high, yesterday had been spectacular, and of course today saw our party finally completed. Nigel C, Abi's dad, was all togged up in his pristine kit and raring to go.

We pulled out onto the A82 and faced our customary uphill warm-up. We had already agreed we were to keep to single file all day. There would be no chitchat along the way, everyone had to concentrate and keep safe. We had allsorts whizzing around our ears and one of the most memorable things for me was that suddenly it was really noisy. Our first 3 days had been peaceful, surrounded only by nature, even if that was the sound of the wind and rain on Day 2, but this was juggernauts, buses and cars. It wasn't pleasant.

We cycled past Fort Augustus Golf Club, and I gave a salute to Rob, who I felt sure was teeing off on the first green. Everywhere we'd ever been with Rob in the car, he'd had his head on a swivel if we went past a potential outing for the clubs. He loved his golf and he was pretty good too, playing off a handicap of 4 at his best. Mind you, he should have been - the hours he spent practising!

The road dipped up and down, the days profile being a really spikey one. There appeared to be only one potentially flattish section between 30 and 38 miles; the rest of the trip was going to be a continuous series of gear changes. If we got lucky it would be the kind of terrain where the downs actually help you get up the ups – if you see what I mean! If we were unlucky, it would be a long day of constantly trying to find the most appropriate cog and chain combination.

The first expanse of water today was Loch Uanagan, but we flashed past that in an early burst of energy; then we dropped down and crossed over the river to ride alongside Loch Oich. At the point where the River Garry oozes out of Loch Oich we snuck off to the left so as not to miss Glengarry Castle. Unfortunately by this point, some 7 miles into our ride, it had started to rain. Where had this weather come from, the sun had been shining down the road? Everyone stopped and foraged around for their waterproof gear. It was a shame, but there was no alternative. I hate cycling in waterproof trousers, they seem so restrictive, but it's best to try and keep dry for as long as possible.

Anyway, nobody was in the least bit interested in Glengarry Castle, so onwards we went. Nicola's bike started playing up, with her chain slipping here and there. We all made sympathetic noises, and hoped it would come to nothing. We found ourselves back on the A82 and onto the lower stretch of Loch Oich. The roadsides were heavily wooded and it was quite dark and gloomy. Through the trees we could see the loch with the rain bouncing off it. There was little wind, and the water was still. It was a shame really that the rain was so distracting, and then there was the traffic to worry about, too. I hope I don't come across as a total wimp? - but I hate it when you get overtaken, especially by a long vehicle. They seem to cut in just a second or two too soon, and their rear wheels come whistling past your shoulder. Everyone is in such a hurry, I guess we cyclists do get in folks way. "Time and tide waits for no man" – and all that!

The road then runs parallel to the Caledonian Canal running through the lochs into Ceann Loch. I would love to do that run on a canal barge; it must be stunning, starting at the coast, running from Inverness, along Loch Ness, then down through the various lochs, finishing on the west coast of Scotland and Fort William. I had picked this route especially to follow the route of the canal, because I thought the road would be flat; well, it wasn't too bad! I also knew it would be stunning; unfortunately, the view was fast disappearing! The Scottish weather had arrived again; it's a real show stealer!

The second fall of the tour was along this next stretch of the A82. Only the group of "elite" cyclists witnessed it, but by all accounts it was a classic. They'd just gone past John and Jean who had gone ahead of us in their car to continue their support and banner waving – what fabulous friends! There were some road works and as they approached the traffic lights, they rather inconveniently changed to red. I'm not sure of the details, but there was a bit of gesticulation between Claire and an unknown, unsympathetic driver. She decided to eyeball the said driver and managed to cycle straight into a very large signpost, you know the sort, triangular, white with a big red border, a warning sign, huge!! Everyone, including Claire saw the funny side of it, but she was lucky not to be badly hurt; even her pride only suffered a tiny dent – not sure about the road sign though?

We realised that there was a group approaching us from the rear. We should have known that was because something was wrong and not because we had suddenly speeded up! Nicola's bike was off the road. We were told Terry was with her in the car and they were working through the options. We did have spare bikes on Carl's van for such an eventuality, but Nicola has a dodgy thumb, and needed her own bike, with its specialist electric gear changer. If her bike went down, she was going to be out altogether. As we huddled together in that particular lay-by we all took a second to think about the knife edge we all rode between remaining in the game, and being out. A bit like life in general really – it doesn't take much for your own personal house of cards to come tumbling down. We needed some luck alongside our best efforts and determination if our challenge was to succeed.

As we pushed on towards Fort William we were all a bit gloomy. We were potentially one rider down; nobody wanted that to happen. Despite the torrential rain by this point, we decided to pause at the Commando Monument, with its famous backdrop of Ben Nevis. I think you should always find time to remember those who have made the ultimate sacrifice for our freedom. It is a very poignant memorial, dedicated to the men of the original British Commando Forces raised during World War II. It's near Spean Bridge and overlooks the training areas of the Commando Training Depot established there in 1942 at Achnacarry Castle. It was sculpted in 1949 by Scott Sutherland, who won a prize of £200 for this fabulous work in bronze.

As we stood there, trying to identify Ben Nevis through the heavy rain-dispensing clouds, we thought of Abi's previous visit, a year earlier, on her 3 Peaks Challenge. There was no chance of her recognising it, we laughed. Abi, like Pip, preferred to cycle with no Garmin. These were the small navigational units most of us liked to have strapped to the front of our bikes, to ensure we didn't get lost. Abi, like Pip, didn't really want to know where she was going. They both shared the same focus on Land's End - what else was there to know? Abi wouldn't realise she was on familiar territory, and today she'd steamed off with her Dad, disappearing ahead of us, so we missed the opportunity to rib her on the subject.

The three bronze Commandos looked extraordinary on this day. They appeared to sparkle against the almost black sky, as the car headlights reflected in the rivulets of rain cascading down their metallic bodies. "United we conquer" is the inscription on the stone plinth – oh crikey, welling up again!

As we pulled out onto the main road, Terry screeched to a halt, wound down his window (well he was hardly going to get out of his car in this weather, was he?) to tell us that Nicola had hopefully fixed her bike. Now there's girl power for you! She'd taken her bike apart on the roadside and put it back together, and that appeared to have made all the difference. I'm sure there was more to it than that, but you get the idea. She was right at this moment cycling like the clappers to catch us up; could we dawdle a bit to help her? I didn't like to tell Terry that our top speed was actually already technically a dawdle compared to the speeds Nicola was capable of!!

Our route took us right past the front doors of the Ben Nevis Distillery. I think we could have justified a trip inside for a tasting on many levels:

1. We were waiting for Nicola,
2. Medicinal reasons – doctor's orders for my chest,
3. .... oh well 1 and 2 are pretty compelling reasons!

Anyway needless to say we pressed on. A long dis-used railway bridge took us over the River Lochy and past the entrance to Old Inverlochy Castle. We wiggled past the battle site of the Battle of Inverlochy and found ourselves in downtown Inverlochy proper. The rain was continuing to pour but our attention was caught by a group of excited cyclists exiting a small cycle shop. Of course, no one else would be out on their bikes on a day like this; we had to know them. It was Claire, Antonius and Max, all looking extremely smart, not to mention a little smug. "There's nothing left in Medium, Large or X Large," they declared. The shopkeeper couldn't believe his luck. They'd bought up his whole stock of wet weather gear – and didn't they look pleased with themselves too! It was a totally happy blur of fluorescent kit that disappeared into the murk ahead of us.

We came along the water's edge of Loch Eil into Fort William. The recurring problem of needing a wee was occupying our minds and Elizabeth spotted a Morrison's – unfortunately on the other side of a dual carriageway. I refused to deviate off course, which of course was completely unreasonable of me. Then flying down the dual carriageway, threatening to overtake us, we see Nicola. We are carefully keeping to the designated cycle path running adjacent, and she was obviously in a panic with no idea of exactly how far behind she might be. It was a wonderful reunion. Fortunately not far up the road we found the lay-by we had been expecting to find occupied by Carl and our lunch, but instead it was filled with the participants of a National Scramble Bike Competition. How kind of them to place a row of half a dozen pristine porta-loos for our convenience!

As we pulled out of Fort William, there was Carl. On another day it would have been a very scenic spot. Overlooking the loch, watching the boats coming in and out of the harbour with a fabulous view of the mountains on the far side. I remember thinking that I needed to be especially careful crossing over the road to get into the lay-by. I also remember clocking that there was a lot of gravel lying about. The next thing I remember was landing flat on my face in amongst the rack of bikes of those who had already arrived. Not a very elegant entrance to lunch, and actually my elbow hurt too! (It did take my mind off my cough though!) Anyway, I was helped to my feet, which wasn't as easy as it might sound, as I somehow or another was still cleated onto my bike. I dusted myself down and looked around to see who had been looking, only to find Elizabeth in a similar state of fluster. Apparently, completely separately, she had repeated the performance herself. Well I did say she was a good friend – but really?

More picnic food was consumed, and more banter exchanged. Nigel C was new to all this, and had a go at complaining about how cold and wet he felt. Oh dear, that started it! No one had any grounds to moan unless they had endured Day 2. This was nothing by comparison – you should have seen Day 2!! We all wrung out our gloves, straightened the peaks of our rain caps under our helmets and got ready to depart. Antonius had been darting around with his Go Pro camera over lunch asking folks what they thought of it so far. You can imagine the sort of replies he'd recorded! Claire, Antonius and Max got ready to pull out into the traffic, and gave us all a cheery wave. But that ruddy layby wasn't finished with us yet. Antonius didn't quite get it right and as his back wheel hit the wet tarmac, over he went! Thankfully the road was clear. He is a super-talented cyclist, and almost bounced up as quickly as he had gone down – but there was no getting away from it, Antonius was the fifth fall of the ride.

The next 30 miles hugged the shoreline, tracking Loch Linnhe all the way to Creagan. The cycle path from South Creagan is newly constructed and follows the old track bed of the former Ballachulish railway line. I know it's a bit sad, but I was really looking forward to seeing Pip's face on this bit. He is a complete anorak on the subject of trains, and I knew he'd love being on an old railway route. His reaction didn't disappoint me – he loved it, stopping to read all the wayside information boards. We all enjoyed it, and our group of Abi, Elizabeth, Pip, me and now Nicola, too, took some lovely snaps of this traffic-free section, utilizing Abi's new selfie stick.

The route comes along the banks of Loch Creran, passing alongside Oban Airport and through to North Connel. The single file bridge crossing over to Connel on the south side was a bit of a challenge. The traffic was controlled by timed traffic lights and the pressure was on to clear the bridge before being headed off by the oncoming cars. Mind you, the incredibly fast flowing water underneath us did act as a good incentive to get a move on. I'd looked forward to the promised view across to Dunstaffnage Castle, but I'll have to see that next time too.

Ardmucknish Bay flows in towards Taynuilt; we had 7 miles to go. The A85 was not very friendly, and the weather continued to throw itself at us from all directions. Everyone, but especially me, was totally fed up of the coughing, but the rain seemed to have got right inside me – I actually wanted to be warm and dry so much, I could have cried. This last section was horrible, and seemingly endless. The dark was creeping up on us again, but I couldn't go any faster. I wished our friends would push on and get themselves indoors - I knew Pip would stick with me whatever - but I was actually also immensely grateful for their company.

The Taynuilt Hotel was beautiful. We were now in the county of Argyll and this gastro pub, with its craft beers and malt whiskies was just what the doctor ordered. Our room was palatial, and as quickly as we could, we peeled off all our layers of wet gear. After a day like this in the saddle you are not just wet, you are filthy too. My prized pigtails, the ones Rob had challenged me to grow, were plastered with mud, as was my face – in a funny sort of way I did feel a bit child-like again. As a grown-up you don't get really dirty very often – but of course when you are knackered, hungry, and now surrounded by filthy kit, which ideally you need to wear the next day, it's not so funny! Our room was quickly converted into something out of a pantomime scene, possibly Widow Twankey's Laundry, and we hit the bar.

Terry very kindly bought me a double Glayva, on the rocks, which as Whisky Liqueurs go, is very good for the chest!! We all settled around one large dining table in our own private dining room and shared our day.

There were a fair few of us who had taken a tumble that day, but Nigel C made his first claim to fame - he had taken multiple falls. He was still getting the hang of his cleats apparently – he was still working on that as we approached Land's End!

Looking back I can see that fatigue was beginning to play its part. We were a few days into the ride now, we'd taken a fair few soakings, we had a collected a selection of bumps and bruises and we still had 12 days to go – things didn't seem so funny anymore. I seemed to be bombarded with general moaning and groaning, and every time someone approached me, I, followed by Pip on my behalf, would wince. I knew everyone was weary, but so was I! Pip would look across the table and give me a cheeky wink – it could have been Rob.

I didn't need much rocking that night, partially down to the fact that our bedroom now resembled a sauna due to all the wet washing steaming away on the piping radiators (which was very good for my chest,) the quantity of whisky liqueur I had consumed, and the belief that if it would just stop raining I might stop coughing!

****

July 2011

From: Lorraine
To: Friends
Subject: Rob
Date: Fri, 28 Jul 2011 11:20:02 +0000
Hi,
Rob battles on, we take one day at a time and it is totally horrible! This is a cruel disease, and the treatment is vile. The nurses are wonderful. Loving and kind, everything a nurse should be. The Sister is a dragon and needs stuffing and mounting somewhere. Pip and I hang on by our fingertips and I spread my long rambling emails around so that I don't wear any one person out completely!
When that baby is placed in your arms and you experience that enormous wave of emotion/love, I thought I could imagine how it would feel if I thought I might lose him - it's a good job you can't.

L. x

We are now fairly well settled in hospital routine. Day and night seem hardly distinguishable. We stick to Rob like glue – that is how we are all happiest. Various "people" have been circulating and it becomes clear that we are being targeted – it's just not entirely clear yet, what we are being targeted for. Rob is exhausted, even by his own recent standards of exhaustion. He doesn't want the TV on, he doesn't want to listen to music; he just wants "to be". Pip reads the paper; I close my eyes and try to doze. There is a commotion at the door and two young ladies accompanied by Sister Anne and Rob's Consultant enter. Crikey, what's happening now?

Suddenly quite a lot of energy is being expired. They've obviously been thinking about this and have a plan. The view is that Rob has already potentially become institutionalised, and needs to stop behaving like a patient, by which I think they meant he should get out of bed, get dressed, and embrace the day. Rob also needed to talk. Yes, they had all, in their infinite wisdom, decided that Rob was bottling it all up and needed to spill his innermost fears and feelings – and apparently this young woman, a cancer survivor (bully for her) was the person to whom the spilling was to be done.

Sorry, but another short deviation here. I had been for a number of years an active listening Samaritan. I'm not sure if I was a good one or not, but I did my best. Having spent hours trying to perfect my listening skills on courses (SAMs like training!) and then hours listening to the folks that ring the emergency lines, the one thing I am absolutely sure of is that it is never the right time to talk until the person doing the talking decides it is. So for these folks to barge into Rob's room and dictate the timetable was outrageous.

Pip and I were unceremoniously removed from the room, and Rob was left in the clutches of the young cancer survivor. Well frankly, they should all have been ashamed of themselves. I'll never know exactly what passed between Rob and his "young lady" but her companion determinedly led us off the ward. Of course, having had the benefit of surprise, she'd achieved the desired separation, but then she had no idea where to take us. We ended up on the landing outside the ward, next to the three lifts that came and went discharging patients to the adjacent day unit, and supplies and patients to Rob's ward. It was not exactly quiet or private, although as I mentioned before, from the 10th floor landing the view across the college rooftops of Cambridge is pretty spectacular.

Our "counsellor" rambled on for a bit, although I think to be honest I wasn't listening very hard; all I could think about was how on earth was Rob getting on? He had looked so vulnerable as we had been so assertively removed. It felt like a posse of professionals had taken a hold of my heart and wrenched it out. How dare they think they knew better than us what was good for us – did we look that stupid? How could people think they have the right to decide what was best for our family, most especially Rob, with next to no knowledge of any of us, or the dynamics of our family. She sat too close to me, whilst Pip sat behind me – we were on a bench seat all in a long line – really cosy! And so she began....

With her head slightly tilted to one side, and with a weird nervous smile plastered across her face she started, "And how did you end up here?" I just blinked at her, what a stupid bloody question! I wanted to scream back, "By ambulance you idiot!" But of course, I didn't. I looked her in the eye and said, "You really want to do this, do you? You really want to unravel me, here, on this public landing? I hope you know what you are doing!! Please don't start this unless you are confident you can put me back together!" I felt like a grenade, my finger was squeezing where the pin should have been, but if she pushed a few more buttons that would be it, there would be no going back. Actually by the end of that little speech, I may have been shouting. Pip put his hand calmly on my shoulder, and with that Rob's Consultant scurried across the landing presumably hoping that this was all going to turn out for the best in the end.

A conversation with a friend helped me in the aftermath of all this. As she said "It's hard," and it still is, even now, all these months later, with all that we have subsequently been through, not to still be furious with the insensitivity of some of these professionally "supportive" people. Did nobody, at any stage, think to ask us first? They might have started with "Are we wanted?" They could have begun by finding out about us, about who we all were before trampling all over us, they could simply have made us aware that they were there, as and when and if we wanted to talk to someone.

Anyway, our counsellor was a little shaken. She was young. She definitely needed to go on a few courses, and dare I say it, grow up a bit. After what seemed like an age we were allowed back into Rob's room. He had effectively thrown his "young lady" out. He may have been ill, but he hadn't lost all his marbles. No, she didn't know "exactly how he felt" and no, she couldn't possibly promise him, that "everything was going to be alright, after all, look at me!" He was laying on his bed curled into the foetal position, shaking, with tears running down his face. I felt murderous. I crouched down to put my arms around him and immediately felt the heat radiating off him.

Sister Anne was summoned. Rob was burning up. All hell let loose – he had an infection. Oh, so now she understood why he had been reluctant to raise his head from his pillows earlier – this was our first taste of a "spike"- there were to be many to follow. Basically at the stage within the chemo cycle where you have no immune system functioning, you can easily catch a bug. It can be as simple as a common cold, or more likely a bug that is never actually identified. It might be air-borne, or in the water you shower in. These spikes can be life-threatening, and need IV antibiotics within the hour. You become hooked on the readings of the thermometer.

The main reason for me writing this book is that I have no idea what to do with all these memories. I am plagued by flashbacks, some good, mostly not so good. I, upon reflection, now hold this one episode heavily to blame. I am, by nature, a talker. I think I would actually have benefited from some form of counselling along the way, but these young women spoilt that for me. All people are precious, and I believe should be shown the utmost respect at all times. Our experience of the various counsellors that breezed in and out of the selection of rooms we found ourselves staying in was pretty awful. The statutory opening line seemed to be "and how are you feeling today?" I know it must be difficult to know what to say, or how indeed to start a conversation with a very sick young man, or his distraught parent(s), but really, is that the best they can come up with? Hurrah for the Samaritans I say; people who listen, without making judgements, letting a conversation proceed with no timetable or constraints. I am very proud to have been part of that organisation in the past. I'm sure there are fabulous counsellors out there - you just need to find them and connect with them. Sadly at such a time, you don't have the energy or inclination to go searching – you kind of like to think that they'll find you.

After the dust settled with Rob and things had calmed down a little, Sister Anne and I, had a "bit of a chat". We came to a mutual understanding that whilst we appreciated all the help that was being offered, you can't just treat families all the same. Rob and Pip and I would do it our way, just as other families would do it theirs. Rob had indeed refused all offers to meet other young people with cancer, or to play on the ward Game Station, or visit "The Oasis", a teenage drop in centre run by Teenage Cancer Trust. As Rob said, he'd never played computer games before he got cancer, why would he want to start now? Most importantly he wanted to see his own friends, not make new ones, not sit and look at other young people as sick as him – we are all different. We spent most of the next 2½ years dodging various counsellors – we did talk, but to our friends, our family, sometimes to Samaritans, but for us, the most valuable conversations were with each other. Perhaps that is rare, it certainly seemed to take Addenbrooke's by surprise.

From: A Samaritan Friend
To: Lorraine
Subject: Rob
Date: Sat, 29 Jul 2011 11:17.30 +0000

Hi Lorraine

As was Wendy's reaction so was mine, to cry for you and wrap you up in our love and care. I <u>know</u> that we are privileged in being able to get alongside people and allow them to proceed at their own pace. It doesn't sound as though you've had that experience yourselves. Thank goodness you and Pip are a team even though you would desperately like some of your own space (a very healthy reaction I think).

I've just finished a night duty and without exception everyone I've spoken to has said: "Have you heard how things are with Lorraine?" As I've said to you before, there is so much love and concern winging it's way to you. I know that it doesn't change things but you should feel proud that so many people hold you in such high regard.

In a situation like this I again realize how our callers feel who can't do anything to change things but so want to for those they love and care about. I also am very much aware of how much better it is to be able to speak to someone, you don't have to choose your words carefully with and can convey so much better what you feel (well I can anyway.)

Anyway, Cycle 1 of chemotherapy is nearly over.

The familiar voice heard in the lift doesn't even annoy me any more as she announces, "Doors Closing, Lift Going Up!" I have begun to accept that this is now my life. I had always held tight to the belief that "Things like this didn't happen to people like us". Well that's a load of crap, who exactly did I ever think "People like that" were? Well obviously, it's "People just like us!!"

As Rob said,

"Don't say why me - say why not me."

Carl & Terry

Chapter 7

Wednesday 6th May, 2015 – 9.30am, JOGLE Day 5 Taynuilt to Dunoon (66.9 miles +3152ft)

Our breakfast briefing was rather taken over by Carl on this particular morning. He was worried; some of our bikes were not in very good shape. The weather had been pretty brutal, and any weaknesses were being highlighted; and if you didn't have any weaknesses before you started, you probably did now! Brakes were the real issue; in this incredibly wet weather our brake pads were wearing down much quicker than usual and a few folks were almost down to the metal. Carl was busy trawling through our box of spares, but we had to ask him to go shopping for more stocks; we couldn't risk getting into trouble.

I did manage to stumble outside between my cereal and eggs and bacon to give Pip's bike and mine a bit of a clean. I suggested Abi joined me, but she declined. In fact, since the day she had taken delivery of her road bike, which was back in June 2014, she'd never had anything done to it. Carl was worried, Abi wasn't. Her youthful exuberance and general confidence in life would get her to Land's End – she was certain of it. Thankfully Carl wielded his expertise over her bike, replaced her brakes, swapped the gear cables over, which had been set up wrongly, presumably since the day she'd had it, and adjusted the gears – there would be no stopping her now.

Nigel C awarded the tour moustache to Adi. There was a developing "tension" between these two great mates. Adi had taken Nigel's stock of jelly-babies hostage and a ransom note had been received. The saga continued to entertain us for days, with photos of these poor jelly-babies having been pegged to washing lines, and with various extremities missing causing much amusement.

Thank heavens the morning of Day 5 was dry. I really hoped that if I could just keep the damp out of my chest for a day or two, I'd be fine. I felt stiff and sluggish this morning, but I knew I'd soon loosen up. The ride profile looked unremarkable, which probably meant I was reading it wrong, but ignorance is bliss on some occasions, and I didn't want any further details. There were two sizeable climbs along the way, but nothing we hadn't seen before. We were getting a bit difficult to impress with hills by now.

We headed off on the main A85, following the path of the River Awe. It was a leafy run, and we all settled down for a fun day in the saddle. The road took us right along the riverbank, and we were making good speed. Nigel H had today joined yesterday's "pack at the back", which was lovely, and our first group shot of the day was at a charming little hamlet called Lochawe. On the steep banks of the river, the road runs high, looking down over the railway station complete with an old railway carriage. Once used as a tearoom, this old carriage is now holiday accommodation. What a fabulous spot for a holiday! My train anorak husband would love it, arrive by train, stay alongside the track overlooking the river, and sleep in a railway carriage – I must organise that trip soon!

Across the road was the local store/post office, and Nigel H immediately spotted the opportunity to indulge in a much-needed chocolate fix. One of our ladies was experiencing a bit of a melt down on the picnic bench outside the shop. The dilemma facing us was 1. Do we wade in and try and offer more words of sympathy? 2. Do we dash past ignoring her and deal with the chocolate crisis? 3. Do we turn and enjoy this absolutely stunning view and hope things settle down behind us? I should add, she wasn't alone; there was already a circle of kindness around her.

I know living with Rob's leukaemia has changed me. There was a time when I'd be the first to sit and indulge in a round of shoulder hugging, and "there there's" – but I don't have that in me anymore. What *is* a crisis, has for me, been redefined. There seemed to be shock that families were being missed – well at least their families were still intact. There seemed to be surprise that anyone should be feeling knackered, well at least they were knackered because they'd been cycling at the front of the ride, and thought they may have been pushing themselves too hard. Think how it feels to be constantly trying simply to keep up! There seemed to be surprise that their bodies were racing – well I had warned everyone that those gel energy sachets were evil, and gave you gut rot – did no-one listen or believe me? When we had cycled from Paris to Colchester with Rob's Cricket Club we had all ended up with upset stomachs. Your metabolism speeds up when you live at a repeatedly faster rate, everything speeds up – did they think I'd made that up too? We all had the same problems. Crikey, who's sounding cranky now? That incident actually affected the rest of my day on and off. I suppose actions have consequences – and all that.

How you respond to others really defines who you are; it says what kind of a person you are. If you are patient and kind, that says something. If you are quick tongued and sharp, it says something else. Sometimes I look in the mirror and hardly recognise the person starring back at me – what that says hurts.

In the end, Nigel H's need for chocolate made the decision for us, and so we went to see if we could help. The dearest old Scotsman you could wish to meet intersected us. In full kilt and deaf as a post, but with the warmest smile imaginable, he asked (please read this with a Scottish accent,) "And where are you going?" I explained (with an English accent), "We're cycling from John O'Groats to Land's End, for charity." There was a bit of a pause whilst he computed this...and then (in Scottish) he replied, "Och, that's an awfully long way!!" We all shared a giggle, the old gentleman too.

It was understandable, it had all bubbled up, but we all knew that the best solution for our distraught lady was to get a grip. Dealing with other people's emotions is exhausting. Sometimes, you just need to man up and get on with it, or as Rob would have put it, "Grow a pair!" Everyone had his or her own demons to deal with. Like the rest of us, no one could afford to waste energy on crying; it wouldn't help. Lots of hugs were administered, and she took off. She was a strong cyclist; others of us had more fundamental problems to deal with. She couldn't let her head spoil her chances of success, not when her cycling was so able to complete the challenge. Others made sure that didn't happen. In the end, you ultimately have to sort yourself out. Whilst you have your health, your destiny is usually, although not always, in your own hands.

Having enjoyed the view from Lochawe across to Kilchurn Castle for long enough, we set off once more. Our route took almost a hairpin bend around the river basin and headed off on the A819 towards Inveraray. The pull up from the banks of the River Awe was a bit of a challenge, but I actually managed to cycle the whole thing! My cycling wasn't very beautiful, but I did it. We then hit the River Aray and enjoyed a very pleasant downhill freewheel into Inveraray itself. The woodlands were weird, like something out of a movie set. I remarked to Abi that if you wanted a film setting for a battle scene, this could be it. All the tree trunks, looked scorched and lifeless, the ground was blackened and there was no sign of life. A bit unnerving to be honest – I have no idea why it was like that, something must have been going on, perhaps a recent forest fire?

As you come into Inveraray, you pass through a stone arch. The view of the loch is revealed ahead of you, before you are faced with the decision to turn left towards Glasgow, or right towards Campbeltown. Straight ahead of you on the green overlooking Loch Fyne is the bronze memorial of a Highland

Infantryman. He is stunning with his rifle and kilt, and the inscription reads:

IN MEMORY OF
THOSE,
YOUNG LOVED,
LAMENTED,
HERE WHO DIED
IN THEIR COUNTRY'S SERVICE
1914-1918

I didn't get past "young loved, lamented". There were additional plaques to commemorate WWII as well, with an extensive roll of honour.

We headed left, and cast our eye into the Inveraray Woollen Mill, complete with coffee shop. There was a tell-tale row of bikes shining in the chilly sunshine – no prizes for guessing who they belonged to. Adjacent to that is the entrance to Inveraray Castle, at this moment complete with a real piper, who was giving it his absolute best on the bagpipes. Generally speaking they are not my favourite instrument, but in this setting, the bagpipes were glorious.

Half a mile further down the road we paused on the top of a perfect arched stone bridge. Over to our left was a wonderful view of Inveraray Castle, location for the 2012 Downton Abbey Christmas episode.

Loch Fyne is Scotland's largest sea loch, and we enjoyed a perfect picnic with it as our backdrop. The only blot on the day was Nicola's bike; it was playing up again. Terry had located a bike shop in downtown Dunoon, tonight's destination. The mechanic on the phone felt confident he could sort the problem out, and so Nicola steamed off with a group of faster riders for company, to make sure she arrived before closing time. Hopefully her bike would be fixed once and for all. We could see our route winding its way the other side of the loch – a ferry would have been welcome at this point. Sadly, no such ferry route exists, but we didn't really mind, it was beautiful. A group at a time we set off, Nigel H sticking with us; we relished his company. Pip enjoyed having another fella to dilute us females too. With Nigel's arrival the quality of the singing definitely improved. We steadily worked our way through every Scottish song we thought we knew. Of course, knowing all the words wasn't totally necessary; we believed our own versions were more entertaining anyway.

Our next pause was at Creggans, a welcoming looking gastro pub, on the banks of the loch, looking back towards Inveraray. You felt like you could reach out and touch the castle on the opposite bank and we would have loved to sit on the bench with a pint and a packet of crisps, but we had to console ourselves with a quick visit to their facilities, which the publican generously allowed, and then back to the pedals; we still had a few miles to crack, and as ever when we stopped we all quickly got very cold.

I'm sorry if you are getting a little bored of the geography, and all the lochs, - there were a lot of them! But I really want this book to be, as much as anything, a record of our ride. You never know, maybe in years to come, my route will be talked about like Mr. Wainwright's famous "Coast to Coast" walk! You never know, someone might actually want to retrace our ride some day? On that fifth day, I had no idea of one loch from the next; we actually were probably heard expressing the view that if you'd seen one loch you'd seen them all! That is actually not true; they are all unique and incredibly beautiful, their similarity ends with the fact that they are filled with a lot of water. Well all that rain has to go somewhere!

As our day progressed there were plenty of miles to let the mind wander. I had left home with a long play list of music prepared on my iPhone; my earphones were neatly curled up in my pocket waiting to help alleviate the boredom of hours in the saddle. Music is a huge part of my life; after all, I'm a dance teacher. Rob loved music, Sam is a music teacher, and our house had always "rocked!" You always knew when Rob was awake, because you'd hear him.

Abi had made special Cd's for Rob whilst he spent weeks on the ward for treatment. He would play them on repeat, and we were quickly word perfect. Losing Rob has changed how I listen to music – I hope this aspect of grief will soon leave me. Sam is a talented composer and writes his most powerful stuff in a state of angst. I guess other songwriters feel that power of music too, whatever the genre. Almost any song can reduce me to tears and those tears can flow at the most surprising moments. I didn't reach for those earphones once on JOGLE. My own thoughts seemed to be noisy enough.

On this stretch I began thinking about the background of grumbling that was beginning to take a hold of the trip. It would have been naive to think that you could throw the eighteen of us together and that it would not happen, but I had rather clung onto the hope that there would be a sensitivity to it; hence, the only rule issued over our champagne toast that previous Christmas was: "No moaning allowed!" By that of course I didn't really expect there to be no moans at all – I'm not that daft! - but I had hoped that people would save it for the really important stuff. Everything else they were capable of sorting out themselves. Anyway, maybe it was time to nip all this groaning in the bud. We still had a long way to go and I for one, wanted to enjoy myself.

Lock Eck was our next jaw-dropping stop, on the Cowal Peninsular. This loch, seven miles long, is famous for its "algal bloom" which has apparently been known to kill dogs. However today there was no sign of anything dodgy. It is totally surrounded by mountains, and so is incredibly sheltered. There was a stunning campsite on the banks, and for someone who would rather cut their own arm off than go camping, even I thought it looked idyllic. There was evidence of a children's rope swing hanging from a tree on the beach, and the water's surface resembled a mirror, it was so still. The reflection of the mountains was picture postcard worthy and we enjoyed a very special thoughtful moment in that place. We also ate a handful of jelly-babies each, to spur us on our way. Dunoon was on the radar now, just the final 10-miles to go.

This final stretch broke the mould. It was flat, the air was still, the sun was shining and, as I sit here, I would add we even had a tail wind – well that's how I remember it. I always get excited when I'm heading off to the seaside, and Dunoon was historically a holiday destination. So loch side or seaside, we were in holiday territory. Technically it is on the banks of Holy Loch, a sea loch, which was famously used as a submarine base during WWII. The US Polaris submarine was also based here during the height of the Cold War. In the late 1960's Dunoon was the subject of a song entitled "Why don't They Come Back To Dunoon?" by the Humblebums. I have found it on iTunes; it's quite a catchy little number, although I don't think it will be troubling my playlist! Billy Connolly also was reported as joking during a performance in 1969 that "First prize, at a local competition, was a week in Dunoon, and second prize was a fortnight" – well that seemed a little harsh, but we were all looking forward to making our own minds up about the place!

We were heading for The Park Hotel, at the far end of Dunoon, so we were able to enjoy a ride along the entire length of Marine Parade. First impressions were pretty good; it had that lovely sea-sidey sea-weedy smell, and the gulls squawked convincingly. It felt like the seaside to me. Our hotel had enjoyed better days but our room enjoyed a splendid sea-view, even if it was a little tired. Never mind, so were we, and the welcome was warm. Good news greeted us with respect to Nicola's poorly chariot. The local bike shop had worked their magic, and everything was fixed. I was so relieved; I didn't want to lose anyone, but especially because of a technical issue.

Liz's brother, wife and children lived in Glasgow and so were coming to visit and take Liz out for dinner. She was really excited, but for the rest of us I'd done a bit of research and located a highly recommended restaurant in town for dinner. We'd all arrived in good time, so with little stress, we all strolled, crocodile fashion, up the hill into Dunoon proper, in search of Braes Restaurant.

Various conversations were shared, but one was between Pip and Fossie. Fossie's relationship with us was through cricket; he had watched our family grow and shared matches with our boys. He had watched Rob endure his illness and along with everyone at our club, held his breath as it took its course. He asked Pip how he thought the trip was going, how did he feel about the ride splitting into four distinct groups? I think Fossie was a little taken aback, but he knew Pip well enough to know that if you ask him a question, you'd be wise to expect a truthful answer, so I don't suppose he was truly surprised. Actually I think Fossie already knew the answer – that's why he asked the question. Pip said that he would like to see some of the stronger cyclists occasionally hang back, to help and support those who were sometimes struggling. Pip was missing the team spirit he was used to feeling on the cricket pitch, too.

It turned out to be a bit of a night for clearing the air. I blame myself, but perhaps I hadn't made Carl's role clear. His brief was to drive the support van containing our luggage, carry the bike spares, support us in maintaining our bikes, and provide a picnic at stops, to be arranged. He wasn't there to fetch and carry. His job did not involve making sure everyone's luggage was transported to and from the van; we had to do that for ourselves. The fact that he was a complete star, and continually went way beyond the call of duty, of course, made a rod for his own back. We were all very grateful for his help, though, and I am sure some of the bikes wouldn't have made it without his ministrations.

I also had a bit of a bleat about Terry's role. Terry was a full member of the challenge too; he had simply never wanted to cycle it, preferring to support the rest of us, however that turned out to be necessary. I for one, would have considered a successful trip for him, to be one, where he did nothing. Obviously that was a little optimistic! To begin with Terry looked, and probably felt, a bit spare. As the trip progressed, many had the opportunity to be grateful to Terry, who really did go the extra mile to keep everyone's chance of succeeding a possibility. I shudder to think how many miles he drove on our behalf.

The restaurant was perfect. We were allocated a separate dining area upstairs, which meant our usual banter could continue as noisily as we liked. We could share the briefings for our next day's ride and the various "special" moments could be shared. Abi astounded us all by chomping her way through double fish and chips that night – I'm not sure if that is something to be proud of or not? Adi presented the "Moustache" to Colin aka. Fossie. It was awarded for Fossie's prowess on the up hill sections. "Dancing on the Pedals" he called it. "Come on Elle, let's dance," he'd say. Well, if only I could cycle up those hills as well as I can dance in my studio, or better still in my head, I'd have had a much easier trip!

****

July 2011

In order to try and understand exactly what was going on in Rob's bone marrow, samples were taken on a regular basis – he hated and panicked about every one. The very first test had been done within days of being admitted to Addenbrooke's, and Rob had found it excruciatingly painful. A young doctor called Fisal was deputed to take the sample and he looked as nervous as Rob did anxious. He rolled his sleeves up, tucked his tie into the front of his shirt and rolled Rob onto his side. I knelt down next to the bed and clutched his hands in mine. "Come on Rob, we can do this together, look into my eyes and concentrate on my voice."

The local anesthetic was injected into the right hand side of Rob's lower back; this alone made him cry out in pain. The next bit is not for the squeamish, but then the digging around started. Try as Fisal might, he could not manage to get any kind of sample. I concentrated on trying to help keep Rob calm. I employed a relaxation technique that had been of some use to me during my three labours, where you basically allow your mind to take you somewhere else; that was of course until I yelled for the gas and air.

As a family, we have a favourite spot. It is a tiny village in Greece called Stoupa. The mountains come down to the sea, the beach is sandy and tree strewn, the water is crystal clear, dotted with freshwater springs, and filled with fish; it's fabulous snorkeling and beach cricket territory. I talked and talked about this place, even Fisal said he thought he'd like to go there. But this bloody test was taking for ever, and despite Fisal's furrowed brow, now covered in perspiration, we still had nothing for the scientists to work on. Pip was waiting outside, and it cost him dearly in more ways than one, as without supervision, I promised Rob we would all go there on holiday when he was better. "With Tom and Sam?" he asked. "Abso-bloody-lutely!"

A ten-minute procedure was now clocking in at 40 minutes, and Fisal had to admit that he needed help. Rob's Consultant was called and she too rolled her sleeves up. The pain was still horrendous, but at least her experience, determination, and knowledge that this wasn't going to be an easy sample to get, meant that she went for it with a strength and resolve that actually we all appreciated. The process was barbaric, likened, in my experience only to having a tooth extracted. It's brutal, it's without that feeling of science. It's a lot of painful pushing and shoving, and that's what I felt watching. I shudder when I remember what Rob went through, and know that even in my imagination, populated with vivid pictures of Rob's face, screams and looks deep into my soul, I still can't get close. These bone marrow tests became the very worst of times for him, and for us.

The doctors were apparently surprised. These tests were done routinely on the leukaemia ward, and it was usually a fairly uncomfortable, but reasonably painless experience. Yet again Rob's youth and general level of fitness was working against him. All his sport had ensured that his bones were strong and dense. Yes, producing cancerous cells, but tough and unwilling to be hacked about by anyone. He was promised pain relief for all future tests. I wasn't even sure Rob would agree to any future attempts.

Later that evening, still in a state of shock I became aware that my right hand was throbbing. On closer examination I realized that one of my fingers was swollen; a ring I had worn for years was cutting into my skin. Rob had crushed my ring. Of course I didn't care about that, but it was the measure of how tightly he had held onto me.

At the end of that first cycle of chemo, the bone marrow test needed to be repeated; it would be on day 28 and the countdown had already started. It was the only way to tell if the chemo had worked, and if a full remission had been achieved. One of the nurses, Emma, came to see how Rob was feeling on the subject. She was a wonderful example of a nurse. She said she had never wanted to be anything else – you could tell. "Come on Rob," she said, "I'll get you some gas and air. If it gets women through labour, it'll get you through this." I can't remember what Rob's reply was, but that's probably just as well, as I'm certain it wouldn't be printable!

This time Rob was taken to a designated treatment room in the Hematology Day Unit. A "very experienced" houseman, who turned out to be a gorgeous Australian young lady (which was not lost on Rob!) arrived to "do the deed". I asked if she had been made aware of how painful and difficult the first test had been, and I was assured all would be well. I knelt alongside Rob's face, whilst Pip waited outside. He couldn't have come in this time, even if he had wanted to; the room was too small. "Don't go Mum, promise me whatever they say, you won't leave me on my own." I wasn't going anywhere.

Despite the use of the gas and air, the level of pain Rob experienced shocked the Junior Doctor. She said she had heard of young people suffering due to the strength of their bones, but she was so sorry for Rob, and it was the first time she had ever witnessed it. Thankfully she did get a sample, and we were returned to his room on the ward. She marked his file to suggest that for any future bone marrow tests Rob should be given an anesthetic.

It's weird, but I wondered where these various specimens went. The front page of Rob's medical file was a page of stickers, all computer generated, all with his name, date of birth, and medical number on. Every day file after file of blood, and then the bone marrow samples too, disappeared from the ward – where did they go? Had Rob just turned into a number?

Anyway, there was no time to dwell on such things. Cycle 2 of chemo was ready on the ward when we returned. Wherever all those precious files ended up, all I could say was that we would be holding our breath upon the results. We would need to wait for those.

From: Lorraine
To: Everyone
Date: End of July 2011

We continue to take each day as it comes here - although I could have done without breaking a tooth yesterday, so had to dash back to Colchester to get that fixed. After all that I have witnessed Rob go through I can't even begin to complain about being terrified of dentists, honestly I can't imagine how I ever felt I could make a fuss!

Pip and I are coming at it from two different directions, he operates on a "need to know" basis, and just keeps saying we have to hold onto the belief that "everything will be fine". I need to know everything - I always knew I was a bit of a control freak - and now it is confirmed. Of course, I am totally out of control so ... I want to believe "everything will be fine" and I know, or at least I think I know, that Rob has a 60% chance of a good outcome - but 60% just doesn't seem good enough when it is your child! For every 6 people waltzing around telling you they went on to get married, their fertility recovered and they are now rocket scientists, four poor sods didn't make it! Even then we aren't talking about being clear of cancer for ever, this is keeping our fingers crossed for an extra 5 years. Still I'll take that.

Anyway more test results due back later today, and we've just had the day 28 bone marrow taken. It is hoped that Rob's bone marrow should show signs of regenerating, and we wait with baited breath to see if the Leukaemia is gone. As I understand it, if the blood/marrow tests are good we go on for a further 3 cycles of chemo, if not we go down the stem cell transplant route. I might have felt more reassured if the consultant hadn't bitten my hand off when I mentioned that Tom was coming home from Dubai for a week in August - "might it be sensible to get his tissue tested as it might be more complicated from a distance?" - "definitely - I'll inform the transplant team immediately" - just what I wanted to hear. Apparently there is a 1 in 4 chance of a sibling being a match - even if they are though it's a big ask.

I've stopped emailing too much, as once I start typing I seem to pour out everything and I guess it's not what everyone wants to read. People talk about that feeling of isolation and now I know what they mean. People ask you how you are feeling, but actually they couldn't bear to know really. I've tried to talk to the Teenage Cancer Trust women – but that didn't prove to be very helpful. Anyway, after a little prodding from her I began to talk, and she was so unnerved by the surge of emotion and fear she giggled! Very helpful!! Pip is wonderful, loving, supportive and useless all at the same time. He has this preoccupation with getting Rob out of bed, which when you have a white count of 1, a red count of 8.5 (on a good day), you are waiting for platelets and are full of chemo results in an exhaustion we can only imagine, I can't see the problem in just going with the flow. I've tried to talk to Pip, but he can't bear to hear my fears, so I keep them to myself. He doesn't want to hear about my nightmares, and can't bear to see me cry - so off to the ladies loo again!! I suppose we are back to the Men are from Mars, Women from Venus argument - Venus sounds nice about now!!

A few evenings later we were watching TV – it was the summer of 2011, the one with all the riots in London. Normal, ordinary citizens had been whipped up into a frenzy of rampaging and fighting. Shops and homes were looted whilst people quickly tried to board everything up to protect their property. Rob was enraged. Why was he laying here in hospital fighting for his life, whilst these low lives were behaving like animals? Sometimes as a parent you don't have the answer.

We also watched a program all about Sir Ian Botham. He had just done another of his "big" walks. As a young cricketer, he had visited a children's leukaemia ward, in Taunton, Somerset. The kids were obviously adorable and stole his heart. Moved by their bravery and courage, he returned a few months later to visit again. He asked where some of the little ones were, some of those particular little characters who had made a lasting impression on him. "Dead" came the reply. As recently as 1985, only 20% of children survived infant leukaemia. No real work had been done in this field; the medics could only do their best with the limited tools available. Beefy has dedicated years of fundraising for Leukaemia and Lymphoma Research to try and improve that position. Now much progress has been made, and younger children do have a much better chance of survival. The situation is nothing like as good for Rob's age group.

The program was all about these "big" walks he made for the charity, John O'Groats to Land's End being a favourite route – maybe this was part of Rob's inspiration for our ride too? Anyway, due to Rob's love of cricket, I set to the next day, writing to Sir Ian. It was just a short note explaining Rob's situation. Not long afterwards a card arrived, signed by Beefy himself, wishing Rob a speedy recovery. Rob treasured that card, and now I do.

The first 7 days of cycle 2 were over. We could go home. Rob couldn't wait. He was up, packed and pacing about at the first opportunity. As soon as we could, our bags bulging with medication, lists of telephone numbers in case of emergencies and appointment cards for trips back to

Addenbrooke's over the next 3 weeks, zipped and poised for departure, we set off home. We were all a bit sad that Sam wouldn't be there, but he was off on Cricket Tour with our family's beloved Sou'Wester's Cricket Club.

This Cricket Club only really functions for two weeks of the year, when it tours the West Country. There is the odd exception to this when we squeeze in an extra week or two for an overseas trip, but the rest of the year is all just talk. Meetings held over a pint, where the cud is chewed and the future worried about. Anyway, Sam had gone for two weeks of chasing a red ball, and we wished him lots of runs and wickets. We had all been increasingly worried about him. It was unimaginably hard for him to have been abandoned all those weeks previously; at least for the next few weeks he would have fun, in the knowledge that his brother was at home, and doing OK.

During this time I decided to risk my first visit to my dancing school since all this had begun. Although Bonny and I had spent much time on the phone, me off-loading, weeping, and screaming by rotation, she had been keeping my business going. We had been warned to keep our exposure to other people to an absolute minimum. No young children. No old people, no hugging or kissing. Basically we should keep ourselves to ourselves. Rob was just too vulnerable, and possible infection was all around us. I walked into the office/changing room determined to keep everyone at arm's length. Everyone was so pleased to see me, but it's so strange to be denied that physical contact. Anyway, a look shared between us, said everything.

Coincidentally, in the changing room was one of the pupil's mothers. My school is very near to Colchester Hospital and so I have pretty much mopped up the medical market as far as potential pupils goes. This oriental mother obviously wanted to chat – I wasn't sure I was in the mood. She asked me if I knew that her husband worked at Addenbrooke's? Did I know that he worked for Cancer Research UK in the huge CRUK building I walked past all the time? Rob was one of his cases. All of Rob's samples, specimens and tests went to her husband, the father of one of my little students, for analysis. He was the person responsible for trying to work out exactly what should be in those bags of chemo – each one personally prescribed for Rob. He was the person looking down the microscope at slides of Rob's bone marrow. Rob wasn't just a number after all. This father knew me, and by association knew Rob, and she wanted me to know how deeply all the scientists and researchers cared about everyone whose treatment they were part of. So, Rob wasn't just a number after all. Every time I walked past that huge CRUK building after that I would look up, with no idea where that lovely man's desk was, and send out a virtual wave.

Rob's thrice a week blood tests and the subsequent hours of blood and platelet transfusions were now taking place at Colchester's Haematology Day Unit. It was a huge help to us that Cambridge and Colchester were prepared to work hand in hand. Rob had already become adept at acquiring the TV remote so as to be able to control the programme selection on the communal screen. The Unit was always heaving, but that just needed to be tolerated, and Rob hated being stuck cheek by jowl with so many sick people. Rob would carry his hand disinfectant everywhere, and get me to open doors so that he wouldn't have to touch handles. He was sorry for everyone else, but I have to say that he just looked so out of place, and so young. It brought it home to me just how unlucky he was. You'd get to see the same people every time, and whilst most folks just got on with it, there were always the same few who would be moaning. Rob had names for them all, everyone too rude to include here. Actually it mostly wasn't the patients themselves moaning, it was the people supporting them. I could relate to their frustrations. I could see my life ticking away too. We spent hours and hours in that department. I look back and remember hating myself for wanting it to stop. That seemed tantamount to wishing Rob dead. He had to have this treatment, all of it. He had to get better. I look back now, and realize that I rather naively never, not once, stopped to consider that it wouldn't work. Perhaps that's just as well.

The day came for us to return to Addenbrooke's. Routine bloods would be taken, our chap over in CRUK would be waiting to receive them and process them. Then we would go through to see Rob's consultant and hear the results of today's tests. But on this occasion, we would also hear the results of the day 28 bone marrow test too.

I can still hear the cheer that went up when I phoned Sam who was in Devon. He was sat in front of a sunny cricket pavilion watching someone else do all the work with the bat. A full remission had been achieved. There was no sign of leukaemia to be found. This was as good a result as we could have hoped for. Cycle 2 was already doing its stuff, and we were looking ahead to the final two rounds of chemo to be endured. It was the first piece of good news we had received in a while.

The final dose of cycle 2 was finished on the morning of Pip's 60th birthday. There had been a big party planned, it was due to be held in our garden, with lots of friends and family invited. That grand plan had been cancelled weeks previously, but at least we would manage a bit of a special dinner at home. Tom and Julie were meeting us at home. They were visiting as part of their holiday from Dubai, via India. We'd had to send them to Julie's family in Lichfield, a sort of quarantine, before we'd let them near Rob, and we were even going to risk getting my Mum across too, with some hefty rules about hugging in place. The fatted calf was in the oven, and despite my mum and I managing a bit of a row, Pip had a birthday celebration of sorts; actually, it was probably the worst birthday of his life. Sam had gone off to Corfu, news that had gone down like a lead balloon, which just left the rest of us to do our best.

From: Lorraine
To: friends
Sent: August 2011

Of course we are all feeling the strain of Rob's illness - sometimes I feel like we are in a very lonely place. People keep inviting us out, because "you deserve a night off with all you are going through" - they just don't get it.

Rob is really tired after this course of chemo. We have had a lot of tears from him over the last couple of days, often sparked off by the simplest of things - like he decided to try and change the grip on his cricket bat, and simply has no strength - it was pitiful to watch him sob clasping onto his bat. He had two units of blood on Tuesday, and although he looks better on paper it hasn't made much difference to his energy levels.

He has terrible mouth and throat ulcers and is now on morphine for the pain of that. Feeding him is a daily challenge, we have found that sandwiches made from fresh white bread with the crusts cut off, filled with chicken chopped finely and mixed with mayonnaise is edible, it's agonizingly slow progress though. We keep eating slower and slower to keep him company; otherwise he gives up.

One day I hope we will laugh at some of this.

Anyway, we are half way through the planned chemo now. We already seem to have been at this a lifetime, I can't believe he has so much more to go. Of course it must work, and then all this can be filed deep inside us all somewhere and we can concentrate on happier things.

****

The Rob George Foundation:

One of the things that constantly surprises people, is the financial difficulty cancer patients can quickly find themselves under. But particularly students. Rob was a clear example of this. Once the initial furore of diagnosis had died down, Rob began to worry about how he would exist. He had become used to the mind-set that he was now a young adult, working towards being independent. We had tried to impress upon him that he had to try to manage within his budget – of course, he wasn't doing too well on that front, but then not many students do! I remember saying, with complete confidence, that I was certain that there must be state benefits for people like him. After all, there appeared to be state handouts for just about everything else, and it was clear that he couldn't support himself.

I need to be clear here, we were "lucky". Rob had two parents both able and committed to looking after him. We were "lucky" we had the resources to be able to do that. But that didn't alter the fact that Rob really wanted to remain independent. Pip had a chat with MacMillan Cancer Support, who advised him that Rob would indeed be eligible for ESA (Employment Support Allowance.)

Phew, well that seemed like good news. After all, in our caring society, I think most of us would assume that there would be practical and financial support for someone like Rob. As it turned out, that was wildly optimistic!

The initial application was made by Pip on Rob's behalf at the end of July 2011. The form was a tortuous affair, and needed my husband's legal brain to deal with it. On the 15th August 2011 – Pip's 60th birthday - Rob's application for ESA was turned down on the grounds that he "remained in full-time education".

It's true to say that Rob had not left his course; he fully intended to return the following October to resume his studies. However this year off was not a matter of choice. He was fighting for his life, and on medical direction had been told to take time off his degree. The University was incredibly supportive, and of course this wasn't the first time a student had fallen ill, but the rules stated that Rob would need to take a calendar year out. The system did not allow for folks to come and go when they pleased. A full year it was going to have to be. For the benefit system to use the fact that he didn't want to totally and irrevocably abandon his studies as an excuse to reject his application is awful. Rob's degree was his future.

On the 18th August 2011, Pip on Rob's behalf requested, as was Rob's right, an informal reconsideration. On the 27th September 2011 the decision to disallow the claim was confirmed and so an appeal was lodged to the Tribunal service.

We were informed that any tribunal was unlikely to be heard before March 2012.

Pip decided to go and see our local MP, Sir Bob Russell. In October 2011 Sir Bob suggested that actually Rob should be applying for IS (Income Support). We wondered why MacMillan had not told us about this? So an application for IS was made, and guess what, in November a lady called Joy, (you are not allowed to know their full name, or indeed have any form of direct communication – you never know someone might actually want to talk to them!) called to say that Rob wouldn't be entitled to IS either. She advised Pip that Rob should make an application for DLA (Disability Living Allowance).

And so, on the 4th November 2011 an application for DLA was made, and that didn't get very far either. So, we would have to wait for the ESA tribunal. In the meantime, Pip set up a monthly allowance into Rob's bank account. We all pretended that the money wasn't coming from bank of Mum and Dad, and we all thought "The System Stinks!"

Elle leading Pip – why I hate main roads!!

Chapter 8

Thursday 7th May, 2015 – a sluggish 10.00am, JOGLE Day 6
Dunoon to Ayr (57.7 miles +1580ft)

We set off all together that morning. Departure had been a bit of a fiasco. It had seemed to come as a complete surprise to the hotel management that we actually all wanted to eat breakfast. One poor young waiter was left chasing around like a headless chicken. The only guest to get served with any speed seemed to be the very large owner of a very large dog; yes, the dog was at breakfast too! If you woofed very loudly, and disturbed everyone else's breakfast, not to mention left some of them slightly scared to even approach the buffet table – your eggs and bacon arrived pretty promptly. I obviously wasn't making enough noise! Anyway the talk of the morning was around our imminent ferry ride. Did it count as cheating? Should we cycle around the deck during the crossing to appease our consciences? As we all set off the views from East Bay across Holy Loch were stunning. It was a gloriously sunny day and we were all determined it would be a fun one. Today had been billed as our "rest day" being only 57.7 miles and pretty flat. It is surprising how quickly your definition of a long cycle ride shifts – suddenly 57.7 miles didn't sound so bad.

McInroy's Point to Hunter's Quay car ferry was very efficiently accomplished. A dear old lady approached Pip during the crossing and asked all about our ride. She was lovely, and before leaving rather tearily crushed a £10 note into his hand. It transpired that her husband, who was sat in the car, was too ill to get out and speak to us, and had sent his wife to ask all his questions. He had leukaemia.

We followed the road around Lunderston Bay and then around into Inverkip Bay. This was a main road, but the traffic was light and didn't cause us any problems. What became clear was that us "folks at the back" weren't too bad on the flat. In fact we seemed to be able to keep up pretty well; it was the hills that sorted us out. Anyway, this section was flat, and we looked forward to a sociable day.

As we hit Castle Bay, I found myself cycling with Claire at the front. We were enjoying a lovely catch up. The tarmac road turned into a tarmac path, and then into a stony path. We carried on quite happily; actually neither the bikes nor us were worried by the conditions. It seems though that folks behind us were not so happy. The grumblings got louder. I think Antonius may have suffered a puncture, and after a few shouts, folks decided to turn back and look for the main road. So that left Claire and me. We were quite happy and so carried on merrily, confident that we would all meet up further along. I love being "on the edge", and cycling along, literally almost on the beach was beautiful. I loved nattering to Claire too; we were well overdue a catch up. We found ourselves in one of those swanky new developments - you know the sort, low level flats with sea-views and balconies; and a new harbour filled with a very smart selection of yachts. It was quite a surprise to stumble across it stuck in the middle of nowhere. As we hit the main road again, there was the rest of our party.

We picked up some speed down the A78 - so much so that the scheduled right hand turn was missed. Yes, we would be coming back onto the main road in about 1½ miles and whilst I couldn't remember exactly why I'd selected this particular deviation, there would have been a reason. Looking at the route now, I see that it was on a designated cycle path that takes you past Hunterston Castle, famous for its Ha-Ha Wall. The Castle looks out over the loch, and I would have liked to see it. Anyway we sped down the main road – I'll visit on my return trip - you remember the one, in a car! This slight change in the route did, however, mean that we stumbled across a beautiful bench. It was right next to the main road, facing a gorgeous view across the countryside and out to the loch. It was simply inscribed "The Remembrance Bench". It sat in a sea of forget-me-nots; what a very special spot!

The main road hugs the water's edge down towards Ardrossan and Largs. Although we all needed full cycle kit on to keep warm, the clear blue sun was a lovely addition to our day, and I seemed to have lost the cough – hurray! With its strong historic links to the Vikings, and a suitably impressive statue of a passing Viking to admire, we found ourselves gathering on the greensward overlooking the sea, complete with coffee kiosk, which we all enjoyed together. It was my only coffee stop of the whole trip. It doesn't matter too much; I generally prefer tea!

As hot drinks were finished groups departed, Fossie, Kevin, Nigel C and Abi joined our group. We'd made good progress, it was late lunchtime and we had already fitted in a ferry crossing, and social 33 miles – this was shaping up into a good day!

I'd been particularly looking forward to the next section of today's route, which ran parallel with the railway along the waterfront at Saltcoats. I'd spotted a BBC news clip back on the 15th January 2015, which I posted on our group's Facebook page, showing a storm raging, and the sea crashing in over the cycle path and the railway track. Massive damage had been done by the storm, and I wondered if the cycle path would actually have survived. Well it had, and a fine mile or two it was!

The next section wiggled its way, avoiding the main A78, taking in views of the River Garnock and various parks and general wasteland. It was not especially memorable. As we emerged through one particular section, we were to see our way littered with upturned shopping trolleys, bricks and various other items of debris. I nearly jumped out of my skin as a couple of little traveller boys appeared from no-where, brandishing sticks as guns. As they stood in our way I explained that I didn't think that was a very friendly thing to do! I bet the others ahead of me hadn't been so polite!! The little ruffians soon moved aside, but I wouldn't have wanted to be on my own; safety in numbers I suppose. We all shared a laugh about it over dinner. Held up at "gun-point" - that needed to go into my book!

As we headed into Irvine we came past the Golf Club. There he was again, warming up on the practice green - Rob was never far away! The River Irvine was pretty; winding it's way through the town. We had a number of towns and cities to negotiate on our bikes and we managed to utilize many cycle paths alongside rivers and canals. If there is water, there is usually a way!

As we headed out towards the coastal path again, we hit Irvine Bay on the Firth of Clyde. We cycled alongside the links golf course at Gailes and then the Kilmarnock Golf Course north of Troon. We kept to the sea wall and as we came along, the sight of Troon Beach was splendid. There were children on the beach with their buckets and spades; folks were walking their dogs, and families were generally enjoying the late afternoon sunshine. There was nothing for it - with 10 miles to go, Nigel C declared it to be ice cream o'clock, and so double Mr. Whippy's with a chocolate flake were ordered for each of us. After all that cycling we could all afford the extra calories; I'd have had the ice cream anyway though. We sat on the sea wall, and whilst we

Liz, Fossie, Pip, Nigel C. Elle, Abi (Kevin behind the camera)

dangled our feet and enjoyed the views looking out towards the Isle of Arran, Abi came out with:

"Did you know that an Oyster is male for one year, then female the next?"

Surely that can't be true? However if it is, it's pretty nifty! We also kept a keen eye peeled for the Sea-Cat service to Ireland. If we were two short this evening at dinner it would be because Paul and Hazel had decided to call it best, and hop off home!

We followed the sea wall until we finally hit the Royal Troon Golf Club. I had to stop. I just had to text Tom in Dubai. Golf was a passion that Tom and Rob shared. Tom agreed that Rob would have been salivating at the prospect of all these wonderful courses, but especially the Royal Troon. I felt very close to Rob right then; the route wasn't an accident. I had made choices about the route, at every turn. If something had winked at me from the map, we'd be going to see it. I wanted to feel that Rob was close by. I wanted to see the things that Rob would have wanted to see. I wanted to cycle through his eyes. "Forever, Together" my gift from him says. Absolutely! We cycled right across the course, on a proper track of course, Rob and I both loved it; after all, it was supposed to be the ride we made together.

After the majesty of the Royal Golf Club we had to take a quick detour around the not so majestic Prestwick International Airport - but it was interesting in its way too - before we arrived in Ayr. Cycling along the Esplanade was magical and the cycle track was excellent. Pristine houses look out across the greensward to sea. We were nearly there, and it was still daylight! Ayr feels grand, and it wasn't difficult to see why Robert the Bruce had established the first Parliament of Scotland there in 1315. He'd made Ayr into a citadel, surrounding it by a huge wall, much of which apparently still remains.

Then, the track disappears, we are on the beach, we are 0.7 miles from our hotel, and our route has vaporized! Claire and Antonius related over dinner how they had manfully carried their bikes along the beach, totally determined to "do the route" and then up some steep storm defences back onto the road –

good effort! We wiggled about a bit, and I squirmed at the demise of my precious route, but we all arrived safely not long after, at The Chestnuts Hotel, Ayr, via the road.

Now I've stayed in a few hotel rooms in my time - I'm a lucky lady - but this was easily the largest hotel room I've ever seen! The bathroom was the size of our lounge at home, although there was a distinct lack of hot water in the bath. Anyway, it's easy to find something to complain about, and the shower worked perfectly.

Carl removed our bikes for the night, and we all settled down to a relaxing evening. I actually had time to drink my recovery shake and do all the exercises and stretches I knew I should have been doing daily – Pip had his eye seriously focused on a pint of local real ale. That was all the recovery he reckoned he needed.

Once unpacked, we actually did commence some of the exercises we had been advised to do each and every night. This was actually the first time we had arrived with enough time to even think about such contortions. Now I wouldn't ponder on this particular scene for too long, but you can, I am sure, imagine it; Pip and I starkers, trying to drink our recovery shakes, whilst laying on the floor with our legs up the wall! Not a pretty sight!! We were already giggling away at the ridiculous sight we made, when there came a knock on the door. We were lucky no muscles were tweaked with the scuttling around to find towels, fleeces, anything to hand, in order to preserve our modesty. It was Claire kindly delivering the magnesium spray for the back of our legs. Bless her kindness thinking about anything she could do to help our tired legs. Actually the laughter was the best therapy of all!

Terry for once had had a fairly relaxing day too. There had been no bike issues to worry about, in fact no issues to worry about at all! He was in charge of sorting out our dinner arrangements each evening, and as we'd all arrived in good time there had been no groveling required in the restaurant. We were a party of at least 18 each evening, and that takes some forward planning. Every night we were starving and it's no good then trying to make a decision by committee about where and what everyone wants to eat. Terry had managed, yet again, to negotiate one large table in a private section of the dining room – spot on Terry! Let tonight's party begin.

Colin (aka. Fossie) enjoyed his moment in the spotlight at dinner as he took his turn to present the moustache. He set a "quiz" for which there would be a prize. Q. "What was Colin head of?" We all knew he was a retired teacher, and had over his career taught a range of subjects. Various answers were fired at him – but it was to be a rollover! The moustache was awarded to Claire, for her general strength and stamina on the bike. I'd have awarded it to her for the fabulous way she had wrapped herself around the huge triangular warning sign on Day 4, but perhaps I take a different perspective?

****

September 2011:

As the summer of 2011 rumbles on, each day is a mixture of celebration and stress. Every time Rob reaches for a tissue, coughs or looks particularly tired I reach for the thermometer; when I don't, he does. We act under strict instructions to keep our car full of petrol, and be packed; ready to dash for Addenbrooke's if Rob spikes a fever. We have thrice weekly appointments at Colchester Hospital, which regularly take from 9am til 6pm. Filling the hours sitting whilst blood and platelet transfusions take their course is a challenge; there is only so much daytime TV anyone can bear! Of course we are on first name terms with all the nurses at the Day Unit, and we know that every blood test result is being phoned through to Addenbrooke's from where Rob's treatment is being guided. We know that Rob's future is being cherished. Every one wants this to work. We are so grateful to the two teams, separated by 60 miles, who are trying to make this whole process as manageable as possible.

Rob and his laptop are never far apart. It's either blaring out music, of which we all enjoy his rich and varied taste, or he's messaging his friends. He is word perfect for just about everything that plays.

Suddenly it all goes quiet. Social media can be and is a wonderful thing, but it can also be dangerous and hurtful. Rob and his mates had been in close contact all through the summer and the messages had never stopped piling in. We had a selection of get-well cards to challenge the largest of stores. But of course, it was all a bit of a mixed blessing. Rob's friends had never forgotten him, they had supported him through the initial diagnosis and hair loss, through the weeks and weeks of chemo, and we loved them all for it. Actual visits weren't really encouraged, as we needed to protect Rob, but he managed all that himself. He wouldn't see his Nan, because of hospital warnings, for which he hoped she'd forgive him, but also, he was nervous of seeing his own brother Sam. As a secondary school teacher, Sam couldn't avoid contact with hundreds of young people – it all served to add to the emotional turmoil. I know Sam felt it too – how would he feel if he was the reason Rob caught an infection, it just seemed easier to keep his distance. Maybe we were being too careful, but it was what Rob wanted. Only he truly knew what he was going through, and we had to do everything to try and make sure his treatment had the best possible chance of success.

It all came to a head as everyone started returning from their various fabulous summer trips. Photos of friends on sun drenched beaches, at the top of amazing mountains, at music festivals, at parties, in exotic locations; you name it, everyone of those messages hurt just a little more than the one before. And then his friends all turned their minds to the new year at University, and that was about as much as Rob could bear. He slammed his laptop closed and wept. It was one of only a handful of occasions we saw him even slightly display a sense of feeling sorry for himself.

The chemo seemed relentless. The third cycle was underway, and the noisy building works going on beneath us was the only thing to interrupt our weeklong stay in Addenbrooke's. Teenage Cancer Trust were financing and sponsoring the conversion of a ward into a specialist unit. All the nurses were talking about applying for jobs on the new ward; even our lovely Emma was tempted. Everyone enjoyed speculating about who would get the job of Ward Sister – that was going to need to be one special person. After all, nursing 14 – 26 year olds would be a real challenge. The needs of young adults, is very different from those of little younger patients, or indeed older patients. Watching them not only dealing with puberty or the loss of newfound independence, but cancer too, was a real emotional hotpot. Of course, a space to call their own was appropriate. It all goes back to treating people as individuals, and trying to address their specific needs. Youngsters at the slightly spotty, oily, smelly, angry stage usually do, in my experience, benefit from space.

The nurses talked about all the facilities that were being included. The common room was a big talking point. Pool table, plasma screen TV, computer games, a parent's room where we would be able to make toast and a sandwich; you name it – they made it sound like a holiday camp! Rob wasn't impressed. As he said, "It'll be too late for me, I have no intention of ever stepping inside it!" I could see his point.

I plotted into my diary the next 28 days, the countdown to the start of the 4th and final cycle clearly marked. For Rob, of course, it marked the end of treatment – the beginning of the rest of his life. His hair would grow back, his taste-buds would return to normal, indeed he would simply be able to eat normally, social contact re-instated, fun... Rob, understandably became really low; in fact his specialist nurse Linda, was concerned that a real state of depression was setting in.

And that is how that 3rd cycle of chemo, in one simple conversation, was launched to a new level of stress. Linda came to visit Rob, and of course, as usual, he was the adult, so it all came as a bit of a surprise to Pip and me. A potential trial had been identified, that Rob might like to consider joining. The trial was comparing the different outcomes when only three rather than the four cycles of chemo were received. What did he think? This could be his last cycle of chemo forever? By Day 28 - and that was just over three weeks away - he could be looking forward to a life, with his main treatment behind him.

OK, so the immediate reaction might be, "Fabulous, where do I sign?" But stop a moment... I could have screamed, Pip turned white with shock and fear. We had always had such a clear plan. Full remission after the first cycle, then three further cycles to consolidate the position already achieved. Everything was going well, why change plans now? We could see that Rob was low, but we'd get him through that. Don't move the goal posts now. But of course, the decision was Rob's.

The level of angst that that choice delivered was unimaginably cruel. He was only 19 years old; it was only natural that he would be tempted. I think I felt just a little bit mad at that moment. "No!!" was the deafening scream in my head. "Take all the treatment that's on offer!" We didn't know what the future might hold, we can't walk away wondering if we've cut the treatment short.

As Pip and I walked out of Rob's room we were met with an atmosphere you could cut with a knife. Even Sister Ann gave me a look filled with compassion. The Junior Houseman, was leaning on the nurses' station with a file open in front of her, she looked close to tears. These young doctors weren't much older than Rob; they must have felt it all so deeply.

Pip and I sat in the Addenbrooke's Food Hall, staring at yet another ghastly selection of fast food. Neither of us was hungry, but you felt you had to try and eat something. It was always expensive, always lukewarm, always highly processed but there you go, at least we were close by. I didn't know how to start.

Pip broke the ice, "What do you think?" It all spewed out. I just felt so completely that we all needed to know, for the rest of our lives, that we had taken every chance on offer. I hardly dared utter the thought that the leukaemia might one day return, but how much worse would that be, if we'd opted out of the planned cycle 4, sort of in search of a quick fix? Pip wholeheartedly agreed. But what could we do? We knew we couldn't try and influence Rob's decision; he had to make it himself.

The day wore on and the chemo was hung up on the drip stand, the 6 hour dose ran its course. Rob looked in some kind of living hell, his eyes wide as he struggled to know what to do. The doctors and nurses hardly spoke to him, presumably all terrified of being seen to exert any kind of influence, one way or the other.

Towards the evening our young lady houseman caught me in the ward corridor. "We need to know," she said. "His treatment plan needs to be co-ordinated, has he decided yet?" Her poor stressed face spoke volumes. This was a bad situation - that had been made worse.

As I entered Rob's room, he blurted out, "Mum, Dad, what do you think I should do?" Pip replied, that it didn't matter what we wanted; he had to decide. He was an adult now; it wasn't our decision. We would completely support whatever he decided. "OK, so what would you two do in my situation, I want to know?" he asked.

Pip and I exchanged glances and we knew we had to be honest. I tried to make it sound as if I wasn't pleading with him, although goodness only knows if I pulled that off. Of course, we understood how tempting it sounded, but please, in his situation, we would take all the treatment. None of us knew what the future held, but how much worse would we feel if we'd dodged the very bit of treatment that might just make the difference – his life was too young, too precious, too full of potential, to roll a dice for the sake of a trial. "Please take the chemo!" It was a big ask, we knew that, and we understood he wanted to get on with his life, after all it wasn't us that would have to endure it, but we could only promise to support him all we could.

"Please bring the doctor in," he asked. She was standing right outside. "No trial this time," he informed her. "OK," she replied and left the room. We all cried. It seems completely ridiculous that we were relieved that Rob would have to endure a 4th cycle of chemotherapy, and that we were pleased, but we were.

I left for one of my private sobs in the ladies' loo, to be faced by all the nursing staff standing around the nurses' station. They were obviously talking about Rob, and they were obviously relieved. As one of them said, we just couldn't be seen to influence him, and we've all watched your pain all day. We do believe he's made the right choice, and we are so relieved by the decision. Nobody knew if the fourth cycle would make the difference, but then that's the point – nobody knew!

The date for admission for Rob's fourth and final cycle was imminent. I began my daily phone calls to the ward to try and agree a specific date. Nobody would commit. Time ticked by and every phone call became increasingly strange and alarming. The days came and went; the stress levels at home rocketed. Rob paced about like a caged animal, and promised return calls were never received. We all understood the importance of keeping to the plan. Each round of chemo was planned on a 28-day cycle; there shouldn't be a delay. The whole point was that if even one single leukaemia cell had survived previous chemo it would be found, and snuffed out. We couldn't risk leaving any random remains of the disease time to re-establish itself. The days ticked by and it was unbearable.

Rob was shouting at us in frustration. The old dilemma of even having this fourth cycle reared its ugly head once more. From the lounge I could hear Rob roaring at Pip, and I could see Pip, eyes full of tears, scared to speak. I rang Addenbrooke's, insisted that I spoke to the bed manager, and when he was finally located I shouted at him in total frustration. "Listen! Do you hear what this is doing to Rob, to our family – find him a bed. I don't care where. I've watched the process so many times I could hook him up myself out on the landing – just find him a bed! If my son tops himself, I'm holding you personally responsible!"

From: Lorraine
To: a Friend
Sent: On 18 Oct 2011, at 18:20,

Hi!

Thanks for getting in touch. It's been a rotten couple of weeks waiting firstly for Robs counts to recover and then for a bed. Stress levels have been running high culminating yesterday with Rob going into full meltdown.

The final straw was Colchester General signing him off for a week - no point in continuing to monitor him as levels all now ok - just waiting for a bed - Rob just felt totally forgotten. He started saying he was just feeling like giving up - what was the point - his life was horrible - he hated every day! I think we had months of bravery covering up all the emotions, and the stress had finally caught up with him.

Anyway it is absolutely horrible. It ended up with me on the phone to Addenbrooke's crying totally pathetically telling some bloke/bed manager called David that if my son topped himself because he couldn't find him a bed I was going to hold him responsible....we were on our way in by 6pm!! None of it is pretty but chemo started today. The final countdown has at last begun. Hopefully end of Nov should see us done.

That afternoon we were admitted onto a men's surgical ward. C10 was closed, with an outbreak of sickness and diarrhoea. All Rob's familiar nurses kept popping down, as they were the only ones qualified to administer the chemo drugs. The ward nurses were friendly enough, but treated us like some kind of aliens. The other men and their visitors all had a jolly good gape at this young man with no hair, who needed other, special nurses to sort him out, and the whole thing was a complete endurance test – but we got through it. Rob was paranoid that he'd catch something; it was so far from the isolated world of the leukaemia ward he was used to. He was frightened to even use the loo.

We made good use of the Karen Morris Flat Pip and I were staying in. It was kept "hospital" clean, so that patients could enjoy some time off the ward too. With the lure of a bacon sandwich made by his mum, and a better Internet connection so that the cricket could be streamed to his laptop, we got through it. Somehow or another it was done, and at the first possible opportunity we all legged it for home.

The four cycles of chemo were concluded by a final bone marrow test, and then a few days later an appointment through Outpatients with Rob's consultant. He is himself a dad, with a clutch of young adults at home. He is also a human being and with a tear in his eye told us that everything was as good as it could be.

There was no leukaemia to be detected and we should go away and get on with our lives. We would return to Addenbrooke's once a month for the foreseeable future for blood tests. The first two years were critical. Rob would be monitored for the rest of his life, but we were off. We skipped out of Addenbrooke's that day, everything seemed possible again.

From: Lorraine
To: All our Friends
Sent: November 2011

Dear Family & Friends,

Please excuse the "Round Robin" nature of this short thank you and up-date, we really hope to see you all as soon as possible to express our thanks in person now that we are officially re-launched into society!

The all important update on our Rob... treatment has now finished and the news is as good as it gets, he is in full remission, and we are now to get on with our lives, even if with a new high definition of just how important life is!! Addenbrooke's will continue to monitor Rob for the next 5 years, (probably for ever actually,) monthly to begin with, and the first two years are vital, but we are determined not to be overtaken by the natural worries that do tend to creep up on you, we will absolutely live life to the full and have a lot of fun.

Those words from Rob's Consultant never left my head, and determined how we lived the following 19 months.

"Go and make lots of happy memories..."

Glorious traffic-free cycling – Saltcoats
(this is one of Adi's 700 photos)

Chapter 9

Friday 8th May, 2015 – a keen 8.30am, JOGLE Day 7
Ayr to Dumfries (65.1 miles +3284ft)

We'd had such an enjoyable day yesterday, that us slow coaches were determined to try and keep up today. Our confidence had been slightly restored and we'd been up since the crack of dawn, oiling our jockey wheels and cleaning our chains – perhaps it should have been the other way around and that's where we went wrong?

Fossie's friends came to give us a bit of a send off, and you could see Fossie's mood soar to receive the support. The mileage today was fine, it was just the return of the undulations that was a little alarming; never mind, one hill at a time! All 16 of us headed off, and began to negotiate our way through the streets of Ayr. Exactly 1 mile from the hotel we cycled over a level crossing, and Liz's chain came off. "Go on" she said, "I'll sort myself out and catch you up". Well that's not how it works, how would I feel if everyone cycled off and I was left alone to sort myself out? We hopped off our bikes and wheeled them into the curb. Her chain wasn't just off; it had broken.

I got on the phone to Carl, who had already hit the local supermarket and was half way through shopping for lunch. He'd be with us as quickly as he could. So, I nipped into the local

Post Office and purchased two chocolate bars, and we sat on someone's front wall, dangled our feet and waited. I rang Pip to let him know that we were in a spot of bother, but that we were fine, and together. Phone signals had a life of their own up in Scotland so I actually had to settle for leaving a message. Anyway I wouldn't have wanted him to fall off his bike trying to speak to me – we all know how men can't multi task! Is it illegal to use your phone whilst cycling I wonder? It should be!

Carl arrived and decreed that Liz's bike would "take a bit of sorting out". This was when I gave myself a big pat on the back. We'd discussed taking spare bikes quite late in the day. Space on the van was at a premium and Carl thought he'd find it difficult to cope with extra bikes. He already carried one spare for emergencies, but it was a full sized man's bike. Well that's all well and good but what if mine, or Elizabeth's, or Liz's bike went off the road? We are all rather vertically challenged and we wouldn't be able to reach the pedals, let alone the road! I had managed to persuade Carl to squeeze in my old bike, just in case.

Carl quickly got the spare "kiddies" sized bike off the rack, swopped the pedals over, adjusted the saddle and we were off. Poor Liz had no idea what was going on with the gears, and I tried to give her a crash course from behind. It all got a bit confusing as my current bike and my old one operate differently, so I was trying to give instructions to help her, and do something completely different myself at the same time. See, no bloke would even contemplate that!!

After a couple of miles we found Pip and Elizabeth. They had both stopped, and cycled slowly back to meet us. I think I kissed them both; if I didn't I wanted to. Elizabeth said that Nigel H was loitering a bit further up the road for us too, and so our group of 5 was formed for Day 7. Everyone else was well ahead and totally unaware of our trauma.

We followed the main road, A713, towards Hollybush. We were quickly in open countryside, but the road was busy, and we were on a 10-mile pull up. Liz clattered through the unfamiliar gears, occasionally finding the right one with a yelp of delight. We were following the path of the River Doon; unfortunately we were cycling upstream. We passed through the village of Patna, where the river is wide and clear and our route levelled out for the next 5 miles. The countryside was lush, and vibrant. Suddenly the landscape resembled the fields we were used to from home. We'd temporarily lost the mountains and the Highland scenery, and it felt like we were definitely heading in the right direction - for England. Perhaps the end of Scotland was finally approaching?

As we cycled through Dalmellington the road began to climb once more, a punishing 5-miler taking us to our highest point of the day. It was gorgeous scenery, with a babbling brook to our right hand side all the way to the top. Pine forests come down to the road, and as we climbed beyond the tree line, the walled pastures were replaced by the tufty clumps of grass we had seen so much of on previous days. The sky was clear, and the air nippy, but everything was good. Hopefully by lunch Carl would have had time to sort Liz's bike out, but in the meantime we were making good speed.

It's a wonderful feeling - reaching the top. You immediately know because all the pressure in your thighs is released. The bike begins to take over and gravity pulls you along. We looked ahead to a wonderful vista opening out before us, and Loch Muck and the tiny collection of homes known as Eriff down to our right. The following 18 miles were a joy. Basically down hill, with the odd little pull up to keep us awake and warm, but fun, fun, fun! The traffic was no longer troublesome, and we kept each other company along the way. Elizabeth and Nigel were happy to cycle either together or apart, but as two close friends, it was lovely for us to share the day with them both.

It was the day after the General Election. The SNP had totally washed Scotland yellow. Every lamppost and Working Men's Club was strewn with yellow posters or banners; many homes displayed flags of support. The Scots were very pleased with themselves. As conscientious citizens we had all cast our votes by post before departure. We were a group with mixed political leanings, but we all knew that politics is a dangerous subject. Carl had warned us that the group he had supported on the Coast to Coast route a couple of weeks before us, had strayed onto the subject on their last but one night. Discussions had got so heated, that on the final day of their cycle, hardly anyone was talking to each other! We treated the subject with the respect it deserves.

The view was huge, the skyline enormous; we could see for miles. The visibility was perfect; it was a vista to feed the soul. We found ourselves on the banks of a new river, rather romantically called the Water of Deugh – it looked rather like the previous one. As we entered the tiny village of Carsphairn we spotted the Carsphairn Village Shop and Tearoom. This was it, we were all set to stop and sit for a minute or two. Anyway, that idea didn't last long; it was the prettiest, but shut, tearoom for miles! We did however share the facilities with a family on their way up to the north of Scotland, for their holidays. Looking at the load on board, I have no idea how the children all fitted into the back, but they were delightfully quizzical about our group – they probably thought we all looked way too old to be riding bikes. The usual conversation followed and as their car pulled away we could still hear the kids asking for the explanation one more time, "They are cycling from where to where?" – all in that wonderfully incredulous tone of voice that children manage so well. The kids obviously thought we were certifiably nutty!

The Water of Deugh developed into a rather lovely wide bubbling river flowing into Kendoon Loch at Knowehead. By this point we had moved onto the B7000 and were pretty much traffic free once more. Following the course of the Water of Ken, we reached our halfway point overlooking Earlstoun Loch. We briefly touched the A702 before returning to one of my preferred B roads and continued southwards towards Balmaclellan. This tree lined country lane was a relaxing ride and we began to talk of spotting Carl and lunch. We'd decided to split the mileage unevenly with lunch 2/3rds of the way along. The hope was that the psychology would be helpful - stopping knowing that you were more than half way. Right now though our boilers needing stoking and I was getting grumpy.

Balmaclellan is a very pretty little village with a cluster of white-washed houses clinging to a steep high street. Its only real claim to fame is that apparently it's famous for curling. It even boasts the oldest constituted club, formed on the 3rd Dec 1841 in the Black Bull Hotel; it has an unbroken history. Everything was white, even the church had been painted white. I'd have loved to pause and take a wander around, maybe even find the grave of Elspeth McEwen, who had been found guilty of being a witch. She was the last witch to be killed in Scotland, burned to death in 1698. Sitting on the front wall of the churchyard, impossible to ignore, sat a curious stone couple – Robert Paterson, immortalised as "Old Mortality" and his mule. The statues date back to 1768. Robert Paterson was a Stonemason by trade, and apparently spent 40 years of his life searching out the unmarked graves of the Covenanters and carving their tombstones for posterity. The Covenanters were those people in Scotland who signed the National Covenant in 1638; they opposed the interference by the Stuart kings in the affairs of the Presbyterian Church of Scotland – they basically refused to believe in the Divine Right of the Monarch. The millennium saw the locals of Balmaclellan restore and re-site these statues back to the village – Old Mortality's descendants are apparently still to be found living near by.

Anyway, it's never a good idea to stop half way up a hill for too long, and we rather hoped lunch was at the top. I did smile though, as I gasped for breath, how even the church seemed to have slithered down the hill. Perhaps over time everything would end up at the bottom, and save everyone all this effort? Up we ground, my knees creaking badly.

It was one of those cheeky hills where you think you can see the top. You are nearly there, it's tantalising, and then you turn a sharp corner to see the road disappearing upwards into the distance. Well, cycling up through Balmaclellan isn't funny. Every twist, and the road not only stretched out before us, but also managed to get steeper. The solution was simple; some of us got off and pushed. Elizabeth however continued as she had started – she just kept going, steady but sure, totally focused on the top, or possibly lunch.

As the road left the village, climbing sharper than ever, even our conversation stopped. This was getting silly. Then we spotted Carl, parked up in a lay by - and what a lay by it was, with a view to match all views! As we parked up and turned to look behind us, we looked down into the village and up and across to the Rhinns of Kells; it was quite a sight. Everyone else had finished lunch some considerable time previously. That hour sat on the wall in Ayr waiting to get Liz rolling again had cost us dearly – c'est la vie!

Liz's bike was in bits, a work in progress, but the big news was that Claire had taken a nasty fall. Coming up the final assent, with the whiff of sausage rolls in the air, she'd pushed too hard and found she was unable to get into the correct gear due to the gradient. Her thingame what'sit had sheared off the back, and she'd found herself up close and personal with the road. Thankfully she'd limped away, but her bike wasn't looking so chirpy, and was currently strapped to the rack on the back of the van looking mightily sorry for itself. Claire had set off on the other spare bike. Fortunately for her, the Good Lord had seen fit to equip her with a full sized pair of legs and so all was well. So now both spare bikes were rolling – good call Elle!

We made ourselves a hot drink, then stuffed our French sticks with whatever we could lay our hands on. I then took a stroll towards the sandstone war memorial overlooking the view. It is Scotland's oldest known civic memorial to the Crimean War (1853-1856), and names the five soldiers who had been inhabitants of Balmaclellan, all five of whom had lost their lives. There they were listed: surname, rank, year died, regiment, place of death, forename, manner of death, age of death. It made a startling and gruesome read: James aged 20, Joseph aged 27, Thomas aged 22, James aged 33, William aged 28. Not an old man amongst them. There have been and will continue to be, I guess, so many young men and women lost in war. So many mums, dads, brothers, sisters, wives and girlfriends, who face futures full of grief. I wondered if that would have been better or worse, or just another permutation of vile, compared to my own grief? I don't think there is an answer to that, but to stand and think about death is something we should all do from time to time. Maybe the moaning and griping would be less quick to our lips. At best we hope our lives will be long enough, but even then I'm guessing it doesn't feel so. How many of us make the best of every moment we have? How many of us leave it until it's too late and stand wishing we'd taken every opportunity to live our lives to the full? How many opportunities do we allow to pass us by? I'd promised Rob I'd live his life for him; he wanted us all to do that for him. At his funeral the Rev. Rob had cast that challenge down to the hundreds of his young friends who came to pay their respects. Don't waste a moment, don't spoil a moment, live with care and excitement – "Be Happy!"

Feeling stuffed, we gathered our select group together, gave our stiff legs a bit of a shake out, and straddled our bikes. Dumfries was in a south easterly direction, and off we went.

Quick progress was made to the village of Corsock, just 8 miles down the road. As we sailed through I cast my eye to the left to see Corsock and Kirkpatrick Durham Church – it was a stunner. Then the weather took a turn and the black clouds that had been circling decided to dispense their worst. The rain fell steadily. We zipped up and lowered our gaze; here we go again.

We followed the main 'A' road, even with a brief visit to the treacherous A75, but we soon found the Old Military Road heading down to Milton Loch. Back on a National Cycle Route, I felt safer, and despite the weather I was enjoying myself. The hills were manageable and I afforded myself the luxury of occasionally stopping to enjoy the view. Adi was our photographer in chief, but I wanted my own record too. I got quite proficient at the "selfie". Adi by this stage had gained himself quite a reputation. He seemed to enjoy his own company, maybe even preferred to cycle on his own. He darted about, appearing when you least expected him, but always when you most needed him to. He just seemed to love every turn of his pedals. He was photographing everything – he too didn't want to forget an inch. I don't know how he managed it, but sometimes, having been behind us, he'd appear, always in a bus shelter, and on his phone, up ahead. He was trying to keep his work life going too. Adi totally "got it". He seemed to have really connected to the loss of Rob; he was going to enjoy the trip for Rob too.

Our route meandered through Lochrutton, and into Cargen. We paused to watch a young farmer rounding his flock of sheep, in the pouring rain, into a pen. The main work had been completed, and his beautiful sheep dog, job done, was sat bolt upright on the seat of his open tractor, whilst the farmer dashed around in the field finishing the job. I asked if I could take a photo. The young lad said yes, but on behalf of the dog, not him. "What's your gorgeous dog called?" I asked. "Rob" came the reply – of course!

By now the rain was teaming down, and we were soaked through – again. We'd done well with the navigating, but Dumfries proved to be a bit of a struggle. We were tired, cold and wet to the skin. The Garmins bleeped and buzzed their little heads off - so much so that it was difficult to know which one to believe. All we wanted was to find The Premier Inn, Dumfries. At this point in time a full tour of the town was unnecessary. There seemed to be little to commend Dumfries for a thorough visit, especially in this weather. I remember it as a very grey place – that may well be totally unfair. Obviously, a painful amount of time later, we did find our hotel. No one came out to meet us except Carl. Well who can blame them? We were miserable, it was nearly dark, and the rain was bouncing off the car park. Still, there was always tomorrow to look forward to.

****

November 2011

And so we took Rob's dedicated Consultant at his word.

Rob began to make plans, and one of the first was to go and visit one of his old school mates, now studying medicine in London. "Be careful!" I couldn't help myself.

Off he went, rucksack on his back, spring in his step. Pip and I allowed ourselves our first night out since June, and visited Nigel and Elizabeth for supper. We even had a couple of glasses of wine. After all, we had promised to get on with our lives; Rob was, and so must we.

We took a taxi home, promising to collect our abandoned car in the morning. It was around midnight when the phone went. Pip leapt to answer it. On the other end was a policeman. "Do you know a Robert George?" "Yes, he's my son." The conversation went on, there was a lot of noise in the background. The policeman obviously thought Rob was off his head. They were near Camden Lock, London, Rob had been mugged, and after a scuffle whilst he tried to get his phone back, unsuccessfully, he'd been knocked to the pavement. He was bleeding, and was hysterically trying to communicate to the officer that his "counts were low, and he was in danger of bleeding out." Well you can see how it all looked. Of course, our Rob had been drinking too, and with his bald head, you can have some sympathy with the officer.

Pip explained he was newly out of chemo, and the policeman's approach immediately changed. He took Rob to the nearest A & E, and made sure he was checked over. I couldn't wait for him to get home the next day. Our first experience of "living life to the full" had not gone too well.

Christmas 2011 saw Sam cooking the most splendid of Christmas lunches, and then we all flew out to Dubai for New Year. Rob, Tom and Sam would be together, Pip and I would take my mum too, and we would all join with Julie's family for a New Year's celebration to be remembered. We would say goodbye to 2011 and hello to 2012 on board a privately hired yacht, with a backdrop of Dubai lit by as spectacular a display of fireworks as you can imagine.

One of Rob's great sadnesses whilst in and out of hospital, was that for many months he feared he would never see Tom again, but also, that he would never see Dubai where Tom and Julie were now living. Another promise had been made that we would get him there, at the first opportunity. The trip was deeply important to us all. We did everything we could. We sipped cocktails under the Burj Kalifa, had dinner overlooking the famous musical fountains by the Dubai Mall. We visited the Grand Mosque in Abu Dhabi, and went off road up in the Wadi.

Tom and Rob managed a round of golf, under floodlights, and Rob delighted in ribbing Tom mercilessly about how many balls he had lost. It was a wonderful trip, and we managed on many occasions to forget our underlying nerves. The trip was over too soon.

Our close and dear friends, Terry and Nicola, had kindly offered us the use of their chalet in Switzerland. We had enjoyed many such trips before, and in fact Rob and I had learned to ski together there just after my 40th birthday. We spent a wonderful week there over the February half term, Sam managing to join us too. We enjoyed a whole range of weather, but the best memory is of us sitting out on deck chairs on the top of Chaux Ronde, music pulsating from the tiny hut serving Vin Chaud and beer, and deciding that we would both "like" olives by the end of the trip by trying out the theory that if you ate 4 a day for a week, by the end you would love them. (I'm not sure that actually works, but I can at least now eat them to be sociable, rather than heave at the sight of one!)

Rob enjoyed being on skis, but didn't need to be going fast off piste, or even on a black run to achieve that. He loved just being in the mountains - all our boys do. He also enjoyed skiing well, by which I mean in control and with style – he was pretty fast, too, sometimes. He loved to disappear off the piste edges, going around a few trees, up and down a few mounds of snow and then re-appearing, airborne from the side, when I least expected it. He loved encouraging me to follow him. "Come on Mum, let's find that inner child. Just relax your knees and go with it, and try not to squeal." Thank goodness I was wearing my helmet, I bashed my head on so many low tree branches, but we didn't half laugh!

And then we would sit on chair lifts, being carried up effortlessly, dangling from some cable way above our heads. "Listen to the mountains," he'd say in the hush, "Look at the snow; it's sparkling like glitter in the sunshine." I also loved to watch Rob and Sam at the end of the day, chatting up the beautiful young girls serving in the bar. They were a right pair of Casanovas!

Soon, Easter-time 2012 came around, and the four of us headed off to Cape Town, South Africa. Our Sou'wester's Cricket Club were off on one of our rare overseas tours, and our two young men intended to be an integral part of the proceedings. This was a huge milestone for Rob. He'd spent the winter going to the gym, desperately trying to regain his fitness. Chemotherapy had had a devastating effect on his body; muscles had disappeared, washed away with the leukaemia.

Rob had spent day after day in the gym with a cricket friend Iain. As a young officer in the army, Iain had stood on a land mine whilst serving on his first overseas tour to Afghanistan. He too was fighting for his fitness after multiple operations to save his foot. I'd regularly picked them up after a training session to find Rob in tears, "I can't even lift as much as the girls," he'd groan. Iain would come out with some string of expletives to demonstrate how shocking his own performance had been, and we'd all manage a laugh.

Sam & Rob

After breakfast on the day of our first fixture,

the 43 tourists gathered in the hotel reception to await our coach. Sam and Rob appeared, doing their 118-118 impressions, although I have to admit I have no idea what the significance of the banana skin was. We set off, with Pip's brother Pe, his pen in hand. As the tour scribe, he was trusted to record anything of note, or even not really of note, but vaguely amusing. Knowing Pe's slightly acquired sense of humour, his account was sure to be entertaining.

It was April Fools' day, and we were as ready as we'd ever be, to play the Cape Town Wombats. Scribe Pe was to be found at the bar purchasing his first pint of the tour, and our Captain proudly picked our young Ollie Bocking and Rob combination, to go and open the bowling attack. In honour of Rob's wonderful return to good health, he was handed the shiny red ball to deliver the first over. The tears were already trickling down my cheeks; he looked so handsome, so alive, and lots of our dear friends were there to share the moment. Rob stormed in and took a wicket with his very first ball. An almighty cheer went up; you'd have thought we'd won the Ashes, rather than bowled the first ball of a tour! The Wombats were 0 for 1, but most importantly Rob was 1 for 0 – Pe came scuttling out from the bar demanding to know what he had missed. Despite Pe's aching thirst - well it was hot - he stood with us and watched the next few deliveries disappear in different directions towards the boundary, and so turned to complete his transaction at the bar as Rob began his run up for the final ball of his big come back over. And that is how our tour scribe missed batsman number 2's dismissal - bowled neck and crop! Rob was 2 for 8 – my young man was back!

Later that night in the bar the Wombats captain alongside our own made some awards. Rob was presented with the match ball, and I remember him standing in front of everyone and adopting the Usain Bolt pose, you know the one, like a lightning bolt. For some strange reason the Wombat's captain also saw fit to present me with his team shirt, I think because I was the mother of the leukaemia survivor. He wanted to make sure that I too had a reminder of this momentous day. Of course, I would never have forgotten it anyway, but it was a sweet gesture. Pity he hadn't washed the shirt first, though!

We had a great tour, finding time to explore some of Cape Town and the surrounding countryside too. Rob struggled with muscle cramps which Debs, our on tour physio/masseuse/friend, helped with, but the worse bit was the heat. Chemo had left him with his internal thermostat shot to pieces. If he got hot, it took ages to cool him down again. We had to take it carefully, a cold shower was no good, too much of a shock to the system, it was just another challenge of our life. Wherever he stood fielding, I'd go and place a bottle of drinking water on the boundary rope. People probably thought I was fussing and over anxious - well they had no idea what Rob was trying to hide, and how well he was coping. Rob would say, "Mum, we are a team," and give me a wink. Everyone else could think what they liked! Only once did he have to admit defeat and ask for a replacement fielder. His heart was racing, pumping nearly out of his chest. The veins on his neck and forehead were standing proud, I had to insist he came off the field. I think even Pip thought I was over-reacting – this simply wasn't cricket! I knew how bad it was, and so insisted that our Captain find a sub for him. Deb's young son was sent on, as keen as mustard, and Rob staggered off. "Get me out of sight" he said.

That particular ground was way up in the mountains, at Groot Drakenstein. Around the back of the pavilion was a swimming pool. Apparently it was where everyone would jump in, if the forest fires, that often lit up the mountains, got too close to the wooden club house. We sat for ages, just dangling his feet, drinking water, and then finally wading, then swimming, in that pool. I had been terrified. When Rob was ready to return to the match, to watch the close of play, he just gave me a look and said, "We're good to go, it's over, relax Mum."

We visited the penguins on Bolder Beach, and monkeys on the Cape of Good Hope. Rob and Sam managed to visit a few other local delights themselves too, which Pip and I were not invited to join. We all had a totally fun time; it was a spectacular holiday and cricket tour.

Somewhere around about this time Rob received an invitation to return to Addenbrooke's. Not as a patient, but as a guest at the opening of the new Teenage Cancer Trust ward. Whilst Pip and I thought it was quite a nice thing to receive although perhaps a little bit odd, Rob was aghast. Why would anyone possibly think that a 20 year old, busy trying to get on with his life after treatment for cancer, would want to go and eat vol-au-vents at the opening of a new teenage cancer unit? The invitation sat on the kitchen worktop, awaiting a response. When I looked closely, the invitation had come from the same young lady who we had shared such a disastrous meeting with Rob all those months ago. I could still see her inappropriate wonky smile, and hear her nervous giggle. I think this was another rather dodgy call on her part. Needless to say Pip replied to say that Rob, and indeed his parents, wouldn't be accepting their kind invitation.

As the English cricket season got underway, so did Rob's attempt to gain full membership of the MCC. He had already been accepted as a probationer, and whilst he had taken a year of absence the previous season whilst in chemo, he was now ready to play his matches, and hopefully fulfil the requirement. It was wonderful to watch him pack his kit bag, and head off, full of life, full of optimism. MCC matches are always rather gentlemanly affairs, and I knew he would have a good time.

August 2012 was upon us and the cricket season was interrupted for our promised family trip to Stoupa, Greece. I'd promised Rob all those months previously, during the first of his many horrendous bone marrow tests that we would all go, and so we did. Pip, Sam, Rob and I set off from London bound for Kalamata airport, and Tom and Julie flew into Athens from Dubai and then drove to meet us.

Our flight was pretty unremarkable. The boys behaved like a pair of excited 5 year olds, and Pip and I rolled our eyes a lot. Once at Kalamata we hired a taxi for the 2-hour trek over the mountains. We sat Pip up front, and he nodded knowingly to our driver as he rattled on in Greek. I sat sandwiched between Sam and Rob, trying to ignore the sweat running down.... well everywhere! The sight of Stoupa and the beautiful beaches was a bit of a home-coming, and we were all incredibly excited.

Tom and Julie were already there; they greeted us alongside our hostess. As I began my stagger up the outdoor staircase to our apartment overlooking the sea, I found the breath to order four pints from the bar. A quick turnabout and we were heading for our first sip of something long and cool. As I looked up Julie was sipping her ... SODA WATER! Wow! she was pregnant!! I am extremely proud of the fact that at that moment in my life, perhaps the only moment in my life, I kept full control of my mouth. I necked half my beer, the boys slapped their lips and then Pip, yes Pip, put his foot in it. Well, Tom had to confess, "It's really early days, and Jules is taking it quietly, but yes, we are expecting our first child." I've had a few feelings in my time, but this was up there with the best of them. I was going to be a Granny – this was going to be fun, fun, fun!

We had a lovely week. The boys played pat-ball in the sea. Julie took it easy on the beach and Pip and I watched our family. Happy days!

Over the summer I began to get out on my bike, and Rob started to talk about joining me. He didn't actually have time of course, and before we knew it, he was back off to Loughborough University - time to start year 2 of his degree.

To say we were proud of him would be a total understatement. He was now a year behind his friends, and his confidence in life had taken a massive knock. Rob totally committed to student life once again, he returned with a clear picture of how precious life was, how every moment had to count. He wasn't going to miss a beat. I made numerous neurotic visits, Pip and I didn't like to miss more than a couple of days without a phone call, but we knew we had to let him go. He had to feel that we were confident in the future. We had to allow ourselves to feed off his energy and determination.

****

All through these months, Rob had been retaining some sense of independence due to the money Pip and I paid monthly into his bank account. It allowed him to put petrol into his car. It allowed him to pay match fees, buy some golf balls, and even the odd pint of beer. Due to the timing of his diagnosis, right at the end of the academic year, he wasn't liable for rent on a university flat. Obviously that was a simple matter of luck; we know that with most young people in Rob's position, this is not the case. Rob didn't need to worry about feeding or clothing himself, he didn't need to worry about the expenses of getting to and from Addenbrooke's. Ever since his first application for state benefit back in July 2011, Pip's wrangling with the DWP had rumbled on.

On the 15th December 2011 Pip was due to have his day in court. Rob's appeal was set to be heard and Pip was ready to have his say, and argue Rob's position. Another father, Ian Leech, had crusaded back in 2010; after watching his own 20-year-old daughter Melissa, die penniless. With the help of his MP, he had campaigned for students like her, and by implication Rob, to be supported by the State. The House of Commons was forced by Helen Goodman, the then Under-Secretary at the Department of Work and Pensions, to acknowledge that money would be found to make it an automatic right for students like Melissa and Rob to receive automatic benefits. Sadly, this change in policy was never properly or fully communicated at grass roots level.

As a fully paid up member of our great nation, I don't think anyone would begrudge this handful of our young people financial support. They are not scroungers, they are simply young, and have had no time to build up any kind of resources. We know that Rob, and before him Melissa Leech, are not alone. They are young sick adults, suffering not only an horrendously bad hand in the health stakes, but terrible extra worry and hardship financially. I would challenge our politicians to commission research into how many of these young adults die, simply because they can't afford to get to their treatment, and then try and sleep easy at night! Shame on them!!

Anyway on the 15th December 2011, Pip was doing his legal press-ups over his porridge when the phone rang; it was a Court Official. The Judge had considered the appeal papers, submitted in advance of the actual hearing, and had reached the view that Rob's appeal should be allowed. Pip was consequently advised that the Judge would be finding in Rob's favour. His claim for ESA would be met, since his student loan should, for this period, be disregarded. Rob was to be considered not in full-time education at the date of the claim. Rob didn't actually receive any money until February 2012, by which time his treatment had finished, and typical of Rob's character, he was busy working both for payment and voluntarily. No further claim was therefore made.

On the advice of our MP at the time, Sir Bob Russell, Pip had also lodged an application on Rob's behalf for DLA – that too was unsuccessful.

****

The Rob George Foundation:

The current reality is that if you take an enforced gap in your education - in Rob's case due to his treatment for leukaemia - you are no longer eligible to draw on your student loan. That's not unreasonable, as for that period of time, you are not studying, and in any case you'll need your loan to live on when you return to your course, when you are better!

In Rob's case, on both occasions he was taken ill at the end of an academic year. But others may well be part way through the year, and on top of all the other normal expenses of living that don't go away simply because of illness, they may find themselves obligated to landlords for rent for their accommodation. Unless you are prepared to totally abandon your course, you will, at the current time, continue to be considered a student and therefore entitled to your student loan. But of course you have been forced to take a year out (which the benefit department are determined to call a "Gap Year", which carries totally different connotations in my head) so you are not entitled to any benefits. You are penniless and fall totally back on the mercies of your family, if you have one. And even if you do, they may or may not be able to support you.

At the RGF we have already helped many young folks who find themselves in this lamentable position. We have helped pay their rent so that they can retain their independence, keep a roof over their heads, and not get into debt. We have helped pay for fuel or fares so that they can get to their appointments which will often be miles from home. We help with some of the household bills that quickly mount up when you suddenly find yourself without any income.

Pip, a lawyer, continues to try and get the law changed. We believe that the spirit of the benefit system would want to support our young people in such desperate times. In fact the Government claims the "Spirit of the benefit system does just that"! After all we are not talking about so many youngsters that it would bankrupt the system. This "Forgotten Tribe" seems to fall into a black hole – and they are too ill to complain or make a fuss. I wonder how many of them actually die because they can't afford to get themselves to hospital? It's a disgusting situation. We have a whole folder of letters, each one more eloquent that the one before, and each one yet more skilled at dodging the issue, and not actually answering Pip's questions. If you want to read Rob's whole disgusting experience of the DWP take a look at our website www.therobgeorgefoundation.org where you can read the whole story.

****

Aim 2: To financially support young people who demonstrate commitment and/or talent in the worlds of sport or performing arts, who can show that they are being held back by their financial position.

Aim 2 comes from Rob's love of life, music and sport. He wanted to protect us - that's especially his family - from only being exposed to sick young people; as he put it, "People just like me! Get involved with some bright, healthy young things too!"

The one thing having a serious illness can give you is time. Time spent being treated, feeling shitty, but also time waiting. Rob sat for hours waiting for test results, waiting for appointments, waiting for various bags of stuff to be dripped into him, waiting for them to work. He spent much of that time looking around him and thinking about all the things he was going to do to improve what he observed once he was better – top of that list being to re-organise Addenbrooke's Outpatients Department! (Perhaps one day I'll share with them his observations.)

Whenever Rob could find the energy, he'd pop along to Colchester Golf Club. I bet that after the hours he used to spend practising on the putting green, there are many members who, whilst walking up the 18th hole towards the clubhouse, could close their eyes and still see him there. Rob wondered what happened to all those friends he'd shared sport and music with over the years. Where had they gone? Some had demonstrated more natural talent and enthusiasm even than him, but they'd fallen by the way side. What would our world be like if people didn't participate? It didn't much matter in what, but without clubs, teams, orchestras, competition, performance, life was pretty grey, possibly even meaningless.

Rob came to the conclusion that, in many cases, young people were robbed of the opportunity of realising their full potential simply because, as you get older it gets more expensive. You become less cuddly, and it's more awkward for families to share in your progress. Family finances become ever more stretched. So many young people simply fall by the wayside. The team members, the potential treasurers and captains, maybe even our medal winners of the future, find that giving up is their only option.

And so Aim 2 was added to the Rob George Foundation's first aim. Young people who demonstrate exceptional commitment and/or ability in the worlds of sport or the performing arts, but who are held back by their financial position, can apply for funding.

We have already helped a whole raft of young people, many of whom are striving to represent our country and, all of whom are also juggling impossibly tight financial burdens. We have been thrown into the worlds of Badminton, Hurdling, Judo, Boxing, Athletics, Duathlon, Fencing, Karate, Trampolining, Ice-skating, Swimming, Underwater Hockey, Skiing, Rifle shooting; as well as worlds already very familiar to us like Cricket, Golf and Football. Then there is the Pianist, the Singer, Magician, Clarinettist, Ballet dancer, Actor... the list goes on and on. All these young people are battling against the odds, and grateful for being given the chance to progress to the next level. Maybe, some day Rob's name will be linked, in just a tiny way, to an Olympic medal or two, and then what good might those young people do, inspiring those younger than themselves to strive to reach their full potential too. We have already been thrilled by the efforts of some of our Aim 2 grantees, who have themselves, raised money for the RGF. It is a rolling snowball that our society needs to cherish.

Chapter 10

Saturday 9 May, 2015 – an excited 7.45am, JOGLE Day 8 Dumfries to Penrith (63.3 miles +1937ft)

Well, this morning we leave with a spring in our step, and possibly a tear in our eye too. I also left with my feet wrapped in plastic bags and stuffed into my still sodden cycle shoes, but let's not think about that for too long! At dinner last night I had suggested that some of us slower riders leave a bit earlier. My intention had been to give us a bit of a head start and take the strain off possibly missing our own party, which was due that evening. I also hoped to try to relieve the pressure we were feeling, being constantly behind. I arrived at the agreed 7.45am to find just about everyone else also raring to go – well that was lovely, but not quite what I had had in mind! Perhaps I'd been a little too subtle – not like me at all! In honour of the fact that today would have been Rob's 23rd birthday, Claire awarded the Moustache to Abi. Fossie's quiz is another roll-over and some very special friends are meeting us either along the route on their bikes, or at tonight's hotel for a bit of a knees up. The other big news is that we will finally be leaving Scotland – England here we come!!

The hills don't look too bad on the route profile, and the weather isn't looking bad either. Terry has set off bright and early bound for Penrith with Claire's battered bike on his roof rails. He has a date with a bike shop that will hopefully sort it out. We set off, bound in the first instance for Gretna Green, where the plan is to meet up with Max's family and our dear fellow Trustee David and his wife Julie. Pip and I had had months of build up to this moment, with the extended experience of David and Julie's bike purchases, and training. We couldn't wait to see them, and hopefully they would provide us with some much anticipated and appreciated company and encouragement for a few hours.

Though sunny, the roads were still damp from yesterday's downpour. The skies were now pretty clear, and wrapped snuggly in our cycle gear we were all keen to be off. We soon settled into an elongated group of 8, us slow coaches managing to keep Claire and Antonius vaguely in our sights – it must have been flat and they must have chosen to take it steady! We soon picked up our trusty National Cycle Route and the countryside began to anticipate becoming England. Fields with hedgerows appeared, it began to look all rather encouragingly English. We nattered away and the miles ticked by. We quickly passed through Bankend, and then Ruthwell, Powfoot and Annan. We'd picked up the route of the local railway line, and began to talk about how our friends had driven to Penrith and then caught the train this morning to meet us at Gretna. There was a definite buzz.

We passed through Eastriggs and Rigg, following the course of the Channel of the River Esk, and looked across the channel to Bowness-on-Solway and one end of Hadrian's Wall. Abi kept the nattering at full tilt with her latest little gem, gleaned from our chocolate biscuit wrappers:

"Do you know that kangaroos have three vaginas?"

Well, I'm not sure what one is supposed to say to that?

It was delightfully dry and flat. By this stage we were on National Cycle Route 7, which was a very enjoyable run. We seemed to arrive at Gretna Green in no time, 28 miles on the clock and everyone in high spirits. We had great fun standing by the sign marking the border with England and taking our group selfies using Abi's stick whilst drivers passing by tooted their horns. We laughed that Gretna Green was the venue chosen for around 5000 weddings per year, and we still hadn't managed to get Nigel H and Elizabeth there simultaneously! Now a wedding on Rob's Ride would have been worth a chapter on its own!

We stuck to National Cycle Route 7, heading south for Carlisle. We had our fingers crossed that Max and her team had successfully found the agreed Costa's in Gretna town centre and we would all meet up at any moment. It didn't take us long to reach Carlisle which was originally a Roman settlement, developed to serve all the forts on Hadrian's Wall. Pip enjoyed a few little reminiscences of his walk shared with his sister Cath along the length of the wall a few years previously. It is a great sadness to me, and possibly to Pip, that I am not much of a walker – or alternatively it is a great relief to him that I don't enjoy a "good" walk and he can at least find some peace! I blame the excessive length of his legs; I have to run just to keep up!

We entered Carlisle along the banks of the River Eden and then muddled our way through central Carlisle. We should have seen the cathedral, but that seemed to elude us, I think others saw it more than once! Then, out the other side on the banks of the very swollen River Caldew. We followed that river path for the next 6 miles, and thoroughly enjoyed the traffic-free stretch. Route No 7 then takes you onto a string of single-track roads; they were perfect. From about the 40 mile mark things started heading a bit more uphill, but all manageable. There was still no sign of the others, which was a little strange. We pushed on through Skelton to Laithes, which was pretty much the top of the

Elle arrived – phew!

climb. Picking up the River Petteril we fairly painlessly manoeuvred our way into downtown Penrith, and found our hotel, The North Lakes Hotel and Spa. There to meet us, were our friends Iain and Tony, Nicola and Terry's friends Pat and Mike, Elizabeth's old college friend Seema, Abi's Sister Harri and her friend too, and Emma, Adi's wife. Also, already arrived, were all the other cyclists. I have to confess I was a little confused, and just a tad disappointed. Of course, the explanation was simple - they had selected a different way. Presumably a more direct route, also presumably on main roads. Hey ho! - their bike, their ride and their choice. That night our bikes were stored in the ballroom. Well how appropriate, they too were going to a party!

Iain and Tony's enthusiasm was wonderful to experience. Tony took loads of action photos of us all pulling in, in various states of flushed faces. It was a moment full of energy and love. We heard how Terry had been disappointed at the Penrith bike shop with Claire's bike, so had actually completed a round trip to include Crewe. Everything had gone well and the repair was complete. Fortunately Terry had even managed to do an emergency stop to save Claire's bike from a complete write-off by ploughing into the car park's height restriction barrier; the bike was on the car roof – lightening reflexes Tezza!

We arrived in our room to the most beautiful bouquet of flowers. Rob's three best mates from school days had sent them to mark our "half way mark" and Rob's birthday. Dobbsy, Tuckers and James were and are a very fine example of Rob's mates. The flowers were gorgeous, and the challenge then was on to work out an appropriate recipient, as flowers on the bike weren't really going to work. There was also a bottle of champagne from Pip's sister and her husband David. It was all very exciting.

We quickly invited Nicola & Terry, Nigel H & Elizabeth to come and share the champers with us and I hurried off for a massage, that had been kindly arranged for me by Claire. I loved it, although try though the therapist might, I didn't really manage to relax. She pronounced my legs "shot to pieces" – well I knew that!

After a glass of chilled champagne our little party went down to meet everyone. It seemed strange to see everyone dressed up; I had even put my well-travelled party frock on. A private area had been set-aside for us and the Prosecco was on ice. Making sure everyone had a glass in hand I made the most heartfelt speech of my life. After all, today we should have been raising a glass to Rob on his 23rd birthday. It was a big day and an emotionally charged moment.

I can remember very clearly what I said – I meant every word. Whilst laying face down on the massage couch an hour earlier, looking at the floor through the hole these contraptions have, I experienced one of those moments of clarity. It wasn't any real surprise that Rob had yet again pulled off a masterstroke; it was becoming increasingly obvious that Rob was wise, way beyond his years.

Whilst he couldn't have begun to realise - or perhaps more accurately, would have been far too modest to anticipate - how deeply we would all be affected by his death, he knew he wanted to reach back and help me. I can only speak for myself here, not for mothers the world over, but losing Rob for me, truly felt like a part of my core had died too. A thread of ice runs through my soul, and no matter how happy we manage to be, no matter how exhausted I am, no matter where I go or what I do, nothing quite reaches that steely vein. Rob knew that I would need to do something extreme to reach that place so deep inside me. Hence his challenge: Rob's Ride, through his eyes.

Going the fastest route between John O'Groats and Land's End wouldn't hack it. Going on the nice surfaced main roads wouldn't hack it. He wanted to see the country. He wanted to see the countryside and villages. He wanted me to go and see them for him. He knew it would take patience to wiggle from view to view. He knew it would mean extra hours out in the weather. He knew it would mean sticking with a tough brief. He knew I would have to dig deep inside myself; if not, the challenge wouldn't have been fulfilled, and my promise to him still outstanding.

The thing about cycling until you are totally knackered, having pushed yourself way beyond a place you feel comfortable, in kit that anyone in their right mind would chuck out rather than dry and put on again the next day, is that in order to stay with Rob's challenge, I would have to feel again. I mean really feel right in my soul, that I was truly still alive. That was what Rob was banking on - that I would prove that I could live my life with all my light bulbs burning; I could live my life laughing to my core; I could live my life puffing and panting but at full throttle – I could find that place again where every cell is throbbing with life, mine and Rob's too, deep in my heart. It takes me by surprise when I feel like I am living without my grief "spoiling" the moment, and I do still feel guilty, almost like it is being disloyal to his memory. But that is wrong and unnecessary, and makes the life I have before me meaningless, wasted. He knew what he was doing with that promise – clever boy – thank you Rob!! I asked everyone to join me in raising their glasses and making a toast:

"To living!"

"To living!" everyone replied.

I looked up to see Fossie with his first drink since New Year, and Carl, our man Friday, with tears coursing down his cheeks. He got it - Carl totally got it! We had persuaded him to join Pip and me for dinner, to share the birthday party; it was fun to have a chance to chat and get to know him a little better. Every night he had refused to stay in the hotels with us. No matter what the weather was dishing out, he had gone off either to camp, or sleep in the van. He wanted to save the trip as much money as he could - that was his personal contribution to the fundraising of the Rob George Foundation. I'd love to share a trip with Carl again, although I'm not sure about riding a bike. I might need to volunteer to drive his van!

Pip finished the formalities off and everyone went through for a sumptuous dinner. A wonderful picture was presented to us after our meal, signed by every rider. It is a picture of a champagne bottle and the label reads:

"Tonight we shall sip champagne and be spectacular!"

****

April 2013

As we approached Rob's 21st birthday, we yet again asked the question. "What about a party Rob?" May 9th 2013 wasn't far off. It was a special milestone for anyone, being 21, but perhaps especially so for Rob. As it happened, Tom and Julie along with our new baby grand daughter Ella, would be visiting from Dubai. It seemed too good an opportunity to miss. The plan came together pretty easily in the end, with the love and support of a family friend Jenny; it actually turned into something verging on the spectacular. Jenny's partner Mac was the games master at Colchester Royal Grammar School, and had been part of all of our boys' school lives, but our friendship went deeper than that. Pip and Mac had played very serious cricket together as young men, and co-incidentally Jenny and Mac had been holidaying in Cape Town when we'd been out there on tour at Easter-time the previous year. Over a natter, Rob had shared with Jenny that he really wanted to get into Sports Events Management once he'd finished his degree, and had his eye on a company called IMG. Jenny immediately leapt in with, "I might be able to help."

Each year IMG ran a pre-Wimbledon warm up tennis tournament at The Hurlingham Club, Putney, London. Jenny, as Head of the Sports Executive of the Club, and also as an ex student of Loughborough University, wanted to help support Rob and his total commitment to getting on with his life, and so had helped with some work experience. On top of all of that, at very short notice, Jenny went on to arrange for us to host Rob's 21st birthday party in the Orangery at the Club.

We started with champagne on the terrace overlooking the River Thames, and the Croquet Lawn. All the lads gathered. Black tie was the dress code for this special occasion. The only ladies invited were Julie, Sam's then young lady, (who also happened to be a very talented cake maker – which was handy!) and baby Ella - oh and me!!

Rob had selected the menu - Roast Beef with all the trimmings, followed by a trio of chocolate puddings. His speech had us all weeping with laughter, sadness and total pride too. This young man was obviously wise beyond his years, and to see all his friends listening so intently, whilst managing to also interject with their usual brand of heckling was an honour to witness.

After the formal party was over the real party kicked off. Rob, and the lads headed off for a local nightclub, where Rob had organised a private booth. He said afterwards that it was the only time he had ever played the 'Cancer Card.' When he had rung to try and book the private area he'd been told that it was fully booked. So he'd laid it on thick, about how he was in remission from leukaemia, how it was his 21st, how surely they couldn't not find him a private booth, under the circumstances – this particular young lady had obviously had the full benefit of Rob's not insignificant charms; they had a blast!! It was with some degree of relief that parents weren't required for this bit of the proceedings!

****

June 2013

Then everything came crumbling down. We found ourselves back in the Haematology Day Unit of Addenbrooke's Hospital. It was exactly two years to the day since Rob's first diagnosis and he couldn't even sit to wait for the doctors to come and examine him. The pain was excruciating. He paced. He sat with his head in his hands. It was appalling. Pip and I sat on the edge of our seats, willing someone to do something. Willing this nightmare to go away.

It wasn't long before the nurses took pity on him and ushered us from the chairs in the corridor where everyone waited, to a bed at the side of the unit. At least here I was able to draw the curtains across, and pretend that life wasn't trundling on as normal around us. We all knew that the cancer was back. We all knew some of what lay ahead for us. Rob knew that all the life gained from the previous months of chemotherapy, all the fitness gained from all those hours in the gym, all the plans dreamt of during those months back in the real world, were gone. All of that, he was going to need to fight for all over again. We didn't need an audience of old sick people whilst we tried to come to terms with it.

Bloods were taken, another bone marrow test was taken and it wasn't long before Emma popped up at the end of Rob's bed. "Hey Rob! Bet you wished you weren't seeing me again; you're going to come and stay with us again, for a while. We've got a swanky new ward now; I've already got your room ready; we'll get you transferred down and get cracking with a plan." It was like meeting one of your very best old friends, except we had hoped never to see her again.

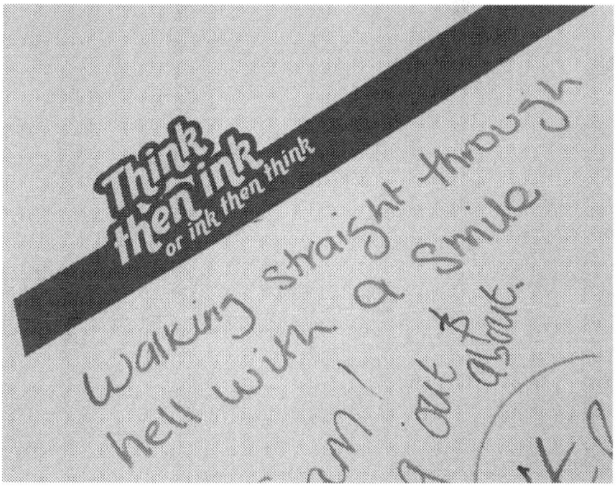

As the porter arrived to wheel Rob downstairs, the pain emanating from his back so crippling that he couldn't walk, he grabbed my arm,

"Don't leave me Mum, promise me!" Pip and I managed a weary smile – we weren't going anywhere.

The Teenage Cancer Trust Ward was indeed sparkly and new. Everything was shiny white and navy blue, big picture windows looked out across Cambridge, countryside views in one direction, the roof tops of the famous colleges in the other. It had the feel of being on a swanky Ocean Cruise Ship. As we passed the youngsters "Chill Out Zone" there on the wall was a huge graffiti board. "Walking straight through hell with a smile," someone had written.

Sister Hannah came to say hi, Emma calmly did all the necessary stuff, and Rob shrunk into the bed. He had fought for weeks and weeks with the increasing certainty that the leukaemia was back. Everyone had tried to convince him he was mistaken, but it was now confirmed. Our little friend over in the CRUK building had looked down his microscope, and all those vile cancerous cells had waved back.

Rob's consultant swung by, to share his clear plan. Rob would have another three cycles of chemotherapy, the final one supported by a massive dose of radiotherapy too. This course of treatment would be followed by a stem cell transplant - then the rest of Rob's life. We didn't have any options, there wasn't a plan B. Chemo would start immediately. Apart from anything else, the chemo would destroy the activity of Rob's bone marrow, and this would in turn take away the horrendous pain he was experiencing.

We already knew from Tom's tissue match taken the first time around, that he wasn't a match for Rob, and so now Sam was hot-footed to Addenbrooke's for his test. The odds weren't great, 1 in 4 for a sibling, but he was the best shot we had. Failing that the National Register, and then possibly the International Register, of willing donors would be searched. The Consultant was pretty confident though; Rob was young, strong, from an uncomplicated European/white ethnic background. The register was bound to find a suitable match for him; there was nothing to worry about.

Immediately it became clear that Rob's chest was full of infection once more. As the weeks ticked by, the chemo, combined with the yellow bags of anti fungal medication, kept us close to the ward. This time Rob wanted to see his friends. Perhaps it was as simple as, that on this ward his friends would be welcome, but also we had to make this time around, somehow different. Busloads of Uni friends turned up, armed with the sorts of gifts that only young people could bring. One was a multi-coloured large, stuffed, legless "creature". When I asked what it was, I was told it was slug; to remind Rob of his room at University! Apparently his room had been so damp, Rob regularly had to remove the slugs from the walls. Rob had done battle with his landlord, but the problem had not been sorted. He'd never uttered a word to us. That Landlord should be hung out to dry for taking rent for such a place, and now Rob was fighting off another humungous chest infection, no wonder!

Pip and I were back going up and down in that wretched lift every day, the dulcet tones of the anonymous female etched in our minds, "Doors closing – lift going up."

We had another visit to our chirpy chap for a second Hickman Line. He was soooo pleased to see us. "You're getting to be one of my best customers," he quipped. It hadn't been that long since he'd removed the first one.

Rob just lay back in his bed; he didn't eat, hardly drank, it was all so hard. We tried to tempt him with small tit bits of food. Pip had gone off to the local supermarket and we'd stocked up on small salty crackers, pots of jelly, fresh pineapple (good for neutralizing the metallic flavour chemo leaves you with). I tried to remember what it had been like when I was pregnant, and that constant feeling of nausea couldn't be shaken off. I had used to make up a plate of Ritz biscuits, spread with a variety of toppings and leave them in the fridge. Then, the second I felt like eating, it was ready; those moments didn't last for long! I suggested a lolly, "Callipo," he replied. Pip leapt to his feet and dashed off to the food hall on site. For days the only things Rob ate were ice-lollies and Burger King ice cream.

Sam's tissue test was still outstanding, and we were all still holding our breaths. Almost every day I'd bump into a mother in the "Parents Zone" brandishing her computer print out of how many matches had been found for her child, how many 10 out of 10 matches, how many 9 out of 10... Rob's phone rang; it was Sam. Dear Sam was so distressed, he could hardly speak. "Don't worry buddy, it's not your fault, I love you," we heard Rob say. He hung up, and wept in our arms. Whilst we had all known the odds, we couldn't help but hope. Now, all our hopes lay with the national register.

Years previously, whilst we were still newly weds, Pip had been a member of our local Round Table. At that time, the Anthony Nolan Bone Marrow Register had been launched, and Round Table nationally had supported it. Recruitment drives had been organised, awareness campaigns championed, Pip and his mates had got involved. It seemed ironic that here we were, all these years later, turning to that very register, hoping it would unlock the key to saving our Rob's life.

We plagued the transplant team for news on how the search was progressing, and were told that nearly 40 potential matches had been identified. They were though, already looking internationally. We celebrated, phew; one of them was sure to be the one.

The infection gradually subsided, the medication was to be continued as a precautionary action for the foreseeable future, and we were allowed home for a week or so before round 2 of chemo. No visiting Colchester's Haematology Day Unit this time though. Everything would be done in Cambridge. At least three times a week we would make the 120-mile round trip. I would get up early on these days, dash over to our local Co-op and come home to prepare our lunches. Rob wouldn't touch hospital food; he didn't know who had made it, what germs they might have inadvertently contaminated it with, he was totally focused on healthy eating, fresh ingredients – that was fine by me.

The Day Unit was functioning way beyond its capacity. Patients were squeezed in cheek by jowl; space was at a total premium. Rob would sit there terrified of catching something. I'd watch him pull up the hood on his sweatshirt, zip up the zip, put his earphones in, close his eyes and try to take up as little space as possible. On a good day, he'd be allocated a reclining chair in a corner, where he could share as little air as possible with anyone else. On a bad day, he'd be sat in an upright chair and get knocked and jostled as his neighbours received their treatment too. We'd arrive by 9.00am and would regularly still be there at 6.00pm. The process of blood tests and the consequent blood and platelet transfusions, and the anti fungal medication took hours.

On one of these days, Rob sat next to quite a young girl. She looked awful, but then everyone did. In the middle of the afternoon this young lady had a terrible coughing fit, "Well that's me done for!" Rob stated. Within the hour he was feeling unwell. Within the next hour he had taken himself over to a vacant bed, set aside for people who came in to donate their stem cells. He didn't ask permission. I chastised him and said he couldn't just put himself to bed. He replied, "I'm ill alright, they'll catch up soon." He knew he was ill. When the Day Unit Sister asked him why he was there, he just replied, "You'll see."

At these appointments Rob's temperature was taken every hour. At the next visit, his was on the up. Within 2½ hours of that sneeze, he was burning up. By this time it was 6.30pm. "Sorry sweetheart, but you're not going home tonight." Back to the TCT ward we went, Emma was waiting to welcome us. In fact we went back into the room we hadn't long left – home from home.

Bit by bit the infection took a hold, and his chest was a mess. The subject of a repeat bronchoscopy was broached. As Emma told me the suggestion had been made, I just said, "Well good luck with that one." Whilst I could understand the need, I also remembered all too clearly what Rob had gone through before. He was not going to be keen to sign on the dotted line to go through that again.

Anyway, somehow Emma and Hannah, and I suppose Pip and I persuaded him that this time it would all be different.

He'd been unlucky before. We would all ensure that history didn't repeat itself. A new respiratory consultant came to visit and after a lot of arm twisting, convinced Rob that the procedure was vital to try to get this infection under control; that the stem cell transplant needed him to be infection free; and that she would absolutely make sure that it was nothing like last time.

Off we all went to the Endoscopy department, Rob wheeled on his own bed, by now too ill to even manage a wheelchair. Indeed the reception and care of the nurses was a wholly different experience. Sadly, yet again the sedation had no effect. Rob was awake throughout the whole thing, he felt tricked and totally traumatized. Rob said he felt physically and mentally abused by that procedure.

Yet again, nothing much was forthcoming on the results front. The nurses even went down the route of isolating his Central Line, in case the infection was there. A cannula was inserted into his hand, with a triple access so that the line could be checked out, but no joy. Rob's breathing deteriorated, and he was put on oxygen. Physio's visited, to try and help him clear his chest, but nothing helped.

Sister Hannah was worried; he looked awful, and nothing seemed to be helping. Before we knew what was happening Rob was being transferred to the Critical Care Unit. It's one step down from Intensive Care and it was a total shock.

He had wires and monitors attached everywhere imaginable, an oxygen mask going at full pelt, and horribly painful Venus blood tests were being taken regularly. But the worst bit was looking around him. Everyone was unconscious. The only sound was that of the machines, and the rustle of the staff as they all moved around in their plastic aprons and disposable overalls, their steps masked by their rubber Crocs on the polished lino floors. Nobody really spoke. That's not to say they were unfriendly, just unused to their patients actually being awake, and especially having a mother and father in tow.

A nurse was positioned at the end of Rob's bed, with a huge tilted desk like a draftsman's. It was covered with charts, where every reading was recorded, and any slight fluctuation was monitored. Emma popped down to visit on her lunch break; it was so good to see her. She said how they would try as best they could to keep Rob's room available for him; she was sure he wouldn't be down here long. Well she was right, Rob hated it and by close of play that day he was being removed back to the ward, much improved. Perhaps his infamous Positive Mental Attitude had worked a miracle.

That night I elbowed the other mothers out of the way for one of the only two camp beds on the ward, I wasn't going anywhere. Politeness be buggered, our need was greater than anyone else at that time.

It was a long night; Rob tossed and turned, coughed, hacked and wheezed. Every time he woke, we'd go through the rigmarole of manoeuvring Rob, whilst attached to his drip stand, to the loo. He was even persuaded that a pee bottle in bed would be preferable, but in his temperature induced haze, combined with the exhaustion, frustration and coughing, the contents of that ended up all over the floor, resulting in the added humiliation. It was an awful night and every minute seemed to be a struggle.

6.00am obs. came around; Rob's stats were not good. The night doctor was summoned, and before we knew it we were off for a chest x-ray. Rob's left lung had collapsed. Then we had the meeting to end all meetings in Rob's room. His Haematology Consultant, the Respiratory Consultant, the ICU Consultant, shadowed by Emma and Sister Hannah, it was cosy. Come to think of it, the most amazing feat was that it should be possible to get all those big wigs in the same room at the same time. They wanted Rob in ICU, and quickly. Rob needed breathing support, and that couldn't be provided on the ward.

Rob didn't want to go. In the last 24 hours his same hospital bed had had 4 different locations, and he felt like a piece of meat being passed from department to department. Whatever they needed to do, he wanted it done on the ward. All their gear had wheels, why couldn't they bring it here, to the room he was so familiar with? Sister Hannah was in tears; Rob needed a level of care she couldn't provide on her ward, she pleaded with him to go. Still he resisted, "God knows what I'll catch surrounded by all those sick people." And then there was the problem that he didn't want to go alone.

The ICU bloke was completely unused to patients speaking up - after all his patients were usually unconscious. I lost the plot big time, and yelled at my captive audience that if Rob went, then Pip and I went too. One of us would be by his side at all times, that was the deal. Did they all understand that Rob was neutropenic? Could they ensure that his leukaemia treatment plan would also be kept up with?

I stand by every word I yelled, and if you could have seen the look on Rob's face, you'd have been cheering me on too. I took Pip's silence as his support – it wouldn't have been his preferred approach, but anyway, it got the result Rob and we wanted.

Within 20 minutes, a separate bay in ICU had been cleared and was being deep cleaned. A reclining chair that I could sleep in, had been located, and as Rob was being wheeled down to his new location, a TV was being dusted off and re-tuned so that he could watch Wimbledon. They were miniscule and meaningless victories, but it served to help us feel some shred of control. It seemed unbelievable that things had deteriorated so quickly. Rob was fighting for his life, and the statistic I had read so many months ago - that more leukaemia patients die of an infection during treatment than of their leukaemia - rang in my ears.

As Rob was wheeled off the TCT ward his eyes were brimming with tears; I think everyone's were. Emma came down with us, but that unspoken question of whether we would ever return hung silent and heavy in the air.

It was action stations once we arrived in the Intensive Care Unit. All the expected things happened; the oxygen was at 100% and Rob was armed with a suction tube. Every time he coughed, we were to stick this to the back of his mouth and try and suck out the gunk; copious quantities of the stuff were collected. Then the nurse appeared with the CPAP mask. It was like some instrument of medieval torture. This would be strapped across his nose and mouth, half an hour on, half an hour off. A suction seal would grip his face, and oxygen would be forced into his lungs on every breath in. The aim was to re-inflate the collapsed lung. The longer he could bear it, the more chance of success we had.

It was truly awful to watch. With the backdrop of the tennis commentary, we watched Rob fight with this mask. Every breath saw his eyes bulge from his face as the air was forced inside him and his chest resisted the attempted inflation. We could only hope it was working. He said afterwards that during those hours he had reached a depth into his own self that he didn't know existed. The feeling of claustrophobia was almost overwhelming. The Positive Mental Attitude, or as he called it his PMA, had never been more evident or tested.

The nurses from the TCT unit popped down, and when they couldn't fit that in, regular messages arrived as they checked on Rob's progress. It seemed odd not to see the Haematology team, but I suppose at that time Rob's breathing had to be the priority.

Day 2 of the CPAP, and during one of Rob's horrendous coughing episodes, the nurse on duty as usual came flying across to release the mask and let Rob get rid of all the phlegm and catch his breath. As she lifted the mask away, she dropped it in horror. Rob's hair had started to fall out, for the second time. She cried out in shock; I later wept in the corridor for Rob. We knew this would happen, but hadn't been expecting it quite so soon. Pip was dispatched for the clippers. I'd done this before, and I could do it again. ICU had never seen anything like it, but hey, that was their problem – welcome to our world!

During the following hours, every time the mask was released it would be caked in the bristles from Rob's face. The nurses would tenderly wipe them away with wet wipes, before it was replaced across his face. It was hideous, messy, itchy, an unnecessary twist. Rob was incredibly brave. He regularly refused to have the mask removed when the allotted time was up. He knew the longer he could tolerate it, the better his chance of recovery was - this want on day and night. The staff of ICU quickly thawed towards us. Having arrived under a label of 'unreasonable, noisy and demanding', they could see with their own eyes what a strong team we were. Rob wanted us, and we wanted to be with Rob. He was going through hell, and the way he was coping was a lesson for us all.

I do remember one particularly low point whilst in ICU. It was the weekend, and the Haematology Consultants covered them in turn, working, in theory, one in four. I dare say they worked many more than that in reality. This particular Consultant was one that we had not really had many dealings with, and in any case Rob was now under the transplant team, so there was no need to build a relationship with him. He was a total buffoon of a man (obviously that's my opinion.) After a couple of visits, he announced on the Sunday afternoon, "Goodness, you two are always here, why don't you take a break, pop off into Cambridge and have a nice meal or something?" I wondered what planet this bloke was living on? Did he really expect us to toddle off, maybe crack open a tasty bottle of plonk, whilst our youngest son did battle with a CPAP mask – I don't think so!

Gradually the treatment worked and, not a day too soon we were allowed back to our ward. Everyone was so pleased to see us. If Emma could have played the trumpet, she'd have been tooting it.

As often happened with these infections, the labs came up with a label for your bug some weeks down the line. Rob had contracted the Rhino Virus – a common cold!

The following morning, I was making myself a cuppa in the Parents' Zone. Another mother was sitting there nursing her coffee, and I broke my golden rule, and started up a conversation. A normally chatty person, you'll be surprised that I hadn't nattered to many of the other parents. We all had enough troubles of our own; generally there wasn't a lot of "sharing" going on. This mum though, wanted to talk. She'd seen Rob return, and having also witnessed his departure had to say how much better he looked. She had been sure he was going to die!

Her 15-year old daughter also had cancer and wasn't doing too well. It turned out that the family were Jehovah's Witnesses, and as such were not permitted to receive transfusions of blood or platelets. When I looked back at how many blood products Rob had willingly received and how they had kept him alive to this point, I simply couldn't understand her. She was waiting for the chap in charge of her Kingdom Hall to pitch up with his "black book". He was going to meet with her daughter's doctors and tell them what was permissible. Bloody Hell! Wasn't all this difficult enough? How could you tie the hands of these amazing humans in this way? "I'm right to stick to my beliefs, aren't I?" she asked me. I couldn't possibly answer that question, we have to respect everyone's beliefs and decisions, but I couldn't actually agree with her either. I couldn't help but wonder if the positions had been reversed, and if her daughter had been the 21 year-old reluctant adult, and Rob had been the 15 year-old "child", whether we'd have been having this conversation. I have no idea what became of that lady's daughter. I don't suppose it ended well.

In amongst all this, I left a message for Elizabeth back at home. We were due to be going to cycle Cuba that October. All being well, Rob would be slap bang in the middle of his transplant then, so sorry, but I was going to have to cry off. Of course she wouldn't and didn't mind. I knew Elizabeth would deal with everything, and I didn't give it another thought.

Abi made regular visits, always armed with a gift to keep us all amused. She'd left Rob with a CD of favourite tunes, and her selection was played on repeat. He hated the absolute quiet, and whilst we tried to steer him to other playlists, he always returned to that CD. Abi made Rob a book, full of homemade puzzles, "interesting" facts, "funny" jokes; she must have spent hours on it.

"Did we know that 1 in 10 European babies are conceived in an Ikea bed?"

Rob loved it. Abi's family supported her visiting Rob, and whilst she is a very competent driver, one night when the weather was particularly filthy and she refused to cancel her visit, her

Granddad Trevor came across with her to Cambridge, and sat and waited whilst she visited. He joined Pip and me for supper, although whilst we did our best to eat the hospital food, Trevor strangely managed to resist. Well in our case, needs must. Abi needed support too, and we were at full stretch.

No sooner had Rob just about recovered from the whole chest infection debacle, Cycle 2 of chemo was waved under his nose. Emma couldn't believe it, surely they would at least give him a week off to recover some strength, but no, it was straight on with the show. We couldn't deviate from the plan.

We began with a renewed vigour to pursue the transplant team for news on a possible match. The news couldn't have been worse. Whilst Rob had been doing his grand tour of the hospital they had been wading their way through the 40+ hopefuls. Possible donors, all over the world, had undergone more detailed blood tests and analysis, and one by one, each had been struck off the list. There was nobody left. I just couldn't help but wail to Pip, "Come on, surely we were due just one lucky break?" At every turn, the cards seemed stacked against our dear Rob.

It turned out that on closer examination, Rob's blood carried a really rare extra protein. Apparently, every now and again the human race throws out these proteins randomly. It is how our species has kept itself strong. I guess the dinosaurs didn't work that one out! The conclusion had been reached, that the search, at best a needle in a haystack, had suddenly become futile.

News spread quickly amongst our friends, and Nikki, a dear friend through the Cricket Club, who also happened to be a nurse, decided to organise a recruitment drive at the club, with the help of The Anthony Nolan Trust. Social media was utilized. Local radio got involved. The local press ran a piece – it was all systems go. Anthony Nolan pitched up with 250 spit tests; a simple spit being all they need to make an initial record of tissue type. That's 100 more kits than they had ever needed at a drive like this before.

Nikki had advertised 6-8pm, but as we looked out of the front of our pavilion at 5.30pm, youngsters were already gathering. Of course Rob knew a lot of young people in Colchester, but that wasn't the reason they were there. They all realized that "There but for the Grace of God..." The queue of handsome, life filled, optimistic young people went down the front steps, across the car park, through the gates. So many of them wanted to be the one that would make a difference for Rob, but they all understood that it wasn't just Rob they were signing up to potentially help. There were others like Rob either waiting for a donor, or who would wait in the future. We estimate in excess of 450 young people showed up that evening. Every spit test was used, and then we sat those that had missed out down on the outfield, plumbed them into the Club's Wi-Fi and made sure each and every one of them registered online, so that they could do their spit tests at home.

To our knowledge, eight of those young people have gone on to be retested as possible donors so far, and four have actually donated stem cells already. What a wonderful chance of life they have donated and of course, it's all part of Rob's lasting legacy.

The second cycle of chemo was finished, and we returned home for the 3 weeks of waiting. We resumed our thrice-weekly trips to Cambridge for blood tests and products, and after a week or two we were sent an appointment to meet with Rob's consultant.

The recent bone marrow tests had confirmed that a full remission had yet again been achieved. As we were aware, a match for stem cell transplant had not been found, but never fear, they had a plan. It was all a bit cutting edge, but had we heard of a "Cord Blood Transplant"? We had read up on it, but believed it to be only really useful for infants. The consultant confirmed that the limitations were that there was only a limited quantity of cells available to be harvested from the discarded placenta after a baby's birth, unlike with a live donor, where a second harvest could be made, if necessary. The volume required for an adult - say someone of Rob's stature - would normally mean that there simply would not be enough stem cells in a Cord Blood Harvest to make a transplant viable.

However, they had found two matching cord blood donations, one in Spain, and the other in France. Both had been purchased by the NHS, had Rob's name on them and were winging their way to Addenbrooke's as we spoke. The two combined would give the required volume to give the plan a chance of success. Due to the immaturity of the stem cells slightly less of a match could be tolerated. "Right then, let's do this," was Rob's response. In fairness there wasn't a whole heap of options on the table.

We went home armed with a list of appointments and assessment dates in preparation for the transplant. There was hope in the air, sheer terror too; but definitely hope.

Rob and I spent a very long day in addition to our normal visits, whilst he had x-rays, tattoos, and breathing assessments. We roared with laughter about the tattoo, one on his front and one on his back. They were for the Radiographer, so that the radiotherapy could be lined up in precisely the same spot each time. All his friends joined in the fun, everyone wanting to see this "tat". "It was of the World" Rob said. "Come on then, let's see this work of art," I ribbed. They were the size of a dot made by a ballpoint pen, "There you are Mum, if you get a magnifying glass out, you'll see, each one is a tiny map of the world. I'm going to visit every place on there once this is all over."

Then came the sting in the tail. Sadly, when we reached the lung capacity test, it became clear that the previous chest infections had taken their toll. Despite the fact that, on a bike, I still couldn't keep up with him, Rob's lung function was down. Well that set the cat amongst the pigeons! The Radiotherapy Big Chief didn't think Rob would survive the doses he would need to tolerate, not on top of the final cycle of chemo to prepare his body for the transplant. There had to be something they could do?

Another gathering of the brains of Addenbrooke's took place and a revised plan emerged to put Rob through a new, cutting edge, method of radiotherapy. Usually the radiotherapy would be given to the whole body. The aim after all was to wipe out Rob's system, to prepare it for the new stem cells, which would hopefully graft, and grow into a new revised healthy system, a new revised healthy version of Rob. This new approach allowed for a level of targeting thus enabling the doctors to protect Rob's already damaged lungs. It would involve a mould being made of Rob's whole body, a full head and face-mask too, all of which Rob would be encased in. He would then be rendered totally immobile twice daily, whilst the therapy was given. Rob was only going to be the second person in Addenbrooke's to have received this method of treatment, but the particulars of Rob's case made him eligible. The medics were all very excited. Sometimes you just want to be ordinary!

Unfortunately, though, this grand plan was all going to take a bit of organising. Rob would need to have his own bone marrow harvested, under general anaesthetic and deep-frozen. This was in case the whole plan unravelled, and then he could be given his own stuff back to buy some time. The mould would need to be made for him, and a special team brought together for his treatment. The schedule was going to be blown; they needed more time.

Rob would be given a third cycle of chemo, not as potent as the previous, and then the fourth would lead into the transplant. What was one more cycle of chemo between friends after all? Rob was gutted. He'd done everything he could, he'd eaten healthily, exercised when he could, but still nothing seemed to go his way.

Talk of "when this was all over" had never been more fervent. Rob had to focus on the "light at the end of the tunnel". Our big cycle ride began to take form in our minds, and every time we talked about it, it seemed that Rob had shaved yet another half or full day off the challenge; we were going to cycle from John O'Groats to Land's End quicker than ever. I never really worried about such details, once Rob started talking in single figures I felt pretty sure I'd be in need of an engine!

The important thing was that Rob had a project, a journey to think about.

A wonderful dis-used railway track.

Glorious “B” roads.

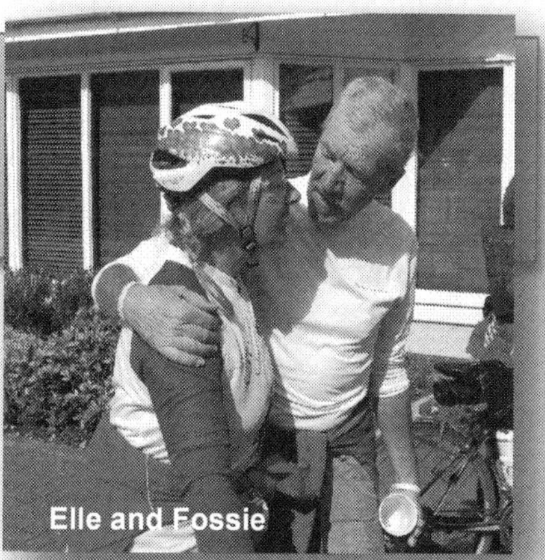

Elle and Fossie

Chapter 11

Sunday 10th May 2015
JOGLE Day 9
Penrith to Preston (77.0 miles, +4875ft)

Breakfast was a sociable affair with our extra riders stocking up on their "Full English" before their warm-ups. They all looked so serious and earnest; I just felt pooped. Fossie's quiz continued to rollover and Abi passed the moustache on to me. I can't really remember why exactly, but probably because we were definitely in this together. I proudly attached it to my bike and our extended party departed. We nattered to David and Julie as we negotiated our way out of Penrith. I was excited to share with David that Dave Deason, the father of one of the RGF's grantees, had sent me a message the previous night. We were supporting his daughter, Emily, who was training to represent Team GB at the World Duathlon Games in Adelaide later in 2015 - that's running, then cycling and then running again. Dave lived in the vicinity and hoped to intercept us on his bike and join us for a few miles. I knew Dave was a marathon runner and keen cyclist; he'd even run the London Marathon earlier in the year in aid of the RGF to show his support. I really hoped we would meet up; he sounded a smashing bloke.

Our cycle route quickly picked up the edge of the local playing fields and took us neatly over the main A66. Pip, Elizabeth, Liz, Claire, Antonius and I paused on a little stone bridge to admire Brougham Castle. It was gorgeous, and Antonius whipped out his camera for a group shot. The sun was shining, the River Eamont was babbling, and the castle looked like a movie backdrop. Photo taken, we looked around us. Well bugger me sideways; they'd all gone on without us! So, it was going to be a bit more of the same as usual then, with our little group at the back, and our own company to keep us going.

Our route wiggled along utilising small single-track lanes, shadowing the routes of the mighty A6 and M6 as they ran parallel at this stage. This part of the Sustrans network of cycle routes did us well, keeping the roar of the traffic just far enough away. I didn't see the waterfall in Waterfalls Road, but as we crossed the River Leith, I certainly heard it. Through Great and Little Strickland we trundled and past numerous fields full of sheep, all enclosed with the sturdy dry stonewalls we would see so many miles of. The undulations of Cumbria were never-ending, and taking their customary toll. I have to say, our progress wasn't outstanding. We should have noted the warning signs when we saw a signpost to Shap off to our right, just 1½ mile's away. Pip now tells me that Shap is famous on the Coast to Coast walk for being so high!! Well now he tells me!

Crosby Ravensworth marked the 15 mile point, and the mile long 500 foot descent into the village had been fun. But there was no time to pause; we had a 3 mile pull up of equal gradient to accomplish. Thank goodness, we agreed - we wouldn't want our visitors to have too easy a time of it! By the top we'd lost the trees again, the earth had returned to moorland, covered in closely-cropped tufts of wiry grass. It was very beautiful, but then our country is.

Just before the 20 mile point we passed through the village of Orton. There, outside a very welcoming looking café, was our trademark line up of wheels indicating that some of our party were there. Our group, though, simply daren't stop. We couldn't afford the time to get involved in being too sociable. The hills were taking their toll and we still had 57 miles to cover before dinner. We simply had to bash on. The weather was closing in and whilst it was not pouring with rain, it was decidedly on the damp side of dry. But the worst of it, was the wind. That punishing head wind was back, and didn't we know it!

Cycle Route 20 took us under the M6 and popped us up on a well surfaced little road running within 50 metres of the motorway on one side, and the main railway line on the other. A peaceful lay by it wasn't, for a quick cuppa with Carl, but we were frozen and the warm up was very welcome all the same.

With the Lake District to our right, and the Yorkshire Dales National Park to our left, we basically shadowed the motorways all day, criss-crossing over and under by turn as we headed southwards. The hills were endless but pretty, and the weather damp, which was just about possible to ignore. Unfortunately the wind was determined to steal the day. We followed the course of Birk Beck to Greenholme, then at Roundthwaite we arrived within 100 meters of the M6. It is astonishing how many times I have driven up and down that motorway, head down, concentrating on the immense volume of traffic that it copes with. Here we were, within touching distance and you could hardly hear it, you couldn't even see it behind the woodland, and the countryside was beautiful. If ever you have the luxury of time to spare, I would urge everyone to ditch the motorway, and explore our glorious countryside. Obviously don't do it all at once, as it'll be a bit of a snarl up!

This section was simply stunning. The River Lune rushed along the base of the valley, a totally vital life force. The M6 carved a route through the landscape, the main artery. Our tiny country lane took the role of one of the many capillaries, feeding the countryside. Oh, and I nearly forgot to mention that the railway was storming along next to the motorway too – it was a very powerful scene. And then there was me, steady but sure, easing my way from north to south, just me and my bike. It was a lot for the mind's eye to compute.

At precisely 26 miles we found Carl. He had parked up in a lay-by, right under the M6. With Borrow Beck, flowing from the River Lune down below us, the traffic roaring over our heads, and the fine stone arches of the railway viaduct 20 meters further on; we cowered from the penetrating weather, eating lunch in the stomach of a monster. Just as we had finished stirring our cuppa soups, everyone else arrived. Farewells had been completed and our visitors were probably in one of those very cars racing over our heads bound for home and the office tomorrow morning. No such mundane timetable for us; we had an adventure to complete.

As we huddled together enjoying the lunchtime chatter, it was interrupted by a sudden burst of Internet connection. It was always a bit of mystery why you'd suddenly find a signal, but with a lot of dinging and donging I managed to find out that our nephew Chris and his wife Sarah were waiting to cheer us on in Kirkby Lonsdale High Street. In fact they'd been waiting for hours already! Somehow I needed to tell them to, at the very least, go to the pub, but possibly even go home. We were going to be hours yet. The signal having again disappeared, all I could do was to send a text to Sam in London asking him to warn Chris. I had no idea if the message had sent but at least I had tried.

Claire and Antonius had pushed on, and the rest of us togged up and set off. We soon became well spread out, the hills quickly sorting the cyclists from the non-cyclists. Fossie and Nicola stuck with us, which was a real bonus. Kirkby Lonsdale was 18 miles down the road, and at this rate it would take us nearly two hours of cycling to get there. As I write all this down, I don't actually think I am quite as bad a cyclist as it sounds; except in a headwind, (oh and perhaps also on hills!!) and then I'm done for. This was going to be one very long day.

It was well into the afternoon by the time we reached Kirkby Lonsdale. I, for one, felt exhausted, and we were only slightly over half way. I thought I'd been pretty abstemious at the party last night, but perhaps not enough. (How could two glasses – oh go on then, maybe three - of Prosecco do this much damage?) Perhaps the champers hadn't helped either? My legs felt like lead, and I was chomping my way through bottles of water faster than ever. As we dropped down into the town there was a sudden whoop from up the front of our little group. Fossie, Nicola, Elizabeth and Liz had stopped and as it would have been rude to plough into the back of them, Pip and I also stopped and dismounted. Turning to look back up the road, there on the tarmac, in the style of all good "Tours" was some wonderful chalk graffiti. Chris and Sarah's handiwork was truly glorious and so uplifting. Chalked all over the road were the words:

Go
Pip
+
Lorraine
X

- followed by a very snazzy little bicycle. It was fabulous. Of course, we needed to photograph that – it was a very special moment. We were hardly going to be mistaken for "La Tour de anywhere" but at that moment I rather surprisingly felt a million dollars.

I assumed it was a kind of "We were here" note and that dear Chris and Sarah had given up on us hours ago. So to pedal on a few hundred yards to find them both, along with Sarah's dad waiting on a beautiful stone bridge to greet us was a very moving moment. I think they had been close to giving up on us - who would have blamed them? - when some of our faster riders had scuttled through. They'd waited for us, their daft Aunt and Uncle following up the rear – what a fabulous family we have!

We had to keep going. Just at a time when I was beginning to consider the possibility that I had bitten off more than I could chew with all this cycling malarkey, two young folks had lifted our spirits – Arkholme next stop. We pushed through Halton Park onwards to Caton, and still the hills kept coming. It was truly like being on a giant rollercoaster all day. I was crumbling. My legs were crumbling. My head was crumbling. This day threatened to beat me. I kept trying to remember my neighbour's words of encouragement the night before we left home "Keep Smiling! If you let your chin go down, you'll be done for." Somehow we all just kept digging deeper and deeper, and managing to find a grimace at the very least!

Apparently Claire and Antonius had also found the day punishing and knew that if they were in a bit of trouble, those of us following up the rear were probably in pieces. In an attempt to raise our spirits they'd gone and bought vast quantities of fluorescent card, felt pens and tape. All along the route they had stuck up notes and signs, versions of the RGF logo, messages of encouragement. I can't believe we didn't see any of them! I think at one point I did see a flash of something on a lamppost, although I didn't take much notice. I barely lifted my eyes from the tarmac. I hope they had a good laugh doing it though; it was a smashing idea and the knowledge that they had been thinking of us and trying to help meant the world. Fossie dashed ahead; concerned that due to the lateness of the hour, Carl may have abandoned our final tea stop. We needed that break, and we were grateful to Fossie for digging deeper still and helping us.

I'd been keeping a bit of an eye out all day for Dave Deason, but no sign. Oh well, it was a bit of a long shot for him to find us; we were a bit of a moving target, even if a slow moving one. Around about Quernmore we found Carl parked up again, the kettle boiled. Terry was also in the lay by; he looked worried whilst chatting to Nicola. It was getting late. It was clear that we were going to miss dinner and that we would be cycling in the dark. We all knew how vital it was to have time to recover, and refuel. Today would have repercussions tomorrow too. We were in bits at the back, I daresay they were in bits further up too, but at least they weren't at the back, and we now knew that they were at the hotel, we had 17 miles left.

We talked about giving up, but only briefly. Terry had made a rather timely visit to a chocolate shop in Kirkby Lonsdale and offered it around. Pip famously said, "If Fossie is finding these hills hard, they must be tough". Even Fossie wasn't "Dancing on the pedals" today; well not with his customary ease anyway. Bugger this, I'd invested too much time, energy and love to be beaten by a final 17 miles of hills and a bit of weather!

With that Adi and his wife Emma appeared from nowhere. Bless her heart; she'd come up especially to share two days of the ride with us. There I was stuffing my face with chocolate, like a broken woman, and Emma bowls up, on her heavy old hybrid bike, with a smile from ear to ear. Seeing her enthusiasm, and Adi's face etched with love and pride – well let's just say I was back on that bike, my lights were turned on and I was off.

We now had Emma and Adi to bolster our group; their company at that time was priceless. Elizabeth had stopped to answer her phone. Nigel H was at the hotel and our former minister from church was there to greet us. Joan couldn't wait much longer; did we have any idea how long we would be? I promise you, if I could I have gone faster, I would have, I'd have loved to share a hug with the Rev. Joan Grindrod-Helm, but those little old legs of mine were not happy. Nigel would have to hug her from us all.

I found myself cycling alone. I could see the other seven folks not too far in the distance and I knew they'd stop and we'd re-group soon, so I wasn't worried. Coming towards me I noticed a van, headlights blazing, horn tooting. I didn't give it a thought; nothing much surprised me anymore, until it screeched to a halt.

Various thoughts flashed through my head. Was I about to be abducted by aliens; or maybe just robbed, raped and pillaged? Well, do your worse, I'm all yours, I certainly won't put up much of a fight, and I certainly can't speed off on my bike! The driver's window was wound down and a lady stuck her smiling face out and shouted, "Are you Lorraine George?" I suppose I must have replied "Yes!" "Don't stop! I'm Dave Deason's wife; we've been trying to find you for hours. He's just getting his bike out of the back and he'll catch you up. We're going to see you into Preston."

I've never taken drugs, but it was like I imagine a shot in the arm might feel. Within moments Dave was by my side, and I'm certain he could see the pain I was in. "Don't think about how tired you are. Don't even think about giving up. Shout at your legs 'Keep going, keep going' that's what I do when I'm running a marathon and my legs feel like lead." I tried, I really did, and with his encouragement I kept going. Everyone loved meeting him, and he was fabulous company. The light had gone by now, and in the dark we were so grateful to have a strong cyclist with local knowledge chaperoning us.

We were still following our trusty National Cycle Route and despite the fact that Dave knew a much quicker way, we all held fast to our resolve to "stick with the route". Four times we crossed the M6 in that final 17 miles – FOUR TIMES! For goodness sake! I'm sure it would have been very beautiful, and kept us away from all the traffic etc. except of course it was by this time very dark and everyone else in the world appeared to be tucked up in bed!

By the time we arrived at The Premier Inn, Preston North, the restaurant was closed. Terry had almost had to cook the take away Pizzas himself, or else see his wife and her nutty mates go hungry. We had done it. The predicted 4875ft of climbing had ended up being recorded on our Garmins nearer to 7500ft, (not sure what went wrong there?) we had cycled for nearly 13 hours, and we were knackered.

In a totally humbling and self-effacing way, Dave simply piled his bike back into his van, said good night quietly and disappeared. I hope that man knows what he did for me late on Sunday 10th May 2015? Without his appearance, his confidence, his determination on my behalf, I'm not sure I'd be writing the same book as I now am!

October 2013

We'd been back and forth to Addenbrooke's as the rest of cycle 3 panned out, and preparations, calculations and measurements had been made. We were told that the cord blood cells had arrived, and the sample that had been defrosted for testing showed everything to be in great shape.

We'd spent another vile day in the Access Unit with the overly chirpy chappy, whilst Rob's second Hickman Line was changed for a third. He would need one with a triple rather than double access for the Transplant. It was likely that the full body radiotherapy would make eating difficult, maybe even impossible for a period, so one lumen would be kept for nutrition. We were also prepared for a feeding tube to be inserted into his stomach – every possible challenge was being prepared for. We were ready, but most importantly Rob was ready!

We enjoyed a couple of smashing conversations with a new lady on the ward, Anita, from Clic Sargent. She was fascinated by our plan to cycle JOGLE, or maybe she just thought us totally mad? Anyway, when Rob said that he would be cycling it on a borrowed bike, the next thing we knew, she arrived looking very pleased with herself. She'd been in touch with the folks at the "Make-a-Wish" Foundation, and they had agreed to purchase Rob the road bike of his choice.

Well, I've told you how Rob liked to shop, and he spent hours pouring over the Internet - we even visited our local bike shop for advice - before he decided which one he wanted. It was a fabulous boost for him.

Every time the sun shone, we'd nip out on our bikes. Rob had a borrowed bike from Nigel H. "Let's give my lungs a bit of a stretch Mum," he'd say. I'd happily puff and pant in his wake.

It was a week before we were due in for the final run up to the transplant. Abi was across for dinner and everything was going along quite normally. Abi was chatting away with her usual enthusiasm.

"Did we know that the ozone layer smells
faintly of geraniums?"

We had cooked a spaghetti bolognaise together, whilst Rob sat quietly watching TV. Looking back the alarm bells should have been sounding. Rob loved to cook and he and Abi usually chatted away for hours; normally I wouldn't have got a look in. I heard Rob go upstairs, and there was a bit of ferreting around in the bathroom cabinet. I nipped up to find Rob with a thermometer in his mouth. "Feel a bit weird Mum, don't panic, we'll see."

Surely not now? But oh yes, over the next hour his temperature took off. Poor Abi, she'd heard about these spikes, but she'd never experienced one first hand before. Pip and I started throwing things into carrier bags, Rob picked up his ready packed bag, and we were out of the front door. "What shall I do?" asked Abi. "Shove the dinner in the fridge. Turn the lights off and close the front door behind you. We'll phone the hospital on route."

Rob was adamant, whilst he knew he needed IV antibiotics within the hour, he also wanted to be taken to Cambridge, they knew him, and with the transplant so close, he didn't want to risk getting stuck in Colchester. So off we flew.

It wasn't exactly plain sailing through A & E, which somewhat bizarrely is the route you have to take to get admitted, even though you have leukaemia and the ward is waiting upstairs for you, with your bed covers turned down. I insisted that we couldn't wait with everyone else, due to Rob's neutropenia, and so we got put into an office. Anyway, after too long, things got sorted and we arrived up in our trusted TCT ward.

All week everyone battled tirelessly to get on top of the infection, and things were pretty soon under control. No worries, the plan was still in place. We were moved into the Transplant room, the one we had watched so many youngsters over the months, get moved into, spending six weeks in isolation whilst they had their transplants, and then go home. Finally it was our turn.

It was the weekend. Tom, Julie and Ella were over from Dubai, and Ella was going to be christened. It was a horrible decision to have to make, but it wasn't really a difficult one. Rob wouldn't be able to go. It was the day before his transplant was due to kick off, and I wouldn't leave him on his own. The difficult bit was that Pip and Sam would need to go, and represent all of us.

Of course it was lovely to see Tom, Julie, Ella and all the family, but poor Pip, Sam and I'm sure Tom and Julie too spared many thoughts for Rob stuck in Addenbrooke's. It was a long day, a family occasion we had hoped to share.

The final radiotherapy rehearsal was scheduled for the Monday morning with the first session booked for 8.00am on Tuesday morning. We knew we were in for a rough ride, and so we all agreed that Pip should nip home on the Sunday after the celebrations, cut the grass, collect the post and sort out his desk, so that our house would be in order to concentrate on Rob; Pip would return to Cambridge later on Monday. All we were waiting for was the final fitting for Rob's radiotherapy mould, and the results of his last bone marrow test. He'd chosen his playlist and left it down in the radiotherapy department ready to be played whilst he lay in the mould for his twice-daily treatments, no prizes for guessing what that was!!

****

More about the Rob George Foundation...

As soon as Rob's relapse had been confirmed, two years to the day since his first diagnosis, all the previous concerns with regards to his finances re-surfaced. Rob had once again been faced with no choice; a second "year out" had to be the plan. As Rob commented, "This could end up being the longest degree in history!" We all thought, here we go again! But of course this time, with all the experience of two years ago, and the ruling from the Court, and then ultimately the payment of the ESA, surely it would be plain sailing?

As it turned out, our assumptions couldn't have been further from the truth. Rob's application was rejected, and Pip requested an informal re-assessment, which was, as before, unsuccessful. The DWP claimed, unbelievably, to have lost its copy of the Tribunal's 2011 decision. Pip provided them with a full copy of all the paperwork, but it made no difference. Rob was going through hell again, and the DWP just seemed to twist the knife at every opportunity. Despite all the difficulties Rob was facing, Pip was left with no choice, yet another formal appeal would have to be made to the Social Security Tribunal.

Despite the previous ruling, the DWP resumed their previous stance; Rob was considered still to be in full-time education. It all hinged on Rob needing to totally abandon his course, "totally, finally and permanently." But Rob still intended to resume his studies in September 2014, after all, it was his future, the one he spent every moment fighting for.

It seemed that Pip would get his day in Court after all! This latest decision was simply immoral.

Yet again we were left feeling ashamed of the way our young people were being treated. We could see with our own eyes that Rob wasn't the only one in financial dire straits – we'd seen it with many other young patients; you just needed to walk up and down the ward.

Chapter 12

Monday 11th May 2015
JOGLE Day 10
Preston to Crewe (71.1 miles +2533ft)

I have next to no memories of the hotel in Preston. I am sure some of you will be heaving a hefty sigh of relief at that piece of news!! It was yet another Premier Inn. It, like all the others, had those not unpleasant pictures of daisies on the bedroom wall, and as you approach the open wardrobe unit, the kettle is to your right and the hair dryer to your left. The significance of a hairdryer took on new proportions on this trip – not for drying my hair, but as a quick way of drying off my cycling shoes – well who'd have thought it?! That morning, as we gathered, I presented the rather droopy moustache to Elizabeth. In my mind there was really no contest; she had been a gold star mate to me. Elizabeth had sacrificed huge swathes of her own cycle ride to support Pip and me and I loved her to bits!

We set off on the A6, which runs between, on the one side the M6, and on the other the Lancaster Canal. It turned out not to be as bad as I had feared, with a rather snazzy marked cycle lane, painted red. These are often not as helpful as you might anticipate, as folks tend to park across them, drive with one wheel over the line, or as we found when cycling in Paris the previous August, place a market over them, but this one was OK, and we made a good start.

Through Barton we went and over Barton Brook. The road was predictably busy, but manageable. As we approached Preston I had decided that we would take a slight detour in a westerly direction to pick up the Lancaster Canal path. This was probably not a universally popular choice; but actually, in the end, it was a very memorable stretch. The photo, at the head of this chapter, was taken right in the centre of Preston. Reaching up above each side of the canal, we could see rooftops of the factories and houses of the city. Here, though, by the canal, was a little slice of peace and tranquillity. Along one side ran the towpath, the surface of which was absolutely great. On the other side ran the most charming collection of aged cottages, all with idyllic and sometimes rather eccentric gardens coming down to the canal's edge. One family had constructed a complete "Bar" area in a little summerhouse. I bet they knew how to throw a party!

Antonius was in his element leaping around taking arty farty photos – well, in fairness, the whole scene lent itself to it very well. The local community of swans were busy with their babies to complete the visual feast. Yes, it was still freezing cold, but Nicola and Fossie had their legs out, so it couldn't have been that bad! It felt like such a special place. I'd been so worried about getting us through Preston. Every road I had looked at had been so intimidating, and yet I'd managed to find this wonderful route. I'd even got Abi with me chirping away – perfect.

"Did you know that cows moo in regional accents?

Did you know that octopuses' have three hearts?"

We proceeded to complete a fun wiggle through Preston city centre. Antonius was a complete whizz with the Garmin and we didn't put a foot wrong. Past the Guild Hall, then past the famous Harris Museum, all stop offs for another day. Without any drama we found the cycle route into Avenham Park, which flanks the River Ribble. The blue sky was stunning, and the river roared along way beneath us. A beautiful tree-flanked cycle path then took us clear of Preston and on our way, southwards. All in all Preston had been memorable for all the right reasons! We waved Claire and Antonius off as they put their foot on the gas and disappeared into the distance – an impressive sight!

We were well and truly into car-building territory now. As a youngster growing up in Swindon when Honda had arrived there, I heard talk of us threatening the famous Leyland and Moss Side for supremacy of car construction in the UK, and here we were. I think Paradise Lane was probably a bit of a stretch of the imagination, but hey, who am I to say? Out into the countryside we headed, Eccleston our next destination.

Eccleston nestles besides the River Yarrow, and the village appears in the Domesday Book of 1086. It is also the home of Bradley Wiggins. We didn't actually cycle along Bradley Lane, but we passed the end of it. Perhaps a little of the Wiggins cycling ability would rub off – fingers crossed!

The countryside was looking at its best, a gently rolling scene, which obviously wasn't going to last all day. The first big climb of the day presented itself – Toogood Lane – well somewhat remarkably I sailed up it – result! We refocused on our next major landmark, Appley Bridge and the Leeds and Liverpool Canal.

The gritted surface of the canal towpath was reassuringly good - although the cobbled lock-sides were an added challenge - and the spectacle of brightly painted canal barges was a sight to behold. Everyone was in high spirits, and the folks chugging up and down the canal were happy to return our cheery waves. They'd regularly shout out, "Where are you heading for?" I loved seeing their looks of disbelief as we replied "Land's End!" I loved cycling "traffic free" and relaxed into the day. It was a great alternative to ploughing our way through the middle of Wigan.

We'd clocked up the best part of 40 miles and were getting ready for lunch. Eyes peeled, we spotted Carl parked up in the car park of the Victoria Inn, Newton-le-Willows. We'd run out of gas for our little stove, but there was a very handy sandwich shop over the road where trays of tea were purchased, and the friendly publican had agreed to allow us to use his facilities – A* lunch stop!

Our next hurdle to be navigated was Warrington. Buoyed by our success in Preston we set off enthusiastically. Yet again I had identified the main cycle paths and looked for water. That usually meant flat and traffic free, and often gorgeous, to boot. We headed for the St. Helen's Canal and picked up the cycle path, The Trans Pennine Trail. It wasn't the most glorious of sections, but we were safe, and the track surfaced. As we approached the River Mersey the area become pretty run down and tatty, but real England none the less. We picked up National Cycle Route 62, which wiggled along and over the River, spitting us out on to the Weaver Navigation section of the River Irwell which, going east, leads into Manchester. We picked up London Road running due south, and truly felt like we were suddenly making real progress on this adventure. These were places I'd actually heard of!

The Romans liked Northwich because of its Salt Brines, and its ability to produce Rock Salt. We liked Northwich because it sits amidst a plain. It sits with water flowing on all sides and is famous for being home to the Anderton Boat Lift. The lift had been constructed to link the end of the Trent and Mersey Canal to the River Weaver back in 1875, and was reportedly looking stunning after its 2002 refit. Someone had also rather thoughtfully seen fit to build a tearoom to compliment the scene – which was a fine attention to detail. Sadly, true to form, we didn't have time to stop. Anyway we found Winnington Bridge, and were able to admire the river at its best before tackling the rest of downtown Northwich.

We stuck to the river, and although progress wasn't swift, (but then when was it?) we emerged to the south, with 60 miles under our belts. Unfortunately a couple of these last miles were on very disappointing cycle paths. Clearly marked as NC5 on the Sustrans routes, it deteriorated to large gravel, which is pretty much unrideable on any kind of bike (although please don't tell anyone I admitted this!) I did actually manage to cycle most of it, but through gritted teeth and only by the power of complete determination - oh and only because I knew I'd probably get it thrown in my face at some point later that evening. If you pedal hard enough and lift your bum up out of the saddle, you do actually make pretty good progress – just saying!

Eventually the cycle path discharged us in the middle of Winsford and once again we crossed the River Weaver. After all that gravel it was a bit quiet in the ranks, but I relied upon my mates forgiving me. I did think there might be a few letters to Sustrans brewing, though. Surely someone could have thought to grade the tracks on the map – simply showing an enticing green line regardless of whether it demarks a fabulous tarmac surface, a rough path, cinder track, earth path, gravel route, or as we were soon to experience, grass, isn't completely helpful. Anyway, all I could think was that it was all part of the adventure. What was the rush, we'd come on a bike ride, there wasn't much to do once you got to the hotel – I was having the time of my life.

71 miles of propelling ourselves forward got us to Crewe – home of Jimmy MacDonald, the voice of Mickey Mouse and our Premier Inn for the night. Crewe is also big into car building, namely Rolls Royce and Bentley. Its industrial expertise had been fully utilised in WWII when it had become the centre for building aircraft engines. This of course made it a prime target for enemy bombs and finding themselves also right on the flight path for Liverpool, the locals had suffered horrific bombing raids. We didn't see much of Crewe itself, but the first impression was of a grey, gritty, industrial town. Anyway we were thrilled to arrive at our hotel in daylight. We even managed to sit down with everyone else for dinner – happy days!

Dinner was fun, the usual unremarkable Premier Inn fayre, but in this instance wholesome and perfect. Terry had masterminded his usual long table and the party started. I grant you, it was a slightly subdued party, but it was fun nevertheless. Emma had cycled for the second day with Adi and was simply glowing. She rather shyly got to her feet after our meal and proceeded to speak in such an emotional way that we all shed a tear, or two. She was so proud of Adi, and indeed of all of us, and so moved by the loss of Rob and our inspiration for the RGF. She, as the mother of four young children, wanted to somehow share what we all felt; that the death of a young person somehow had to be turned into something positive. She was glad to have played her part, firstly by supporting Adi and making it possible for him to do the whole ride, and secondly by joining us for a couple of days. Actually in turn there developed a third way too, when Adi handed the job of collecting his sponsorship money over to her – we all loved Emma to bits. Emma reckoned we were all inspirational – well she was pretty inspirational herself!

Part way through the evening I had a sudden flash of inspiration and asked Fossie if perhaps he had been "Head of Examinations"? Whoo hoo! I'd won the rollover quiz too – a smashing day all around – my prize would arrive at breakfast in the morning.

****

All day on that Monday Rob and I hopped about the Transplant room. We were due to go down to Radiotherapy for the final test run of the mould. Getting into and out of it was becoming a finely tuned process. Everyone was well rehearsed in their various roles, and the timetable would work perfectly once treatment kicked off tomorrow.

We fiddled around on the Internet, looking at various possible routes for our "big ride" and Rob looked lovingly at pictures of the new bike he had selected. Our appointment in Radiology was for 10.00am. Then it was going to be 12.00noon. 3.00pm came and went and still we were sitting in our room. Nurses stopped popping in. Nobody would make eye contact with me when I nipped out to put the kettle on.

Rob and I stopped talking; I think we both began to panic, wondering what had happened.

It was late afternoon, and there was a knock at Rob's door. Rob's lovely consultant entered, flanked by Sister Hannah, and another nurse. Apparently he'd been waiting all afternoon for Pip to re-appear, knowing that we were usually all together, but he could wait no longer. He needed to talk to us.

I have never concentrated so hard in my life; I knew this was news I had to hear clearly. "I'm afraid there will be no transplant. It's very bad news; your last bone marrow test clearly shows that the leukaemia has relapsed for a third time. It is displaying a third mutation. It is extremely aggressive. I'm so sorry but we have no treatment options left."

The silence that filled Rob's room was bone chilling. I could feel my head spinning; it just couldn't be true. I felt like someone had just pushed me out of the open doors of a plane, plummeting downwards, but with no parachute. It's like being underwater. There's a rushing in your ears, but everything's stopped. It felt like all of these things, all at the same time. Everyone had worked so hard, everyone had done everything they could, Rob was so young, Rob didn't deserve this. All the hope that we had survived on for months – disappeared. In a split second it all flies through your head. Rob's eyes fixed on mine, he looked deep into my soul, and the sound that came out of him, will haunt me forever.

It wasn't a word; it was a noise, the sort of howl that an injured animal might make. It was a shocking noise, pain to a degree beyond which it is possible to imagine. The sound of youth dying, it was hideous and haunting.

It was no good asking the doctor if he was sure, was there any chance of a mistake? – he was sure, he was devastated too. "How long have we got?" I asked. "Weeks, a month, but not months," was his reply. At that moment I splintered into a thousand pieces. Rob and I clung to each other both silently howling. I felt like my baby had been ripped from my very womb – a scene from some horror movie. Sister Hannah took me from the room, and Rob was left with the nurse. I guess they felt we would benefit from some space. Ultimately perhaps it comes back to the simple truth, that in the end, you have to sort yourself out.

How could this be true? In the course of a few sentences, so much had been wiped out. No radiotherapy, no transplant, no future for Rob, no future with Rob. I needed to get back into his room; I'd promised to be beside him every step of the way, I needed to hold him in my arms.

Chapter 13

Tuesday 12th May 2015
JOGLE Day 11
A keen 8.00am
Crewe to Stourport-on-Severn (70.1miles +3234ft)

Breakfast was becoming a slightly more sober affair these days. Folks shuffled around, we all looked a bit battered around the edges. As much as anything else I think the constant moving of hotels with the associated packing and unpacking was taking its own toll. It was especially amusing to stay in such a fine selection of, oh so similar, Premier Inns. They fitted the bill perfectly for us, but whilst it was fine when you were actually in your room happily connected to the free Wi-Fi, with your hair dryer to your left and your kettle to your right, as soon as you ventured out of the door, well we'd get lost! We began to forget what our room number was. Was this the one where we turned left, or maybe right out of our bedroom to find the bar? Which floor were we on? It all added to the entertainment.

Pip and I had however fallen into an efficient routine with our overly large kit bags. Most of the stuff we'd brought with us never saw the light of day, but the morning's swift departure depended upon finding the energy the night before to lay everything needed for the next day out in readiness. Then the trick was not to spread your self about the room, only take out what you really needed, and replace it into the bag immediately.

Exhaustion and lots of exercise curiously left me with a very small appetite, so I would take my breakfast, and stash it in all the various pockets of my cycle top to eat steadily throughout the morning. What I couldn't quench was my thirst. My tongue had taken on a slightly brittle feel within my mouth, two pots of tea and three glasses of orange juice suddenly didn't seem in the slightest bit unreasonable for breakfast.

Fossie presented me with my prize. His "roll-over" quiz set all those miles ago in Ayr was over; an empty pot of Sudocrem, (suitably cleaned,) containing a small selection of shells and pebbles from the beach in Ayrshire. On the six carefully selected pieces Fossie had written one of the following words:

Scotland - England - Care
Faith - Determination - Love

As I reopen the pot all these months later to remind myself of that moment - the tiny shells and pebbles now smell faintly of Sudocrem – that smell will always bring back such a colourful selection of happy memories. My Sudocrem pot, labelled JOGLE 2015 in blue felt tip pen, is kept carefully within my pile of memory boxes in Rob's bedroom, packed alongside all the other things I have been unable to, and indeed have no intention of ever parting with. Breakfast was completed with the presentation of the moustache from Elizabeth to Nigel H and then we all hugged Adi's wife Emma goodbye. We'd see her next at Land's End. It was 8.00am and us slow coaches were making an early get away. In order to try and re-establish some of our rather dented self-esteem, we asked for an hour's head start. It did us the world of good to think that at least at some point in the day we were leading the ride, and of course could look forward to being overtaken, and possibly catching a few miles with the main pack later in the day.

You have to keep your eyes peeled when trying to spot some of these cycle paths. As we left the hotel on the main

Nantwich Road, we suddenly found ourselves being diverted off to the right, as the path carves a separate route through the hedgerows. It's always such a bonus to get away from the roar of the engines and all those beckoning rear axles.

Nantwich came and went and we were back onto country lanes. We crossed over the Shropshire Union Canal and allowed ourselves a brief pause on the little stone bridge to admire the view. 16 miles into the day's route got us to Market Drayton, and straight through the middle we went. It had a characterful little High Street with a smattering of Tudor buildings. The lanes of Cheshire, followed by Shropshire, did us very well as we headed in the direction of Telford – with me proceeding with my fingers crossed! I confidently predicted that Telford would prove a bit of a challenge!

The whole route hinged on us picking up the cycle track at Hadley. This accomplished, I could only hope that the Garmins would cooperate, and in turn that we would cooperate with each other. The track was beautifully tarmacked, traffic free, but wiggly. I love this sort of cycling, but others probably felt frustrated by the lack of speed. Anyway we wiggled our way along through parkland, repeatedly crossing the main roads on bridges suspended high above the labyrinth of dual carriageways. At every turn the three Garmins in our little four-some had different ideas. We decided to go with the majority vote at every junction. Liz, Elizabeth and I would pause, shout either left or right and we'd go with whichever two agreed. Pip had displayed a total determination not to have a Garmin at any point on the ride and so took the route of least resistance at the rear and happily let us girls boss him around. To amuse ourselves we devised the game where Pip, our human Garmin, would shout out his predictions as we approached each junction. He was actually pretty good. By the centre of Telford we were totally disorientated as to which direction we were travelling, but hey the sun was shining, the birds were singing and all was well with the world! We were 36 miles into the day and we hadn't had to ride on a single main road!

Telford is huge, with a population of about 155,000. It was built in the 1960's and 70's as a new town, and thoughtfully the town layout incorporated a fabulous cycle network. It now includes the Ironbridge Gorge site too, which is a UNESCO World Heritage Site. I wondered if some of the stronger cyclists might deviate to visit it. Yup, you've guessed it, I'm going there on my return visit too, the one in a car!

Our only slight hiccup came as we approached Telford Central Railway Station. At this point seven cycle paths converge and the Garmins did go a bit potty. With our usual committee approach we tried each possibility in turn and ultimately Elizabeth worked it out. We were off again, and after a few exciting descents down various rather steep ramps, we found ourselves discharged into Telford Shopping Centre. I knew there was a very new and stylish cycle lane running right around the outside of the undercover precinct, so we hugged the outer walls and quickly found ourselves entering Telford Town Park. I also knew by this point that we had cracked it; all those hours studying the route were paying off! Now all we had to do was locate the disused steam railway line and we could all pat ourselves on the back.

It was a simply glorious day. The park was full of students lazing around on the grass, pretending it was much warmer than it actually was. The scenery was dotted with sculptures of I know not what, but we all had our sunnies on, and it did feel decidedly spring-like. We stopped for a selfie and to give time for Pip to imagine the sight of his beloved steam engines puffing into Telford. We were riding high on adrenaline and laughter. We had negotiated Telford and enjoyed every mile.

I knew that we were now sailing along with Birmingham to the east and Shrewsbury to the west. We were heading for the River Severn and Coalport. Our cycle path kept us high up above the road, and we zipped past the entrance to the Blists Hill Victorian Town. The entrance sign says this is a "Fabulous family day out", where children and adults alike can experience the sights, smells and delights of Victorian Ironbridge – definitely next time!

We entered Coalport passing the China Museum and Tar Tunnel – I bet there was a tearoom in there somewhere too! We crossed the River Severn on an ancient narrow iron bridge built back in 1818. It is absolutely beautiful, made up of a lacework of intricate wrought iron. I can't help but wonder on such occasions of all the feet that have passed this way before – well now I have too, Rob and me on our bike, on Rob's Ride'15.

We picked up the cycle track, which utilizes the route of the old railway from Ironbridge and Coalport linking into Bridgnorth and Bewdley. I had thought long and hard about including this section, as it proved impossible to find any pictures of what the track actually looked like, and to assess whether our road bikes would be able to cope with the surface. In the end my attraction to old stream train routes proved irresistible and off we set. It didn't disappoint.

In the mid to late afternoon, (well it was probably more of the late than mid, but hey,) it was simply stunning. The wild garlic was in full flower and the banks of the route were completely lined with it. As the sun sparkled on the river it seemed to draw up the scent of the pungent wild herb. If I close my eyes now I could be transported there again. It felt a total honour to be alive. The track was pretty rough in places, but also included sections of boardwalks, that took you high up the wooded hillsides – it was like cycling on our own rollercoaster track. With its testing twists and turns I could feel Rob smiling inside me; what wouldn't he have given to be here today? I found a reserve of energy and went for it; it felt so good to be having fun.

The route dropped down into Bridgnorth and we knew we were looking out for the cycle path on the River Severn's western bank. The route was barred - closed for upgrading work, and we were being re-directed. Between us, and our route, lay a public playing field, and apparently if we had arrived half an hour earlier we'd have spied a lesser-spotted Adi enjoying twenty winks under the goalposts!

Bridgnorth is a charming little place. Even this early in the season it was full of window boxes, hanging baskets and tubs all planted up with spring flowers. Pip and I have already returned for a short break and taken the time to walk around the narrow cobbled ancient streets and alleyways, reliving our previous visit. In the summer month of August we found it to be a profusion of hanging geraniums and petunias, cafes and quaint shops. It is also the end of the line for the steam train, which runs a year round daily service from Kidderminster. The riverside, is linked by a funicular railway to the main town high above, and there is indeed a stunning tea shop at the top, which we can now recommend.

Our route kept us low, hugging the river, and we craned our necks to look up to the main town, and the steam train tracks way above us. We were on Underhill Street (good name!) when we spotted Carl parked up in a layby, kettle singing on the stove. In we filed, looking to our left down to the river, and up to our right to enjoy the sight of a real live puffing billy steaming into Brignorth Station. Sadly, Liz didn't quite negotiate the slightly raised curb properly and landed face first on the tarmac. It's a painful way to dismount and Liz was left needing a few moments to collect herself. She'd scuffed her face, nose and chin, and one hand. There wasn't too much blood fortunately so we decided tea, chocolate and a couple of steri wipes would do the trick. She put a brilliantly brave face on it all, but it served to remind us that we couldn't relax for a second. As we enjoyed the view, Pip dashed up and down the path trying to catch extra glimpses of his beloved trains (he seemed to have perked up no end) and then we spotted Adi coming back towards us, pushing his bike. The road above was a steep climb and Adi had got his gears in a muddle and his chain had snapped. Carl to the rescue!!

We picked up NCR 45 and headed for Eardington, criss-crossing the route of the railway and the river. The "B" road was a good run and we picked up a bit of speed – yes even us! At Hampton Loade we turned back onto The Mercian Way. Here was another off-road section, still running between the railway and river. The silence you find in these precious places is wonderful. Assuming you are not puffing too loudly yourself, you can hear the birdsong, the river rattling over the pebbles and rocks, and the wind in the trees. It was only interrupted by the sound of laughter from groups of youngsters mucking about in boats, or teams of oarsman training on the water. It's funny how we didn't speak much through these sections; nature did enough talking for us all.

57 miles ticked off, and we crossed the river to enter the Severn Valley Country Park. I wish now I'd had the courage to stick to my riverside path, but I was drawn to the lure of some tarmac, and had felt from the comfort of my computer that the hills would be a worthwhile trade off. If I had known what a stunning day we were to be blessed with, I'd have stuck to the water's edge. Anyway, I rather inelegantly huffed my way up a steep climb - on foot of course - through the Country Park, arriving at the highest point in a car park. There was actually sweat trickling into my eyes, which can make your eyesight go a bit blurry, but there appeared to be two people, not wearing cycling gear, stood waving and cheering. Under such circumstances it did feel a bit like an hallucination, but it turned out to be our friends Vivien and David. They'd driven up from Essex for the day to try to find us, and of course, offer their encouragement. They'd already been to our hotel, and met the others; apparently it wasn't far!! We knew we still had 13 miles to cycle, which felt like far enough to us, although it probably didn't sound so far to David, as he jumped back into his

motorcar! We trundled on, coping with the ups, and enjoying the downs, high on fresh air and friendship.

Pip lovingly cast his eyes to his right at the sight of Arley Cricket Club, which is set alongside the Arboretum. The cycle path takes you back across the river on a modern narrow metal bridge; we nearly missed our trusty blue bike sign nestling in the hedgerow. We proceeded through gorgeous little biscuit-tin like villages, with equally pretty names, Pound Green, Buttonoak, and finally arrived in Bewdley. Bewdley is one of those old towns where the main church has become a roundabout. We entered the one-way system confidently in the early evening; it was deserted. When Pip and I returned on our short break, the bells were ringing and the marketplace heaving. It's well worth a visit. Now in Worcestershire, our third county of the day, I looked down to spot the ancient stepping-stones crossing the river. We, however used the impressive Telford bridge.

Much work has been completed to protect the inhabitants of Bewdley after the devastation of the 2006 floods. The Georgian townhouses have all been prettified and hanging baskets lined our route. We entered our last 5 miles of the day, which, according to the map, looked simple enough. All we had to do was hug the river, keep to the official cycle route until we hit Stourport-on-Severn, turn left, and go through the town to our hotel, where Vivien and David would be waiting, along with Abi's Mum, Gran, our RGF banner and a tray of large drinks. Off we go!!!...

Well, suffice it to say, that I'm a very lucky girl that anyone was still speaking to me that evening. Whoever the local Sustrans ranger is needs his or her knuckles rapped. The track here deteriorates quickly into a barely decipherable narrow, overgrown, path. To our right hand side lay the river dashing along down a steep bank, whilst to our left hand side was a fence, topped with vicious-looking barbed wire. Then there came the stinging nettles, then the kissing gates, then the dog walkers... the list goes on and on. It was hard going and folks decidedly lost their sense of humour! Others sensibly took stock, and trying to decide between falling into the nettles or the barbed wire, chose to dismount and push instead. Me being nothing like so sensible decided to try and do it through Rob's eyes; "what would he do?" Well he certainly wouldn't have walked, so I took the decision to cycle as fast as I could. Somehow or another it worked. I didn't make as much progress as you might think due to having to keep stopping for the walkers and the gates, but we chewed our way through a couple of miles, progress was though painfully slow.

At the point when I allowed myself to think that it couldn't get any worse, of course it did! We were on a wide swathe of chunky loose gravel, with our back wheels slithering about all over the place. Then carving a route steeply up through the deep orangey red rocks we climbed – impossible. I admitted defeat and got off. Apparently Nigel H, not that far ahead of us, had taken the alternative approach and had fallen spectacularly. In the style of Antonius he was on, off and on again so quickly that only his own honesty meant that anyone knew about it – oh, and the passing walkers who hid their eyes too scared to see what he might have done to himself! Abi later referred to that section as "The Valley of Death" which was just a tad on the dramatic side, unless she was talking about me, I suppose? (Good job I was at the back.) We all knew Nigel H's Achilles tendon was giving him a lot of trouble, and I was sorry to have added this to his experience, although he actually has never uttered a moan about that section to me at all.

There then follows a section where we were all totally convinced that we were cycling through someone's back garden. Faced with limited options, we continued. Fortunately no snarling guard dog came racing at our heels. This neatly mowed garden threw us into a plantation of new trees. All the Garmins were beeping and buzzing, no matter which way we tried, signalling that we were "off course". Just in time to save me from a lynching we hear "This way! Follow me!" I kid you not, there he was, waving frantically, smiling from ear to ear - Adi! He was having the time of his life. He had loved the whole run down from Crewe, loved the parks, the trails, the scenery, the sunshine. Perky after his nap in the playing field earlier, chirpy with his gleaming new chain fitted expertly by Carl back in Bridgnorth, we followed him pushing our bikes up a steep footpath. Stourport-on-Severn lay before us.

We wiggled our way through the town, and headed out to our stunning hotel. Stourport Manor was a very welcome sight. The final 5 miles had taken us nearly 2 hours. It was late, but the welcome was immense. The hotel had generously allowed the reception to be adorned with our huge RGF banner and David and Vivien were there to greet us too. The manager had laid on complimentary wine at our dinner table, (which sadly was a little wasted on most of us) and he had even passed our collection tin around his other guests, collecting £120! We didn't see the lovely spa and pool, we didn't walk in the inviting grounds, but we ate well, and we enjoyed a smashing catch up with Abi's Mum Nicky and Gran, and our fellow cyclists.

Apparently Nicola had lost patience with the last bit and double backed on herself in search of a road. Abi's Mum and Gran had found themselves a sunny spot at the nearest pub to the hotel to wave everyone in, and irritated Abi beyond belief (although it made the rest of us laugh heartily) because it was at the bottom of a steep hill. Abi assumed the day's ride was over and had thrown herself onto a bench, only to be told that she still had to get up the hill ahead of her to finish the day. I think it was at that point that Fossie offered to buy Abi's bike off her at the end of the ride, as she was talking about either throwing it into the sea at Land's End, or the nearest skip! Claire had sat down in some nettles. Nicola had got lost, and Terry had discovered a new level of extreme stress having succumbed to a delicious glass of wine and so was unable to drive out to pick any of us up – we wouldn't have got in the car anyway! The final discovery was that, apparently, amidst the stinging nettles and barbed wire, Pip had actually been heard to seriously take my name in vain! Well it's a fair cop; I deserved it! In fairness, I don't suppose it was only him?!! Nigel H, who presented the tour moustache, to Max, topped off our dinner. He was still following his and Elizabeth's ambition to cycle the "whole" way, and remembered fondly Max greeting him at the top of Mount Suidhe overlooking Loch Ness. That seemed a long time ago.

We'd been on the bikes for 11 hours, which for us was an OK day. Smiling and laughing, and possibly slightly wincing we collapsed into a huge and comfortable bed. It is the day that for me stands out as one of my highlights. I would go back and repeat all of it in a flash – yes all of it!

****

Firstly, what do you say to your child when he is told that he is going to die? I no longer believed in God. I don't know how anyone can under the circumstances and I knew Rob had given up on all that a long time ago. My instinct was to be honest; it was the way we had always been about everything. As I cradled him in my arms, rocking from side to side, I said, "Don't be scared. Dying is the most natural thing in the world. It's the one common denominator. Everyone dies sooner or later." I didn't bother with all that crap about God taking the best first. Or going on to some higher place. Or... well what would you say to your precious 21 year old? "I promise Dad and I will make this journey too, one day."

After the storm of emotion had passed, we became truly calm. We'd been fighting for so long, since June 2011, perhaps we were simply exhausted. "Will you tell Dad for me? I don't want to see it – I can't bear to see it." "Yes, of course I will." I went to see the nurses, who were all huddled around the nurses station looking like it was their child who had just been issued with a death sentence, not mine. I knew Pip would need to buzz through from the entrance door to gain admittance onto the ward, and asked if they could let me know when he had arrived. I needed to intercept him, and tell him what had happened. One of the nurses would go and sit with Rob.

We don't talk about death much; perhaps we should? Our old family friend, the Rev. Rob says, in other countries, and in other cultures, death is part of living. It's all around you. We here in the West have managed to separate ourselves from death. It's like if we don't mention it, well maybe we'll evade it completely. Nothing in life prepares you for how to cope with your dying child.

Maybe some of you will be able to relate to that physical ache you get inside when you think about having a baby. The incredible wave of love you experience when your new-born child is placed in your arms. It doesn't matter if you have one child or 10 the love comes in equal measures anew each time. For me, as a mother facing my worst nightmare, I was taken back to the moment I knew I was pregnant.

I'd wanted that third baby so much. And now he was going to die. The baby that had grown inside me, who had spread so much joy, was going to leave us. There was nothing anyone could do to stop it. If ever I had felt my life was out of control, it certainly was now. I knew that a part of me was going to die with him.

One of the nurses came to tell me that Pip had just arrived. I went to meet him.

"I need to talk to you for a minute." Pip's not stupid; he knew something was badly wrong. I don't know how the best way to tell your husband is, that his youngest son is now terminally ill. I didn't think about it too much, I just said it like it was.

"Pip, there will be no transplant, we are going to lose him."

We held each other, but not for long. Rob needed us more than we needed each other at that moment. We went to be with our boy, our beautiful, courageous, handsome, brave son. Later I phoned Tom in Dubai, and then Sam in London. I couldn't be there to comfort them. I couldn't put my arms around them. It was by far the worst day of my life.

Chapter 14

Wednesday 13th May 2015
JOGLE Day 12
An even chirpier 8.30am
Stourport-on-Severn to Tintern
(65.8 miles +3358ft)

Today we were moving south of Birmingham, progress indeed! We gathered out the front of our smart hotel, Abi's mum Nicky and Gran snapping away on their cameras. Us slow coaches took off first, so that was Pip, Liz, Elizabeth and me - and this morning, our numbers were boosted by Nigel H, Adi, Fossie and Kevin too. We were a merry little band as we headed back out of Stourport-on-Severn, exactly the same way as we had arrived; at least we knew where we were going!

Our route was the B4196 and it was perfect. The road regularly carved its way through the signature deep red rock of the area and the wild hedgerows were beautiful in the early sunshine. The quintessential scene of floods of bluebells would occasionally catch my eye, and the bushes covered by May blossom could not fail but cheer us on our way. Everything was shown off to its very best by the clear blue sky and bright early morning. I could certainly get used to this weather.

We went through Noutard's Green, Frogpool and Shrawley, past enticing village pubs and charming local village stores. It was England; it couldn't have been anywhere else. It was sparkling in the spring light, it made me want to explore every turning; I saw so much to return to in the future. All the time we were heading for Worcester, and back to the banks of the river Severn.

We found our cycle path easily, a slick section running along the riverbank. We had made good progress and even our faster friends commented that we weren't actually "that" slow – well it had been pretty flat and it was still early! We crossed the river in search of Worcester Cathedral. It was a slight detour but I really wanted to spare the time to visit. Others in our group equally wanted to take this pause, so off into the town centre we headed, wearing our adventurous hats.

Fossie and Kevin had been in the Cathedral before so volunteered to guard our bikes. In the rest of us pitter-pattered, skittering around on the tiled floors in our cycling cleated shoes. We sounded as if we were all wearing stiletto heels! Worcester Cathedral was breath-taking. It is set up high above England's longest river, overlooking the Worcester County Cricket Club. On the site of a Priory originally founded in 680, Worcester Cathedral was built between 1084 and 1504. Design-wise, it's a bit of everything; it has Gothic bays, a Norman crypt, amazing wooden carvings and modern pieces too. It contains the tomb of King John and was only spared from destruction by Henry VIII during the English Reformation because it was under the control of his younger brother Prince Arthur Tudor. It felt a bright and vibrant place, the main altar decorated by a stunning modern colourful tapestry. We tiptoed around; all lost in our thoughts for 20 minutes or so. The music of Elgar was filtering out from the coffee shop. Elgar, a local chap, had all those years ago visited the Cathedral near to where his dad had owned a music shop. Out in the cloisters we found a group of ladies setting up a temporary exhibition. It was made up of a collection of pieces produced by local school children. We couldn't see all of it, but the willow angels were elegant, majestic and moving. The quote of the day came from Adi as we stood in a huddle gazing up at the awe-inspiring stained glass window, "Well, it's certainly not Everest!" We all fell into a heap of stifled giggles; no Adi, it's definitely not a replacement UPVC window!

We returned to the riverside and continued, bound for Land's End. Worcester has made much of its waterfront and it was a picturesque sight with the locks and cafes, alongside the very smart marina. A very impressive modern suspension bridge transported us cyclists and pedestrians over the river. If I lived in Worcester, I promise you I would never drive my car.

We found NCR 46 easily and passed through the village of Powick, crossing the river Teme next to the old Powick Mill, on the old rather than the new bridge. It is a Grade I listed bridge built in mediaeval times and famous for its part in the Battle of Powick during the English Civil War. The former water mill had been converted in 1894 into the world's first combined steam/hydro electric power station. Like many such interesting buildings, it is now converted into posh apartments.

We meandered our way southwards, through mile after mile of lush rolling countryside. We crossed Castle Morton Common where we paused to eat and drink - in my case a cold bacon roll squirreled away from breakfast. Then off we went again, dodging the sheep, cows and ponies, all of whom happily co-habited this stretch of common land, but none of which appeared to have any sense of the traffic at all, whether that be of the motorised or non-motorised variety. It was fun dodging our four legged friends and their copious quantities of poo, causing cars and bikes to cycle on either side of the road in turn.

Pip and I were struck by the over-whelming impression of open space we had found. Whilst our country does have huge areas of people and stuff, you don't need to cycle very far to find lots of space; green, rich, beautiful, peaceful space. It wasn't that hard to avoid the traffic, you just needed to invest some time, a segment of your life, take a little longer over the journey to find the fresh air. I felt, and still do, very privileged to have been making this trip, in the way I had chosen to do it, the longer and steady way – hurrah!!

At one point, a car overtook us. The driver and passenger were yelling and shouting at us, it was quickly interpreted as encouragement coming out of the windows. Fossie turned to Pip and said, "I think that's my wife!" Sure enough a few hundred yards up the road there was Cee and her friend Clare, frantically waving their homemade RGF banner. Fossie positively leapt from his bike, chucked his helmet in the hedgerow and gathered Cee up in his arms. It was a moment Fossie will never forget, I'm sure; it was very romantic. We all shared a hug and then promised to catch up properly at dinnertime.

We skirted Great Malvern to the west (because it's set upon a mighty hill), and then Ledbury, both places I had visited as a child with my parents. It was fun cycling with a few new faces around. Abi kept up the banter, and the exchanges between her and Fossie were particularly entertaining. Did we know?

"A garden snail would take three years and 2 months to make it from John O'Groats to Land's End,"

(and I bet that's if it goes the direct route.) Then, a particular favourite - did we know?

"All humans start life as an arsehole, it's the first part of the body to form in the womb."

What would we do without her?!

Again, village after village linked by views to fill the mind. Bromsberrow, Ryton, crossing the River Leadon and looking down to see the old cobbled ford into Dymock, and then Kempley. I don't have enough words to describe what a wonderful day we were having. We were now on the look out for Carl and lunch; over half way, we were ready to take a break. I can't remember exactly where he popped up on that day, but I do remember it was a full house for lunch. Abi's mum was there to meet us along with her Gran too. Terry was parked up alongside the van and some of our quicker riders were still enjoying their lunch. Claire and Antonius were long gone, having been charged with entertaining our three visiting cyclists. They were old friends of Carl who had cycled JOGLE with him before, three very serious cyclists – Claire reported later though that they had never done it quite like us!! Well there is a whole new world out there, chaps – I can help you break your addiction to tarmac!!

Rather sweetly, or perhaps with a touch of the macabre, they had looked around at dinner the night before and asked Carl what he thought our chances were of finishing. Carl had apparently replied that he had never been surer. The air of determination that pervaded the group was second to none. Well, I would have had to agree with that. We hadn't done too badly today – things were looking up at the back. Adi pushed on as he was hoping to meet up with a cousin at a local pub for lunch. She was currently embroiled in her own battle with cancer treatment and we all wished them well. He'd pop up later – there was no doubt about that!

Lunch took on a real festive air – it was great to be in such a large group, and to arrive whilst there was still some good pickings left for us – we had got used to arriving to a table of empty packets. But Carl had wised up for us, and was now hiding away a few tasty things so that we could have a feast too. Nicky snapped away furiously on her camera, the various hedges were allocated as ladies or gents facilities and we were soon ready to tackle our next milestone – Ross-on-Wye, and ultimately on into Wales.

Nicola joined our group after lunch, which was lovely, and not much more than half a mile up the road we passed Adi. He was sitting with his friend, enjoying the sunshine of a pub's beer garden, a pint of squash in his hand. The pub was called The Moody Cow – fab name!

My bike was playing up. Carl's diagnosis was that it was just filthy. Nicola, every morning, would be found cleaning her jockey wheels and chain so that they were absolutely gleaming. I really wanted to do the same, but never quite managed to find the time or energy. As I changed into the lower gears everything would sort of stick together and resist, which is absolutely not what you want, going up hill – I already had enough problems. Claire and Antonius had already put their bikes through two car washes and so I decreed that the first one I spotted I would be heading into.

As we entered Ross-On-Wye, I can't imagine why, but I was near the front of the pack. Over to my right I spotted a hand car wash, complete with a group of well-weathered Polish gentlemen keen to help. I yelled I was going in – and as I signalled right, pulled across the traffic and eased my bum off the saddle I cast my eye behind me. Everyone had followed.

It was hilarious; we all queued up and one by one the bikes were jet washed. These chaps obviously thought we were totally mad, but quickly took it in their stride. £2 per bike exchanged hands and my vehicle was working as good as new. Nicola was the only one to resist, due to her electric gears, but then her bike was blindingly clean anyway.

Through the middle of Ross-on-Wye we went, passing all the charming tea shops, book shops, antique shops etc. you might expect from such a famous little place. We cycled right past the impressive Market house dating back to 1650 and we took in the stunning view down to the famous horseshoe bend in the river Wye as it flows towards the Black Mountains in Wales. It's a very lovely place, and easy to see why it is accredited with being the birthplace of British tourism. Apparently it all started back in 1745 when a Rector started running boat trips along the river from Ross. The scenery was thought to be so picturesque that visitors began to flock to the town – they still do.

All was going well, we'd got a tinsy bit miss-guided through the town centre, but nothing to worry about. Having enjoyed the steep descent down into the town, we had made it to the top of the pull up out of town along the Walford Road. We were well spread out and I saw Fossie pull off the road onto the pavement, presumably to allow us to regroup after the hill. Nicola was next and all I can think is that she clipped the curb somehow. In a split second there she was flying over the handlebars, hanging on for dear life, feet cartwheeling over her head. I can remember thinking that this was definitely not going to end well!

There was a fair display of blood about the place, but our resident GP, Elizabeth, who was I suspect wishing dearly that everyone didn't assume she would also be a dab hand at first aid, was hailed and of course leapt into action. Nicola was badly shaken, and immediately talked of not being able to ride any further. Oh no, we were not going to rush into that decision! The conveniently placed Prince of Wales pub, with a very well equipped beer garden was just over the road. We settled Nicola onto a bench, dispatched Fossie, Kevin, Nigel H and Abi off to Tintern, and Elizabeth, Liz, Pip, and I stayed with Nicola. After all, we were well used to coming in late, and despite the fact that this had been shaping up to be our earliest finish of the trip, we had no quibbles about sitting in a beer garden until Nicola had got over the initial shock and was ready to take a calm decision.

We had limited first aid supplies upon our person, the main box being on the van with Carl. A phone call to him confirmed that it would take him ages to get to us, and Terry, also already at the Hotel, wasn't leaping to make the 20 mile drive back to us either – I like to think he didn't jump at the request to try to make sure that Nicola didn't make her decision too hastily, or he may have simply been relaxing with a cuppa, we'll never know! So under Elizabeth's instructions I raided the pub's first aid kit, which was pretty pitiful, and Pip ran back down into the High Street to find a chemist where he could purchase the rest of the required list. The kitchen of the pub proved the most useful, containing new boxes of gloves, and unopened packets of J-cloths, and Nicola soon settled down. Miraculously all her teeth were intact and she hadn't bitten her tongue; she had though hurt her wrist. It seemed to be working OK and there wasn't any immediate swelling, which just left her leaking chin.

Like our Fairy Godmother, Adi appeared chucking various boxes at us containing steri wipes, gauze, and steri strips. We gazed on confused. He'd apparently crossed paths with Pip running down into the town, the events had been relayed and the decision made that once the items had been purchased, it would be quicker if Adi cycled them up the hill, Pip was taking his time on foot. That man just knew where he was needed most!

It wasn't the most exciting round I have ever purchased, but we all enjoyed a bottle of chilled sparkling water, and then we turned our thoughts to the rest of the ride. I repeated what Sam had said to me on Day 2 – "You can only get on the bus once." However, if you are too injured to continue you have no choice. We would wait here with Nicola for as long as she wanted and needed. We absolutely would not be leaving her there, however much she protested that she'd be fine alone! For goodness sake!!

And so with Nicola's chin stuck together with a whole box of steri-strips and covered with a mile of tape, and with a double pair of cycle gloves on her hands to try to support the damaged wrist, we limped on. Adi stuck with us for extra support, and the final 20 miles of the day would take as long as they took; nobody minded in the least.

Those miles were quiet; everyone's mood had altered. We all sank deep into our own thoughts, feeling every bump on the road, knowing that Nicola would feel it doubly. There was nothing more we could do. Keep her company, stick with her, and be the best friends we knew how to be. Ultimately though, we each had to pedal our own bikes.

We headed down to the river and Symond's Yat. The River Wye loops repeatedly, carving out the deep gorge, and the huge stones left standing are an incredible sight. We looked up to admire the eagles soaring above our heads. Perhaps we'd better keep moving in case they were sizing us up for dinner? The scenery rivals anywhere in the world – this trip has renewed my love of our own countryside, for sure.

We picked up the cycle path on the east bank and entered the Forest of Dean. I had such vivid memories of trips here with my parents and indeed a trip Pip and I had made almost 30 years previously with our eldest son Tom as a tiny baby. There is a rope bridge across the river, where my Mum had frozen half way across all those years ago. I'd taken Pip there, and replayed those memory movies. Now I stood by that rope bridge, newly sporting the addition of cycling boards across it, and imagined taking Rob there too. I think the forest does have a slightly mystical feel to it. The surface would, under normal circumstances, have been fine for the road bikes, but it was not very helpful for Nicola. Already well shaken up, her wrist, and probably her head too, were going to be feeling pretty sore by now; we took it steadily.

10 miles accomplished and we were in Monmouth. We found the main A466 and headed for Redbrook. Here I'd offered two alternative routes. Either stick on the main 'A' road and beetle swiftly to Tintern, or cross the main road over the ancient Redbrook Bridge and pick up Lone Lane. This pedestrian bridge would keep us away from the A466, and my research had told me that this was another road particularly dangerous to cyclists. It twisted and turned its way along the River Wye with woods on both sides, and was the only main road serving the area. We paused and had a quick committee meeting. Whilst we would have loved to take the country lane on the Welsh side of the river, we knew that the road surface on the main road would be beneficial to Nicola. It was a no brainer – that little country lane isn't going anywhere – I'll catch it next time.

Others had apparently crossed the river earlier, and enjoyed the delights of The Boat Inn. Some had even found a third option and encountered a hill of epic proportions – for which I got the blame!! Ask Abi - she loved it!! It was early evening now, and the road was thankfully very quiet. We pushed on, and I actually cycled faster pretty much, than at any other time. Nicola didn't complain once, she literally grinned (or grimaced) and bore it.

We too crossed the river and entered Wales about three miles from the hotel. Llandogo passed in a blur, then Brockweir, and finally Tintern. Everyone was sitting out on the front lawn with a gin and tonic or something deliciously similar when we arrived, toasting themselves in the evening sunshine. Terry had almost chewed his fingers to the bone with worry, but Nicola was fine. The Best Western Royal George Hotel would do us nicely.

Pip and I showered and dressed; keen to squeeze in a quick walk down to the remains of Tintern Abbey before dinner.

It was great to be able to walk hand in hand, look at the sun setting over the ruins, and remember happy times when we had pushed Tom through the remains, in the snow, in his buggy. We obviously spared many a thought for Nicola, now being carefully assessed by Dr. Elizabeth, and tried to not go down the route of what if... and we did allow ourselves to think of Rob. The evening sunshine, blue sky, Nicola's accident, our general weariness, all mixed together to stir up our emotions. We hoped Nicola would cycle tomorrow. Of course, it wouldn't be the end of the world if that wasn't possible, but it was potentially going to alter everything.

****

Late October 2013

There were various possible treatment plans bandied about. Rob's Consultant scoured the world for any last treatment that he might not have heard of. At one time there was even briefly talk of us going to America. We'd sell our house, we said, anything. There was a new cocktail of chemo being tried in the States. Rob's Consultant was emailing an American counterpart to see if it might be any good for Rob. We were clutching at straws, he wasn't even sure that the NHS would finance it. We'd have done anything, but in the end Rob didn't want it.

Enough; Rob called time. He would accept no further treatment. We all stood around his bed in silence. Rob was calm, collected and considered. He couldn't see what of the real Rob would be left if by some miracle he survived. It had been hard enough to get back to normal life after the first rounds of treatment. He had, deep down, struggled to see how he would cope after the planned transplant. But enough was enough. He knew he was going to die, and he was going to take control. He didn't want to die fighting to live, surrounded by doctors and nurses feeling they had failed. He wanted to die calmly, and in control of a disease that had the upper hand.

My heart was already broken, and of course I wanted him to live with all my being. But I was so proud of him, and his decision had to be respected. Emma shared how brave she thought we were all being, how deeply she respected us for taking Rob's decision so calmly, so resolutely. She'd seen so many families ripped apart, clinging futilely onto life. Well, we'd remained united so far; leukaemia had taken enough. Rob would have as good a death as we could manage. We would continue to take our lead from him.

Those first few days were terrible. We sat quietly together in Rob's room, the camp bed a permanent feature. I look back now and wonder at how blind, how blinkered I had been. Why wasn't I prepared? Why hadn't I, just once, allowed myself to anticipate the worst? But you see, I'd never given it a moment's thought, not once. That is still one of the most shocking things. Had I been stupid, blind, or just plain thick? I had never allowed myself to give a single second to the thought that we might end up here. That the treatment, that all our dedicated love, everyone's dedicated love, wouldn't work. My whole life, my training as a dancer and teacher, was propped up by the belief that if you wanted something, you just had to work hard, sometimes very hard. I had blindly thrown myself into Rob's treatment and support. I had believed that it was something I could influence. The pouring over his charts, making sure no tiny fluctuation was missed. The medication was always on time, any change noticed. But it had all come to this, Rob was going to die, and there was nothing I could do to change it.

So there we three sat. There was no medication, and so there were no doctors that needed to come in to monitor progress. Even the nurses hardly visited. All the hectic trips twice daily to radiotherapy and transplant procedures we'd been gearing up for didn't happen. There we sat in the Transplant room of the TCT ward. Just hours before all the life saving treatment had been due to start, but now we were silent, numb. It felt like we had the ultimate contagious disease, death.

Rob put his music on... Pip tried to read his paper... I fiddled around...occasionally the TV was turned on...Rob dozed. He slept holding my hand or I climbed into bed with him and cuddled him. We tried to eat. Everything was just so deeply quiet.

Nobody but us knew. Rob needed and took time to think. We had to take our lead from him. But as the days ticked by we all needed the support of our friends. We had to talk to him about telling everyone. Messages of support for the transplant were piling in, thick and fast. It felt dishonest to keep receiving all this love and support for something that wasn't even happening, was never going to happen.

Encouraged by us, Rob sat typing away at the very laptop I'm sitting with now, and composed an email to all his friends. He apologized for the generic nature of its design, but hoped everyone would forgive him. He thanked his mates for being the best anyone could ask for. He said many truly remarkable things, and he said goodbye.

He sent it to Pip and me, "What do you think?" It was incredibly humbling, totally eloquent, perfect. There were no better words to be found, after Rob had sent it to all of his friends, we used his words too.

From: Lorraine & Pip
To: Our Family and Friends
Sent: 22nd October 2013

We have chosen to use Rob's words to bring you all up-to-date with our desperately sad news. Earlier today Rob sent the following message to all of his friends:

"Please forgive the group nature of this message.

Firstly, I want to thank you all for being absolutely the best mates ever. Sadly my news is not great but I feel the time is right to bring you all up to speed.

The last week has not gone to plan. I developed an infection last week and was admitted to Addenbrooke's on Wednesday. The doctors got this under control, which just left the final Bone Marrow Biopsy to come back clear so the transplant process could kick off as scheduled on Tuesday 22nd Oct. Monday afternoon my consultant came to deliver the devastating news that sadly the leukaemia is back, clear to see under a microscope, and very aggressively.

This means the transplant is off, which means I've run out of options. So now the emphasis is to try and keep the pain under control and go home for my final weeks.

I know you'll all keep in touch - words don't really seem to do all this justice but I'm trying to remain calm and hope you'll all stick with me till the end.

Love you all, you've been the best mates I could have ever asked for.

Rob."

As you will all imagine, we are totally devastated. For now we remain at Addenbrooke's. Rob is comfortable at this time, and we will let you know as a plan develops.

With our love,
Lorraine & Pip.

I liken it now to how I imagine it might feel to be a fighter pilot. You fly, maybe for hours to reach your target, your plane fully loaded and armed. You reach the designated spot, perhaps take a deep breath, and release your bombs. Then I imagine there must be a few seconds of complete silence. Of course the roar of the engines is still filling your head, but the deed has been done, there is no going back. What will be, will be.

I wanted to recall that email, the act of telling everyone made it irreversibly true.

We never saw our old consultant again. Whether he couldn't bear to see Rob, or us, I don't know. 2½ years of intensive treatment and care had come to this. As a doctor, as a father, as a fellow human being, whatever his reasons for not saying goodbye, we understood, perhaps it was as simple as self-preservation. We started to get to know a new bunch of medics.

The Palliative Care Team started to call. By comparison to our Haematology bunch they were very gentle. It seemed to be a pre-requisite that they spoke in hushed tones. It annoyed the pants off Rob. They started talking about what Rob wanted, about controlling his pain, about where he might like to die. At that time he was pretty comfortable. The final round of chemo was still working its way through, and so his bone marrow was only just beginning to recover. The anticipated pain would be as the leukaemia kicked off again. It sounded too horrendous for words; we had no idea of how bad it could and would get.

Rob didn't want to move. He knew everyone on the TCT ward. He trusted them all. We had all shared so much. But the truth is that a hospital is not always the best place to be, perhaps especially when cure is no longer an option. On our ward, no one seemed to know what to do with us. They weren't able to try to make Rob better anymore, and I suppose the harsh reality was that he was taking up an expensive bed.

We began to talk about moving to a Hospice. Rob had never really heard of a Hospice, and he wasn't keen. I hated the idea of him dying in Addenbrooke's. I hated the idea of his beautiful body being wheeled down those long corridors in an anonymous body box, being stacked up in the hospital morgue, having a label tired around his toe. I wanted him to be loved to the bitter end. I wanted to take him home, or at least as close to home as I could get. These were all fears that I didn't and couldn't share with him.

Tom, Julie and baby Ella were in England. It had been supposed to be a time of celebration, of Ella's christening, of

Rob's transplant. All our eyes were on the future. Instead they came to share in our grief. It was only the second time Rob had seen Ella, and as she scrabbled all over his bed, fiddled with the tubes coming out of his chest, identified his eyes, nose and mouth for us, the tears cascaded down Rob's face. In that moment he held in his arms the future of our family, and he wouldn't be with us to share it.

Sam came to the hospital too, and the three boys had some time alone together. I don't know what they said, but I can guess at some of it. They weren't brothers that were joined at the hip; they had their similarities and their differences. But they were loving brothers nonetheless. I looked at Tom, now a new young parent himself, and I wondered how he would cope. On the one hand a lawyer in Dubai, with all the responsibilities that brought, on the other a husband and a new dad. He did though have Julie, and I hoped she'd do her best to support him. The one huge sadness though, was that Tom would not be around to support and share in Sam's and our grief. How could we all support each other from such a distance? Whatever Pip and I were able to do for either of them; it would not be the same as the bond between brothers. I knew they were both in for a rough ride, in different ways – and there was nothing I could do to protect either of them, nothing I could do to protect any of us.

Of course, anyone who has ever lost someone close is thinking, oh for heaven's sake, lots of us have been there! Pull your socks up, you just have to get on with it, life goes on. A close member of my family pretty much used those very words. Well, "good for you" and shame on you for your lack of empathy! I'm just telling you how I felt, and yes, people have said these things to me. I was even told that Tom didn't have time to grieve, he had a young family to provide for now. Of course he did, but "no time to grieve?" – there should, and there would, always be time to grieve. There would always be time to grieve for Rob. My relationship with that particular family member may never be quite the same again.

I took a photo of my three beautiful boys. Rob on his hospital bed, Tom and Sam either side of him. "It's just for me," I said, "Thank you!"

After Tom and Sam, Julie and Ella had said goodbye, none of us knew if Tom would see Rob alive again, whether they would all three be together again. It was heartbreaking. Rob scrolled through my phone after they'd gone. "It's a real keeper Mum, post it on Facebook, that's how I want to be remembered, smiling, with my brothers holding me." And so I did. It's a photo that I still hardly bear to look at. He then winked, and said, "Jules is prega's again, and they wanted me to know. It's a secret!" He never could keep a secret from me.

We decided that we needed to try and get Rob home, just for a day. It was a major undertaking. All his drugs had to be signed out, counted out, you name it, the performance was impressive – what did they think I was going to do, sell it all on the black market? Sam was playing in a gig at a pub in Colchester, and Rob wanted to hear him play, one last time.

As we entered the kitchen at home, Rob and Pip exchanged a conspiratorial look, and Rob gently placed a Pandora gift box into my hand. He had no money, so I knew that Pip had done the purchasing, but the gift was from Rob in every true sense. Two charms were inside, a shiny silver heart, and a little scroll, inscribed "Forever, Together." He placed his hand upon my heart, and promised me that's where he would always be, and I think that is exactly where Heaven is.

Heaven is a meaty subject. People traditionally raise their eyes upwards to the sky, but do we really think all our loved ones have departed this world to sit on fluffy white clouds? It's a lovely idea, but no, not really. Heaven is, I suppose, our security blanket. Heaven is a word we use to make sense of everything we don't understand. Using your scientific brain - and mine is extremely small - it feels like a ridiculous notion, that we are all left floating around, chatting to our version of God, somehow keeping an eye on the rest of us waiting our turn to join them. Heaven, to me, feels like the love and memory that is left behind, the feeling that is in my heart, in the core of my soul, the feeling of Rob that he left me with, that is Heaven. It goes everywhere with me. Perhaps that's where God lives too?

During the day Rob tidied his bedroom. We watched the black bin liners gather on the landing, we watched as he lined up the only things of value he possessed. His laptop, which he wanted Pip to have, his prized cricket bat which he wanted to be given to Sam, with the promise that he'd try to use it, his iPhone which I will always keep in my desk drawer and two bottles of real champagne. One was for Tom and Julie, and the other for Sam, both had been given to him on his 21st birthday, and had been saved for when he got the all clear. He gave me a list of all his passwords, and PIN numbers, and he even told me of the folder on his laptop that I could look at after he had died. "Don't be shocked Mum, there are photos there you were never meant to see, but I want you to see with your own eyes what a great time I've had." We watched our brave young man "put his house in order".

We squeezed in a visit to St. Helena Hospice, just around the corner from where we lived. The nurses and staff were so welcoming, so gentle, but also so robust. There was no pussy footing about the subject. This was a one-way ticket. Death was their specialist subject. It was a very honest environment. The nurse who showed Rob around said how well Rob looked, and at that moment he did. Rob warmed to the idea, maybe we had experienced all that Addenbrooke's had to offer us, and maybe it was time for this show to move on?

The gig was great fun. Abi joined us, as did Essie Sam's new young lady at the time; and Rob of course, enjoyed a G & T. As it turned out, it would be the one and only occasion that Essie and Rob would meet. It now of course, means the world to us all, that Sam's new wife to be did manage one very special evening in his company. We had our eyes firmly on the clock, we knew how long a window of opportunity the drugs gave us, and as soon as Sam's set was finished, they shared a hug and we loaded Rob back into the car, and made a dash back to Cambridge.

Addenbrooke's is a huge place, and we were used to being a part of it both during the day, when it was heaving with people, and after hours, when you needed to know the magic words, "C9", to gain admittance through the locked doors. Rob had overdone it, well you couldn't blame him, but the pain that developed took us all by surprise.

I suppose it's like anything, it's easier to keep things under control, rather than try to get on top of a crisis. Of course the crisis we were fighting off was a huge one. Emma was on night duty and guided him back into his room with her arms around him. She could see the pain behind his eyes, "How bad?" she asked, "Not good," came Rob's reply.

Things just spiraled out of control so quickly. Within the hour Rob didn't know what to do with himself. He couldn't lie on the bed, he couldn't pace around his room, he couldn't kneel on the floor and lie across his bed – no position gave any relief. He moaned; he made noises we'd never heard before. Real pain, deep severe pain, is ghastly to witness. To watch our son, reeling around, crashing his fists into the walls, pleading with us, with Emma, with God, to do something, was haunting. We all felt helpless.

Emma knew what he needed, but didn't have the authority to prescribe it. The leukaemia had obviously kicked off again, big time, the pain was coming from the core of his long bones, his legs, his arms, his spine – there was nowhere to hide from it. The Palliative Care Team worked office hours; it was the middle of the night. TCT's night doctor was called, and he too looked horrified. It took hours, but gradually the drugs began to take effect, we were all exhausted. Emma had looked after us all night. By the early hours of the morning and by the time it was her turn to go home, we all felt some progress was being made, and Rob finally managed to sleep.

The next day, Rob's pain regime was majorly reviewed. A morphine drip was put up, with a pump on demand, operated by a trigger that Rob held onto tightly. "Tell me again how the Hospice works," he said. We could all see that we were no longer in the right place. What Rob wanted, more than anything, was to die pain-free. He didn't even care about being fully conscious. When the pain kicked in, it was intolerable and we totally respected his decision.

There is something very beautiful about deciding you want to go into a Hospice. It brings with it a whole world of honesty, and freedom. We were no longer holding onto any vestiges of hope that "everything would be alright." There wasn't going to be some flashy miracle, or magical cure. We could set aside that great British stiff upper lip. We could be sad, we could cry, we could say everything we needed and wanted to, we could say goodbye. Leukaemia was going to end Rob's life, and we were going to watch.

Even now too many people offered us the chance to leave. "You don't need to watch this." "Remember him how he was." "We'll look after him for you." "Don't do this to yourselves." What did people really think of us, I for one wasn't going to leave my baby's side for a second, and I knew Pip for two, was right alongside me.

In the middle of one night, the familiar music playlist rattling away in the background, Rob called, "Mum, are you awake?" "Yup." "That bike ride, doesn't look like I'm going to make it. You'd better promise me you'll still go. If you don't I'll haunt you!" Of course I'd do it. He laughed, "Bet you wiggle out of it." "I promise I'll do it Rob, for both of us." I absolutely meant it.

Twice a day the Palliative lot visited, and reviewed the morphine. Quickly a background dose was prescribed with top ups on demand. The pump clicked away day and night. We were told that the four empty beds we'd seen on our visit to the Hospice were actually closed. The Hospice was launching its new Hospice at Home service, and resources had been temporarily re-directed. It was a bitter blow. Rob was in desperate need of their field of expertise, and yet we couldn't get him a bed. Every day the doctors phoned asking for an update. Day after day the reply came back, "Maybe tomorrow."

Rob was at the limit of Addenbrooke's skills. The Palliative Consultant admitted that she had nothing left to try. It was hideous. What was left of his precious life was ebbing away in a world of pain and frustration. A whole gang of Rob's Loughborough friends came to visit. The "Chill Out Zone" was booked out to Rob, Pip ordered 20 take-away pizzas, and one evening was lost in laughter and smiles. Rob was so spaced out on painkillers that I don't know how he even spoke, but that visit meant the world. He couldn't take his eyes off his friends; it was as if he was trying to suck some life out of them. We couldn't take our eyes of him. It was time to say goodbye, it was heart-wrenching. One of his closest friends left in floods of tears. Mostly they held it together, at least until they were off the ward. Young people and death do not go easily hand in hand.

Two weeks after the cancelled transplant, 10 days after our initial request, we were offered a bed at St Helena's. It's hard to think back to that day, packing all our things into cases and bags. All the things we had brought ready for our six weeks in the isolation of a stem cell transplant, all our notebooks and maps, and all our dreams for a different future than this.

Rob was injected with a massive dose of morphine for the trip, which we hoped would give us a 4-hour window to travel. We said our goodbyes. Everyone was in tears. I remember saying to Emma that I couldn't imagine how she did her job; she agreed that she didn't think she would be able to cope much longer. I asked her how often they all had to say goodbye like this? She looked me in the eye, "Too often, where do you think so many of them go, the youngsters off this ward too often go home to die."

How could I have been so blind? I guess you just don't see what you don't want to see. Getting cancer as a young adult is horrendous. It's as if your body is in its prime, and so is the cancer. It's bright, it's clever, it's full of tricks, just like the handful of young people, the "Forgotten Tribe" that it chooses to attack. I salute all the "Emma's" of this world. She wasn't much older than Rob herself. We heard later that she had moved to ICU – well you couldn't accuse her of taking the easy option!

We walked through the packed concourse, hand in hand. It was the familiar scene of stressed people, queuing for coffees, watching their clocks, on their phones, all living in their rich and various parallel universes. As usual the concourse was heaving, not a seat to be found. We walked past the usual clutch of fag-addicted people propped up outside the main entrance frantically dragging on their nicotine between treatments. We found our car and drove away. We left all our hopes and dreams for Rob's life behind us; we had no choice.

Rob's pain was barely under control. We got to within 40 minutes of home and things deteriorated fast. The rain was lashing down and Rob was crying out, he needed more morphine. I told Pip to stop the car, zipped up my hoodie and opened the boot. "You can't draw up syringes of morphine in a lay by in the rain!" Of course I could. I might be administering a heavily licensed, class A, class B (I don't know) drug, but I didn't much care. Rob swallowed the stuff down, and Pip drove bravely.

St. Helena Hospice, the inpatient section, is based in the old Myland Hall. As we walked through the front door, there on the wall was a photo of our "Best Man". Chris and Pip had been young lawyers together, partners in crime, you might say. They had also participated in the first ever, fundraising event for the hospice, when it was just a dream, an idea. Chris went on to be the chairman for many years, and this photo commemorated the official opening, where the Queen Mother had

officiated. Chris had lost his life to a brain tumor a few years previously, but it was somehow soothing to be greeted by his smile.

Rob's room was ready. It overlooked the front car park, so he could watch the comings and goings, and a beautiful tree. I called it the "Weeping Tree". As the autumn leaves fluttered down, it just seemed to cry for me.

Rob couldn't lie down, the pain was relentless; it seemed out of control. The Hospice Consultant almost immediately arrived. He was a very mature man, I don't want to say old! He exuded confidence and experience. He didn't take his eyes off Rob.

"Rob, you know where you are? Do you understand why you are here?" "Tell us what you want, help us understand how you want to die." The clarity was extraordinary. No talking in riddles, no tarting around. There wasn't time for any of that.

Rob was clear; he understood he wouldn't be going home. He knew he was going to die here. He couldn't bear the pain any longer. At all costs, he wanted to die pain free.

"Even if that means that you might lose consciousness?"

"Yes."

The doctor turned to the nurses who stood listening and taking notes, "Double everything. All the drugs Addenbrooke's have prescribed, double the dose of everything, let's see what that achieves."

He turned to Rob, and to us too, and calmly explained. "Young people like Rob are prime specimens; whilst they are very sick, the rest of their body remains strong. They metabolize everything much more quickly then older patients. Doses that would send an older person into a coma might not even make Rob sleepy. It seemed so obvious, it explained so much.

This man exuded total confidence, and what he was saying made total sense. It just seemed incredulous that the doctors at Addenbrooke's, especially the doctors on the Palliative Care Team, didn't share this knowledge. Yet another example of what a select club Rob had joined.

Our new doctor promised that he would not leave the premises until Rob's pain was under control. They would review every 30 minutes, and he would revisit every hour. When he felt it was safe to go home for the night, the nurses would be free to call him back at any time. The calm that settled was amazing, and so welcome.

Within a few hours Rob was calm too. The drugs were kicking in, a moment for thanks indeed. By late evening one of the nurses suggested a bath. Rob was shattered, comfortable, alert, but also a bit on the ripe side. It had been days since anything more than a "good wash" had been achieved. Frankly we'd had more pressing matters. She'd do everything; he'd love it! They exchanged a wink, and Rob reluctantly agreed.

A wheelchair arrived and off they went. Before long the nurse re-appeared, "Come on you two, it's family bath time, Rob's ready to hold court!"

There he was, in his boxers, his Hickman line carefully wrapped in a towel, up to his armpits in bubbles. His favourite play list was being amplified from built in speakers in the ceiling, and a Jacuzzi of bubbles was massaging his aching body. There was a smile from ear to ear, which was of course totally contagious. "Rob's just ordered a G & T, would you like one too?" "Too bloody right, yes please!"

At bedtime, a second hospital bed was squeezed into the room, right alongside Rob's, "That's for Mum or Dad." They knew we weren't going to leave Rob alone. There was a reclining chair too if we both wanted to stay.

I know that it must have cost Pip dearly to go home each night. He was just 5 minutes away by car, but it was still away from Rob. Rob and I had one kind of relationship, Pip and Rob another. Rob simply didn't want Pip to see everything. He believed that neither he nor Pip could bear it. He loved his Dad so much that he wanted to save him some of the pain. I'm not sure it had the desired effect, but we respected Rob's wishes.

Rob posted a picture of himself in that amazing bath on Facebook, raising a glass to all of his mates. "It doesn't look that bad in there mate," one person posted. Crikey, some folks should think before they post comments online. We didn't look at Facebook after that.

Unusually for the Hospice there was another young man alongside Rob. In the adjacent room was John, aged 30, surrounded by his girlfriend, parents, siblings and the family parrot, dying from bowel cancer. It brought a new level of pain to the place. Death is natural. Life has a natural order to it. This was life off its kilter. This was death out of step with life.

Rob wanted to see very few people; Abi, Glen, James and Tuckers, and he wanted to see his family; that was about it. The boys had been at the Grammar School together; they were a very close foursome. Then there was Abi, Rob knew that his death was going to hit her hard, and there was little he could do about it. He could have tried to distance himself from her, but she wouldn't have gone, even if he'd wanted her to. Her loyalty and love, laughter and buzz kept us all going through those final weeks. Rob also knew that he could count on those special friends to stick together afterwards. We would all need each other.

We talked about "afterwards". That's when the future of the Rob George Foundation was sealed. Rob never said "Why me?" He never demonstrated self-pity. He only expressed sadness that he would be robbed of the chance to "make a difference." We asked him what he meant. He explained that he knew he was unlikely to do anything truly great; he was hardly going to discover a cure for the common cold, or even cancer (maybe Glen would, he mused?) But he had intended to step up, shoulder some responsibilities, to be one of those people that *made a difference*. Perhaps take on the treasurer's role, fixture secretary, he didn't know, but he'd go the extra mile.

Quickly the aims of the RGF took shape. It would be our chance to "make a difference" for him. He liked that idea. He set a couple of ground rules, the best one being that everything we ever did to raise money had to be something he would have liked to join in with. Preferably the bar had to be open, the music had to be blaring out, he wanted to ensure that everyone, but especially Pip and I, had a good time. He never stopped thinking about everyone else.

On a number of evenings that merry group from the Grammar School along with Abi, would gather. The nurses would wheel Rob down to the family room, and they'd watch a Dvd, and rib James. It was always James; apparently it always had been. He didn't mind. Pip ordered pizza and produced slabs of beer and coke. Rob was by now on Ketamine, and joked that he spent most of his waking hours on a legal high.

The days turned into weeks, and it was almost possible to forget that Rob was actually dying. Our world had become very small. Our precious Rev. Rob visited regularly, Uncle Pe visited from Newbury, Aunty Cath visited for lunch, as did Claire, they all said their goodbyes. There was a pattern and rhythm that seemed to be possible to keep going, in my dreams, forever.

Rob had been put on a low dose of chemo as soon as the transplant had been cancelled, as a way of controlling the raging disease, and therefore the pain too. I began to visit the idea that maybe there had been a miracle, and in fact the chemo had worked. Maybe it was all a huge mistake.

Of course, fantasy when mixed with exhaustion, stress levels running so high that they are off the scale, mixed with total despair, is a heady mix. Transfusions had been stopped; this after all was a Hospice. They cared for the dying, they weren't there to try and effect a cure. Rob was becoming increasingly tired. He asked to see the Doctor. Could he have a couple of units of blood? He really felt he would benefit from a bit of a pick me up. He knew his own body, and knew the red cells were struggling to circulate; the myeloid leukaemia was taking over. Blood counts were taken, and whilst they made dismal reading, a transfusion was agreed. It would be a one off, but they understood, Rob wasn't quite ready to say goodbye.

There were a couple of nurses that Rob had taken a particular shine to. He had questions, practical questions. What would happen to him after he had died? What would they do to him, with him? Where would he be taken?

The nurse perched on the end of his bed, and answered all his questions. He would be washed, dressed in the clothes of his choice, or if not, of ours. He would be taken to their "very cold room", wheeled on his own bed, where they would look after him until the undertakers came to collect his body. They would continue to talk to him, as none of us is certain of exactly what happens after we have died. He wanted to see this "very cold room". The nurse didn't miss a beat, "Just give me half an hour, I'll sort it out for you."

He told me he wanted to be put into his Loughborough University Cricket Club trousers, the ones embroidered with his name. He also neatly folded a cream t-shirt with florescent pink stripes and placed it on top of the trousers. No shoes. No socks. He wouldn't need his flip-flops.

He was helped into a wheelchair and I pushed him to the other side of the building, where there stood a wicker screen, and a pedestal with an arrangement of silk flowers.

We paused, "OK Rob?" "Yup." She opened the door and we went into what looked like a little bedroom. There was a bedside table with a lamp turned on; it was strangely welcoming. Other than that, all I remember was that it was cold. Beyond this little room, was another, even colder room.

We returned to Rob's room, and he received his transfusion. He talked about dying; he absolutely didn't want to die like an old person. He wanted his music on, it would all be OK, he just hoped he didn't end up in that cold store with a load of old people!

We knew we didn't have much time left with him. Sam had been able to get a lot of time off work, his school was incredibly supportive, but Rob wanted to see Tom too. "Do you think he might come home Mum?"

I emailed Tom, "If you are thinking about coming, if you want to see your brother before he dies, you'd better be quick, I think we only have days left." Tom read that message when he got up the next morning. Apparently he only went into his office in Dubai to tell them he was coming home. By the time he got back to Julie she had packed his case, and organized his tickets.

I was able to tell Rob that Tom would be there in the morning. His face was a picture of joy, one of our last precious smiles, I seriously hoped Rob would last that long.

Tom arrived, closely followed by Sam. We had 48 very special hours. My mum was about to be 80 and the nurses organized a Chinese takeaway in the old wood paneled dining room of Myland Hall, we took photos of that special gathering, photos loaded with so many emotions. Rob even appeared to rally, but of course he hadn't really. Saying goodbye was simply horrific, it was as if a part of Rob was already dead. Tom left knowing that he would never see Rob alive again, Sam never returned either, I think he wanted to share that with Tom.

The effect of the transfusion didn't last long, and when Rob asked for another, whilst the doctors did check his blood counts, we were told it was useless. As I returned to his room, he looked me in the eye again, "Well Mum, what's the news?" "You're running on empty mate." Rob laid his head back on his pillows and closed his eyes.

Abi continued to visit. During the day, as she only worked around the corner, if Rob was a bit lively, we'd text and say "come now". In the evenings her Dad Nigel would sit outside in the car park ready to drive her home. We'd been at the Hospice for nearly 3 weeks; it was almost 5 weeks since our world had been shattered.

It was early afternoon, Saturday 7th December 2013, when suddenly Rob became really agitated. He sat up in bed, swung one leg off, his eyes were wide and he started talking, to whom I have no idea. "Yes, I'm ready, which way do we go? This way?" he was looking out of the window.

He was trying to climb off his bed, a tangle of wires, tubes… "Whoa Rob, where are you going?" Pip and I pushed him back onto his pillows. Rob sat bolt upright and grabbed, really grabbed Pip's arm; he looked directly and deeply into Pip's eyes, "Be Happy!"

We all sat in a stunned silence for few seconds, Rob's eyes never left Pip's, "Be Happy!" he repeated. "I promise we'll try Rob," Pip replied.

Rob lay back onto his pillows, closed his eyes, and never moved again. I believe that at that moment, in every real sense, Rob died. Our Addenbrooke's Consultant had been right; a month, weeks but not months he had predicted.

Of course Rob's young heart just kept beating. His kidneys kept produce pee; his lungs kept expanding and contracting. The nurses couldn't believe it, "It's OK Rob, when you're ready, you can go." Pip and I would sit on his bed, stroke his face, run our fingers through his hair, and tell him that we loved him and that we would be fine. We would tell him it was OK to leave us. We understood; we knew he would stay if he could, but he had to go. Go with our love. Go peacefully with our blessings.

Abi came that evening and sat with him. It was her final visit.

Pip and I slept in Rob's room, and Sunday dawned bright and breezy. Rob's body continued to live, but it felt like the real Rob was a long way away. All day we watched and we waited. The nurse assigned to look after him all day stayed late. She was sure he wouldn't live beyond the hour; she wanted to be with him, and with us. But the hours stretched into the evening and she had to say her goodbyes.

Somehow another day had passed. Sunday evening came. We were exhausted; you can only stay awake so long. The nurses promised us they would check in every 30 minutes. Any change, if we were asleep, they'd wake us.

We did doze, and every 30 minutes, like clockwork, the door would squeak open, and the flashlight of the night nurse would focus on Rob.

At 1.20am we became aware of the nurse standing over Rob. She hadn't left the room as before. "What's happened?" I asked. Pip and I were up like a shot. "Something's changed," she said. "I don't think we have long to wait now."

We sat either side of his bed, holding his hands, one each. We talked to him, we tried to soothe him, we caressed his slim hands and kissed his forehead, we told him we loved him; we told him it was OK to leave us. We wept tears we didn't know we had left inside us. Life is so fragile and precious, and our baby's life had come to this.

His face turned towards mine, and with a shocking strength, Rob's last breath was blown directly into my face. The velocity was breath taking and its meaning seemed clear.

"Here is the last of my life, take it, live it for me.
Live my life too."

It was 1.30am on Monday 9th December 2013, and Rob's life with us was over.

❖❖❖❖❖❖❖❖

"Can we turn that music off now please?" whispered Pip. Rob's playlist had been on a loop for days. As the silence settled, I opened the window wide – grow your wings and fly my angel. None of us knows for sure what happens after we die, but I wanted Rob to go with my blessing. I wanted him to find peace, not to be constantly called back to this world. Perhaps that's what is meant, by letting someone's soul "rest in peace"?

We sat with him for over an hour. Then the nurses came and I watched whilst they washed my precious boy. It was suggested that I give them some space, some privacy for Rob whilst they dressed him, "What no socks?" "No he liked bare feet." Everything was calm. Everything was dignified. We all continued to talk to Rob, maybe he heard us? Respectful care and love was heaped upon him – in every moment, in every touch.

The next time we saw Rob he looked totally at peace. 5 beautiful yellow roses had been placed next to his face on the pillow, and we walked beside his bed as he was wheeled into the little cold bedroom along the corridor. It is not a walk that any parent can imagine holding their child's hand for.

We cleared everything out of his room, as quietly as we could, and went home. Rob had promised me he would be in every beautiful place, and in every champagne bubble, well I'd better get looking.

We went back the next morning to see him. He was just as we'd left him, with the beautiful yellow roses resting upon his pillow, with the little lamp casting a homely glow around him. We learnt that John had died a few hours after Rob. After all those weeks, just Rob and John laid side by side in the cold room. I think everyone felt, that was as they both would have wanted it.

****

Ironically, on the day of Rob's death, Pip had been scheduled to appear in Court, at the Tribunal hearing for his second claim for ESA. When Rob had been moved into St. Helena Hospice Pip wrote to the court explaining that under the circumstances neither he, nor Rob of course, would be able to attend. He asked for an adjournment.

Their response had been to issue a Direction's Notice, stating that a postponement would not be possible. The Notice went on to state "the appeal has no prospect of success, as [Rob] has not abandoned his university course." How dare they reach a conclusion before they had even heard Pip's argument's; Pip didn't share any of this with me until many weeks after Rob's death.

In a bizarre twist, at 10.00am on the 9th December 2013, 8½ hours after Rob had died, the Tribunal was held. Pip had made a written representation to the Court in his absence on Rob's behalf. The Tribunal once again found in Rob's favour, allowing the appeal on exactly the same grounds as before.

Rumbling on in the background of all this was also an application for the new PIP – Personal Independence Payment. Rob's application for the PIP had been acknowledged back in August 2013, and various forms had been completed about his illness, and how it was affecting him. We'd been advised that a decision would be made by October, which was in itself a joke as this was supposed to be a fast-responding benefit for people in a state of crisis! Pip made countless phone calls chasing the claim up, but was simply advised that no decision had been made.

On the 2nd March 2014, nearly three months after Rob's death, we received the news that his application had been unilaterally cancelled. The reasons given were that Rob had died, and the DWP had been unable to contact his next of kin.

The treatment Pip endured from the staff at the DWP was shameful, and on occasions hostile. We were left feeling that it was the DWP's wish that their claimants would give up in disgust and go away, or possibly die!

In desperation, in March 2014, Pip wrote to the Prime Minister, David Cameron. He asked that a full investigation take place into Rob's treatment, and that the appropriate changes be made to the practice and procedure so that in Rob's case, and in the cases to follow, justice might be done. I don't suppose there is any coincidence that, shortly afterwards, Rob's estate received all the arrears of the ESA, and the PIP too.

We were allowed a few days of "joy". We believed that at least the precedent had been set. We would be able to help young people in the future to get what they needed and deserved. It was a victory of sorts. The payment had arrived too late to make any difference to the quality of Rob's life but others would benefit. It would all be part of Rob's legacy, he would have "made a difference."

A short time afterwards, Pip received another letter from the DWP. It was the cherry on the cake. Addressed to Mr. R. George, commiserating with him on the death of Mr. P. George, they simply wanted to put the record straight. Whilst they would not be asking for any of the money to be repaid, they had actually coughed up by mistake!

Correspondence between Pip and the current Secretary of State, Iain Duncan Smith continues. We now have a new local MP, Mr. Will Quince, and the saga goes on…

The Severn Bridge

Chapter 15

Thursday 14th May 2015
JOGLE Day 13
Tintern to Glastonbury (57.0 miles +3928ft))

We had tormented ourselves with the weather forecast the previous evening, so to awaken to the sound of rain bouncing off the pathway was no great surprise; it's not a happy sight though. Weather is a bit like miles; it takes on a whole new set of meanings after you've been out in it for a few weeks. What starts off sounding like a long way, isn't quite so impressive or worrying after day after day of miles. Weather that from the comfort of your sofa sounds unbearable is not so bad when you've been soaked through on a regular basis. We'd already endured a lot of "weather" and so I allowed myself the view that this was nothing to worry about, I was just going to get wet again and no amount of "waterproof" kit was going to change that. What was a little wet weather between cyclists? As the rain trickled down the windows it reminded me of the "Weeping" tree outside Rob's Hospice room. Perhaps they were tears from heaven?

We nipped across the rain swept garden to breakfast. Folks were surprisingly upbeat. Max presented Nicola with the tour Moustache on the basis that she was now sporting a beard (made of steri strips) on her chin to match it!

All in all Nicola had been pretty lucky. She was well up for cycling, although it was all under review. Her jaw had stiffened overnight having taken such a harsh encounter with the tarmac the previous afternoon, but the gash seemed to be holding together. Dr. Elizabeth was anxious about how the wound was to be kept dry in all the rain, but as we were cycling through the middle of Bristol later that day, if we needed to, we'd detour via A & E. Nicola's wrist was sore, but everything seemed to be working, so multiple layers of cycle gloves were Velcroed on snugly and again, we'd keep talking to each other, and review the situation as we progressed.

Not long afterwards, the early leavers were gathered in the car park, zipped into their fluorescent kit, the weather beginning to whip itself into some kind of fury at our determination to remain undeterred. Off we set, passing the now dreary looking remains of Tintern Abbey. Photos of our departure taken by Abi's mum tell a perfect tale, with our lights reflecting in the huge puddles on the road, and her flash bouncing off our reflective kit – it looks like 10.00pm rather than breakfast time.

The first three miles were a challenging uphill warm-up, guaranteed to leave your waterproof kit confused as the rain is repelled on the outside, and yet you swim in your own steam inside. The lush wooded hillsides protected us from the strong wind but the rain ran down the road, down us, and down my neck – yuk! There was nothing for it, just ignore the weather.

We then "enjoyed" a smashing five mile downhill, which should have been a free ride, but of course the weather played its part. As we sailed past Chepstow Racecourse we kept signs for Bristol in our sights. We easily found the cycle path and as we hit the huge roundabout that leads onto the River Severn Crossing we had to smile as our Garmins announced we should "turn right onto the M48". I love bridges, so was really looking forward to this. The bridge had been opened in 1966, within my lifetime, and as a youngster, brought up in Wiltshire, I vaguely remember the excitement as an alternative route into Wales was offered. Fortunately there is a designated cycle lane running each side of the motorway, and so off we went.

The weather was hideous. The rain beat down upon us, and the wind was so strong as we battled our way across the open expanse that we simply had to keep pushing forwards. As soon as we felt a slight loss of momentum, the fear was that we'd be scooped up by the wind and either deposited in the river raging way down below us or onto the main carriageway of the motorway. Neither was an option with great appeal.

Once on the other side, our little group cowered behind a large electricity box. I think we were all a little wobbly; it had been a pretty scary experience. Anyway, we were all still alive to tell the tale so we'd simply add it to our list of adventures. Nicola had joined our group today, which was to seal our steady gathering of cyclists. Elizabeth, Pip, Liz, Nicola and myself headed off towards Bristol central, feeling brave and determined.

We picked up part of the National Cycle Route, which wiggled on a network of lanes heading into Bristol. As I said, I love bridges and, combined with my desire to make each day memorable and scenic, we were heading for the Clifton Suspension Bridge. Built in 1864 and spanning the Avon Gorge, it links Clifton to Leigh Woods in Somerset. The design of the Clifton Suspension Bridge is based on one drawn up earlier by Isambard Kingdom Brunel. Tragically two men had been killed during its construction.

Bristol is famous as the City of Seven Hills, and it began to feel like we were tackling each by turn. We cycled past Nicola's son's old Hall of Residence whilst he had studied at Bristol University and then we cut through Henbury Park, with Blaise Castle off to our right. A lady hailed us; who was cowering under an umbrella and waving enthusiastically. She was a friend of Liz's who had turned out to greet us. We were so bedraggled, I'm not sure we did her enthusiasm justice, but it was fabulous to receive her support and it certainly gave Liz a real boost.

We stopped and whilst Liz nattered away, I cast my eyes around me, and remembered all those friends and supporters who kept sending in messages of support. Each night we'd check Facebook and emails, and read all the fantastic messages. It makes a huge difference to know that people are cheering you on, wishing you well, and willing you to succeed. If you were one of those people – thank you!

After 21 miles into the day's route, we hit Ladies Mile and I remembered that this was the final landmark before our second bridge of the day. Of course, if you are going to go over a gorge, I suppose a steep climb is to be expected, so upwards we toiled, and then, there we were and there it was. Clifton Suspension Bridge is a toll bridge, but free to cyclists. It's elegant, it's beautiful, and it's a reflection of a bygone era. It was special to cross it slowly, to take in the view, whilst of course ignoring the wretched weather.

As I stopped beneath the sign placed on one of the main pillars by Samaritans I looked down into the gorge and thought of all those poor souls that had felt throwing themselves off the bridge was the only option left to them – it does carry a reputation as a suicide bridge. I would plead with any such desperate person, phone Samaritans; talk to someone, please don't jump. Back in 1885 one such young women had taken that plunge. However, due to the customary dress of the day, her skirts and petticoats billowing out had acted as a parachute, and she had survived.

In February 2014 the Clifton Suspension Bridge was closed due to high winds for the first time in living history. I think we were lucky that Tuesday 14th May 2015 wasn't the second such occasion – there might have been a few cross words thrown at me if we had needed to make the necessary detour in such a case!

On the Somerset side, we headed into Ashton Court Mansion Deer Park – who knew one even existed on the outskirts of Bristol? The view back towards the city was stunning and well worth taking a breather to enjoy. It felt as if we were crossing one of those historic film sets – Miss Elizabeth Bennett and Mr Darcy would appear any second. On second thoughts, no chance – they'd be cowering in the dry and warm refreshment tent! The herds of Red Deer and Fallow Deer were sensibly nestling tightly and timidly together under the huge old trees, watching with amusement as we carved our way past the impressive Mansion in the centre of the Estate.

As we approached the boundary of the Estate, I did emit an expletive or two. Nice cycle path, nice view, nice fence, err nice gate – well and truly locked! And that is how you would have found us, knees up around our ears, climbing over the fence, ready to receive our bicycles as they were lifted over by Pip. All things are possible – well we weren't going back!

As we cycled through Long Ashton, the open countryside spread ahead of us. Bristol had been totally memorable – for many good reasons. It wasn't long before we found Carl, huddled in a puddly layby. All the windows of the van were steamed up, and the kettle was boiling. We knew it wasn't going to be a good idea to settle in, once you are soaked through and stop, you get cold so quickly. We gobbled our lunch down somewhere near Lulsgate Bottom (fab name), listening to the roar of the aircraft at the nearby Bristol Airport. Our boilers stoked, we headed off for the Mendip Hills – now there is a clue in the name as to what lay ahead of us.

It is indeed an area of "Outstanding Natural Beauty" and we coped pretty well with the undulations. Nicola's chin was remaining stuck in place, and I think her aches and pains were loosening up as the day progressed. A last minute change to the planned route meant that we missed out the nearby Cheddar Gorge, mostly because the road leading there is called Cliff Road and that didn't sound like a good name to me. We were however heading off towards Wookey Hole.

At 37 miles the climb was a real challenge. In fact as you look at the ride profile it looks vertical – what was I thinking? At one point, whilst I was still cycling, Liz and I, lurking at the back as usual, noticed an open farm gate. A few meters further up the hill, standing in front of another closed gate, stood a mature lady - I guess the farmer's wife - complete with flowery apron. "You'd better keep pedalling love," she said with a cheeky smile, "We're moving the cattle."

I am pretty scared of cows at the best of times, but chasing me up a hill, when my lungs are already screaming for more oxygen – that's not funny. Strangely I remember smelling them first; the pong preceded the mooing and the distinct thundering of their hooves. I was terrified. Surely I couldn't have got all the way to Somerset from John O'Groats only to be stampeded to death by a herd of cows? For a split second it seemed possible... Liz and I pedalled with gusto and spotted a young farm hand, by now hardly able to stand for laughing at the pair of us. Pip, Nicola and Elizabeth had pulled across the little junction, leaving the gateway clear into the new field, manned by the lad, now wetting himself laughing. Phew, as I wiped the perspiration from my eyes, and my heart settled back into a healthy rhythm, even I could see the funny side.

We enjoyed a stunning ride across the tops of the Mendips, a range of limestone hills, famous for the caving and potholing opportunities. The land falls away in the distance, looking forwards to the Somerset Levels. It was weird to be cycling so high, but with these huge views falling away all around us. Priddy Hill Drove followed by Pelting Drove was the scene of our next encounter, this time with some sheep; the farmers sure were busy today. Our National Cycle Route picked up Deerleap, which carved its way steeply down through Ebbor Gorge. It was one of the scariest descents so far. The lane was narrow, so steep, winding, and wet. Our brakes squealed as we resisted picking up too much steam, and the view wasn't to be missed either. We got to the bottom curiously out of breath, but all in one piece – and there was the entrance to Wookey Hole.

The rain had actually stopped falling by this point, which was a relief all round. Our route had been especially planned to circumnavigate Wells Cathedral. I wanted to see the Cathedral from all angles, and if we hadn't been so disgustingly wet, I'd have wanted to go in too. As we approached through the medieval city, we were indeed awed by the "magnificence of the towering Cathedral". It is described as England's smallest city, and will make a marvellous destination for Pip and me on our next weekend away. With its Roman roots, its Bishop's Palace, and its close proximity to Glastonbury, we'll be sure of a great trip.

As we approached the Cathedral, Nicola's phone rang. It was Terry, who told us to cycle closer, and to stand in front of the Wells Cathedral School. The school orchestra was playing a stunning piece of Bach. Terry claimed he had organised this concert especially for us – nice touch! We got off our bikes, and took in the whole scene. The music, the immense Cathedral, the sense of history; it all combined to form another very special moment for our minds' eye and our memory banks.

We weaved our way through the narrow streets; it was a truly charming city. We left Wells on a very thoughtfully provided cycle path running alongside the busy A371, before heading off again across country. As we headed towards the Somerset Levels our spirits soared – flat, flat, flat... now this is cycling at its best.

Ahead of us, looming upon the horizon, we could see a curious bump in the landscape. It was the famous Glastonbury Tor. It really does stick out like a sore thumb. However, even on the flattest of runs, it seems possible to find a hill, and this was no exception. As we pulled ourselves up the Old Wells Road, we found ourselves being cheered on by a small family group. The woman was particularly vocal. It turned out that none of us knew her, but she had chatted to some of our earlier riders, and had decided to stick around to cheer the rest of us through. It was a random act of kindness by a lovely stranger – I think there is potential for a book title there somewhere. I told her about the RGF and she promised to leave a message on our Facebook page, and she really did. When we finally arrived later that night, her encouragement was waiting for us – what a total star!

We cycled right up Glastonbury High Street, filled with its curious array of shops stocked with Dream Catchers, Crystals, and Tie Dyed long frocks. The Abbey was off to our left, and I duly noted a visit to be undertaken on foot, on another day. Abi was already looking forward to coming for the 2016 Glastonbury

Festival, Pip and I were already talking about returning whilst making sure to avoid the Festival. It takes all sorts!

Glastonbury is reputed to be the site of the first Christian church in Britain; the Camelot King Arthur had been here too. Renowned for its music festival, attracting Hippies of the past and present, it had a unique atmosphere about it. I reckon I could happily burn my bra and settle down here; not sure that was advisable on our current trip though!

Tonight's hotel was another Premier Inn. We'd had a few nights off so we were ready to count the Daisy pictures again. We found our room, cranked up the heaters, and draped our sodden gear about the place. Having turned our room into a mini sauna, we headed off to the bar – a gallon of water followed by a G & T for me tonight. Dinner was totally unmemorable, but absolutely fine - something and chips. Nicola concluded the day by presenting the moustache to Hazel, on the grounds of the outstanding teamwork being demonstrated by Paul and Hazel and their dedication to each other. Day 13 was done; it too had been a fabulous one.

At various points along the way there was just enough energy left to reflect on how things were going. As we now entered our final few days of the ride, the enormity of what we were so close to achieving began to hit home. It also became clear, and never more so than now as I try to write an account of everything, that this book is, of course, only about my ride. There were some folks I had hardly seen.

I can fully appreciate that my approach to travelling from John O'Groats to Land's End would not be everyone's. Living with me takes the patience of a saint at the best of times; so cycling with me can only possibly be an extension of that. I know a few folks made alterations to my route; of course that was absolutely fine. I really did want everyone to have the ride that they wanted. If I am going to be honest though, I was just a little bit disappointed. I was still seeing us as one big united team. Maybe the truth was that actually we were a number of united teams, all with the same aim, but with a variety of methods.

I was lucky that so many friends rotated at the back with Pip and me. To have so many friends that shared the "goings on" at the rear is something we will all dine out on for many years to come. There has already been a birthday party and a Sunday lunch where some of us have relived what seemed like every turn. Even the awful bits sound like good fun after enough wine!

****

Pip and I busied ourselves in the days after Rob's death; putting together a service that we felt would give our beautiful youngest son the goodbye he deserved. Tears did dry up for the most part and were replaced by an exhausted calm. Tom, Julie and Ella arrived from Dubai, Sam came home from London, the days whizzed by with the making of arrangements.

Amongst all this busyness, I couldn't bear the thought of Rob lying alone, without his Mum, without any visitors. Everyone counselled against visiting him, except Bonny, the friend I had worked with for so many years. "Knickers to the lot of them, just do what is right for you." So I did. Pip reluctantly came with me, and whilst I don't know what to do with the memories of that time, I've never regretted for a second, those visits.

Then the day of the funeral arrived. As the hearse carrying Rob's wicker basket, completely shrouded in fresh flowers, approached the front of our family home on the 20th December 2013, I knew he looked peaceful inside. I wanted him to feel as if he was rooting around those hedgerows he'd hit so many golf balls into over the years, and I got my wish. Some will say it was a ridiculous waste of money. Well in the words of Bonny, "Knickers!" It was the right thing for me to do.

Our family and close friends accompanied Rob to the crematorium, where we were forced to say our goodbyes. It was horrendous and if I could have found enough breath to scream through my sobbing, I'd have wanted to stop the service. Stop it in its tracks. Perhaps try and make time stand still. Of course that was not possible. The timetable was out of my control. Rob was carried in, in his squeaky wicker basket, to the sounds of my favourite musical theatre piece "Season's of Love," Tina Turner sang "Something beautiful remains" and we left his body to the strains of Oasis belting out "Paradise". The Rev. Rob was extremely loving and thoughtful, and before we knew it, it was over. As we emerged from the small chapel I simply felt totally lost. I had been forced to leave Rob behind – the Rev. Rob opened his arms wide and somehow gathered both Pip and I into him.

We all shared a traditional wake-type lunch, and everyone attempted to be fairly jolly. After lunch we all headed off on foot to our church. It was the church we had presented all three boys at in turn for baptism, the church I had sat and thanked God for so many things in and the church that I had hardly crossed the threshold of, since Rob's first diagnosis in June 2011.

It's true to say that we expected a fair turn out, but it was over whelming. Pip and I stood at the door to our church and greeted an ever-increasing sea of faces. The church was a picture, in the throes of its annual Christmas Tree Festival. The lights twinkled, and hundreds of friends squeezed in and the watery winter sunshine flooded the sanctuary. We guess maybe 450 people attended.

I'd put together some slide shows of Rob, we played music Rob would have chosen himself and I believe we did him proud. Sam put into music what he was feeling; "The Last Goodbye", and I too wanted my voice to be heard. Just after we had been told that Rob would die, I'd sat in the middle of one night at Addenbrooke's and watched him sleep. I'd written a letter to him, which I wanted to read at this service. Pip had read the letter and counselled me not to put that added pressure on myself, and so it was agreed that Sam would help me to record it. He sat me up in his bedroom in London, the microphone of his home recording studio live, and left me to it. "Have as many goes as you need Mum, I'll sort out the best takes later." And so there I sat and recorded my message to Rob:

Dear Rob,

Before I saw your face I'd place my hands upon you, and wondered what the future held for us, who you would be? I knew when you were awake and when you slept, it made me smile.

Then the day came when I held you in my arms, I felt a sense of completeness. As your tiny fingers closed around mine I silently promised to make the most of our lives together. I watched you whilst you slept and hoped for nothing but happy dreams for you. I looked forward to tomorrow, and felt safe in the belief that it would come.

You smiled your way through our lives together, a round peg in a round hole. You've been sweet and kind and loving, always ready to throw your arms around me. As a little boy, like all mummies, I watched you while you slept, marvelled at your peachy cheeks, and wondered at the peace on your perfect young face. I prayed you would have nothing but happy dreams. I looked forward to what might come next.

You followed your big brothers' every lead, with your humour, energy and always with your special smile, shared easily everywhere you went. We chatted and laughed together, cooked together, skied together, we shopped together – goodness me how you liked to shop! We even cycled together. We always tried to laugh together even during all those miles back and forth to the hospital, we still laughed and smiled. And then finally this random disease has taken a hold that won't be broken. Again I have sat and watched you sleep. Again I have promised you nothing but happy dreams. Dreams of all the experiences you wished for, dreams of your friends that will stay with you forever, and dreams of your devoted dad, beautiful brothers and family that wish you nothing but peace, for as long as any of us can imagine. I held my breath, and hoped with every moment for a miracle, but it would seem that our miracle was that we knew you at all.

In the hours when sleep was hard to find you tried to help me. I promised to believe you when you placed your hand upon my heart and promised that you would stay with me there, forever. You told me you would be in every champagne bubble and in every beautiful place. I can't yet imagine how anywhere will be beautiful again without you Rob, but I promise to keep looking.

I promised you that I would live life to the full, because of you. Thoughts of tomorrow will never be the same, will never feel so safe, but your smile will always linger in every sunbeam and on every rain drop, and always in my heart. We will continue to have adventures together.

Now we will cry, of course we will cry. But as you have made us all promise, we will dry our eyes, and smile for you. We will search you out everywhere we go and see your smile in everything we wonder at.

When I think of you, I feel love, and I rejoice in the enormous love that we have shared and experienced. The dedicated and careful love of every doctor and nurse, the dependable presence and love of your friends and family around you, but most especially, the love that you have spread about you. The love that you have left with me, to keep me strong until the day, I believe, we will hold hands again.

Love is not something we just have, it is something we do and share. Love is what you have left us all, and it is the best gift. We will all keep loving for as long as we can; it will last for ever and will not fade in time. It is a love that will keep me strong, as you wanted.

Now I will see you sleep when I close my eyes. Happy dreams my darling boy; no time would ever have been long enough with you.

So please, let us do this one final thing for you. Let our love ease you into the most peaceful sleep of all.

Together, Forever,
Loving you Always,

Mum. x

"The church recorded a live relay, which was transmitted into the chapel for those that arrived late, or were unable to stand for the duration. Watching it back later you couldn't help but be moved by the ocean of young people, shoulders shrugging uncontrollably, sobbing.

As the final mourners left, some of the lads from the Cricket Club sidled up. They understood that we were exhausted, and in all honesty they were probably going to have a bit of a session, but would we please go and have just one drink with them.

By the time we arrived, they were all waxing lyrical. We'd put a small piece into the order of service about our intention to found The Rob George Foundation. They, well into their cups at this point, had decided they were going to kick off the fundraising. They didn't exactly know what they would do, but it was going to be big! Could they count on our support? Pip and I looked at each other, of course they could. Bring it on. Whatever they decided, we'd throw ourselves into it. Living Rob's life for him, it began now....

Tom and his family quickly returned to Dubai and Sam threw himself into hosting a hideous first Christmas. Well obviously Christmas with Sam wasn't hideous, just the fact that it was Christmas at all! The three of us spent New Year with Nigel and Elizabeth and as New Year chimed, we clinked our champagne glasses, our toast:

"In every bubble!"

Nigel then let off a stonkingly good firework display, and 2014 began. It was the first year of my life to start without Rob.

Rob – “In Every Bubble!”

Chapter 16

Friday 15th May 2015
JOGLE Day 14
7.30am!!!!
Glastonbury to Barnstaple (78.6 miles +4651ft)

Today began with a chirpy exchange of birthday cards, it was Paul's big day, and he got to spend it on a bike, lucky him! Perhaps for his birthday Paul wished for some fine weather, and that wish was indeed granted. According to the forecasts we appeared to be set fair now, all the way to Land's End; what a relief!

We had a couple of very long days ahead of us, and so our little team of 5 were ready and raring to leave at 7.30am. We were actually looking forward to the first 30 miles. The Somerset Levels were just as the name implied, level – pure joy on a bike!! We set off on the dreaded A39, the main road that forms the spine of the West Country, and the road that comes with a huge health warning to cyclists. Actually its track record for cars isn't that great either.

Pip and I loved the Somerset Levels. The roads were quiet, the terrain smooth, the sunshine scorching. Pip announced that he was having the best bit of his ride so far – quite an accolade. We hit a slight hiccup near Othery, when we came to a roadblock complete with security guard and Rottweiler in a cage. Repairs or upgrades were being undertaken on the

Sowy River Flood Relief Channel, which required the road to be closed. What you do not want is a detour when you already have an 80 mile day ahead of you, but I wasn't about to take that dog on, so around we turned and set to navigating ourselves past the offending diggers.

It was an unwelcome extension to our morning, but at least the route was flat. We found our way to Burrow Bridge, and followed the route of the River Tone heading for Creech St. Michael where we picked up the towpath running along the Chard Canal. The surface was a fine, sandy grit, and the cycling easy. We passed under the M5 and onwards into Taunton. The only real hazard was passing under the low bridges, which didn't trouble me being vertically challenged as I am, but Pip, being that bit taller, needed to pull dangerously close to the edge of the path to save banging his head. He was worried he was going to topple in – so he dismounted and pushed at every tunnel – just a tad tedious.

The Chard Canal was beautiful. I took a photo of a swan sitting upon her nest, complete with a clutch of signets. The whole scene was perfectly reflected in the still waters of the canal – I'm very proud of that shot. We went sailing past Somerset County Cricket Club and the "Sir Ian Botham Stand", scene of one of Pip's 100's – no time to talk about cricket right now though!

Before we knew it, we'd negotiated Taunton. We'd followed the water once more, and it had worked a treat. We found ourselves to the west of the town and heading for Devon on National Cycle Route 3. Apparently we should be "cycle fit" by now. Many cyclists had forewarned us about this stage, and apparently there would be nothing to worry about anymore! Umm – time would tell. We would effectively follow NCR 3 to Land's End – the finish line felt nearly in touching distance.

30 miles in, and the honeymoon of the day was indeed well and truly over; the undulations began. They weren't scheduled to stop now until mile 1114 and the chequered flag. The lanes were beautiful, the wild flowers lined our route and every now and again you'd see a field left to fallow, filled will

buttercups and daisies. I love the West Country, and I was grateful to be here. One of the factors in doing the ride from top to bottom was that, whilst I had never really been to Scotland, I have spent many holidays in this neck of the woods. I had laughed and said that at least if I didn't make it to the end a) I'd have seen Scotland, and b) I already knew that Devon and Cornwall were stunning. I was however feeling pretty thrilled with myself for getting this far. Perhaps I should add at this point though, that just in case you are thinking of taking on this little challenge, you might like to consider the prevailing winds, which would encourage any sane person to cycle from South to North! I'm not sure what that says about us all, but what it says about Rob is that he knew all about the influences of the wind, and decreed that he wouldn't be taking the easy option – so here we were.

In the village of Nynehead we found Carl displaying his wears in front of the Memorial Hall. Parked up and enjoying a sandwich was also Pip's brother Pe; oooh, he gives a hearty hug! I think he thought we were both certifiably mad taking on this challenge, but nevertheless had come to cheer us on. A few minutes later, Pip's sister Cath and her husband David arrived, and our family reunion was complete. The only shame was that we couldn't really afford to stand around nattering for too long, but they understood.

We trundled along ticking the various villages off, Langford Budville, Kittisford Barton, Stawley, Shillingford, Morebath, and then we hit the edge of Exmoor National Park. We ran along the banks of the River Barle as we headed for Dulverton. It was breath-takingly beautiful.

From the outset I had a very clear picture of what Dulverton had in store for us. Every summer for many years, as a family, some or all of us have joined our beloved Sou'wester's CC for their annual summer tour to the West Country. One of my favourite fixtures is just up the road from Dulverton at Bridgetown CC, a little, rather eccentric, ground built on a tricky slope, with a tiny thatched clubhouse, and no loo. The entrance to the ground is over a couple of planks set over the river, which everyone fondly refers to as a bridge, and it's a well known fact that you can't score anything other than a single hitting up the slope as the ball just runs back down the steep outfield into the waiting fielders hands. You need a bit of local knowledge to pull off a win there. The teas are legendary though; they still include homemade cake!

Our cycle route branched off the B3222 onto Oldberry Lane, followed by Cottage Lane. It looked something akin to a vertical climb. Pip, Liz and I took one look, and admitted defeat. Nicola dug deep, stuck out her chin in a determined fashion and disappeared into the distance; Elizabeth didn't quite get her gear selection right the first time. Unlike the rest of us though, her approach was then always to turn around, return to a comparatively flat bit, and as she would say "take a run at it". Nothing then would entice her to give up. I think she cycled every hill – I'm proud to have been in her group and bask in the reflected glory!

Once at the top the next 7 miles were breath taking, in more ways than one. It is called Ridge Road, and that is exactly what it is. The National Park stretches off to your right, and falling away to your left, the views look down into Devon; a stunning view by anyone's standards!

Sections of the road venture onto Exmoor, and we returned to a scene reminiscent of Scotland - hilly open moorland, ancient Royal hunting territory, our single-track road carving its way between the sodden peaty bracken-covered moor. It is an area protected from development, damage and neglect; it felt a privilege to be there. What a beautiful place! I looked up and thought to myself, "Where is Heaven?" Well at that moment I felt sure it was here on earth, in the hearts of the living. Heaven was with me on my bike on Exmoor – how lucky was I?

There were sheep, cattle and Exmoor ponies. There were also Red Deer, but I didn't see any of them. I'd read about the Merlin, Peregrine Falcons, Dippers, Warblers and Ring Ouzel's – but I always make too much noise to see any birds! The perils of talking too much! There used to be Black and Red

Grouse too, but apparently they are now extinct – presumably too tasty for their own good? Fortunately my talking obviously scared off the Beast of Exmoor too, which is regularly sighted – it's reputed to be a phantom cat.

High up on the moor we met Carl and Terry in a layby. We had achieved 60 miles already, but still had nearly 20 to go – Crikey, who knew a Friday could last so long? The sun had disappeared, and we were all freezing cold. Most of us just had to suck it up and do star jumps in the layby to get warm. Nicola, however, dived into the back of Terry's car and delved into her pink suitcase for extra layers. Where was my Man Friday with my bag? Of yes, he was on a bike shivering alongside me!!

Terry was worried as the day was ticking on, and we were yet again going to complicate the dinner arrangements. All we could do was to ask him to tell everyone else to carry on without us, and order slowly – they were all good at that by now! We'd be there, but probably no time soon.

We left Exmoor and headed through North Molton, where Pip's brother had threatened to buy us a pint; presumably he had meant much earlier in the day? I think it was hard for some folks to understand just how long it took to cover some of those miles. Stonybridge Hill followed, then Filleigh, Swimbridge, Landkey and finally Barnstaple. During those final miles of the day Terry kept popping up in laybys, cheering us onwards. He helped keep us going, alongside some deep strength that continued to drive us onwards. I think by this stage I might have walked to Land's End. Whilst my cycling didn't get any faster, my determination just became stronger.

It had been a long day, and we arrived well after everyone else had finished Paul's birthday Prosecco; but fortunately Nigel C dashed to the bar for a new bottle and we were still in time for dinner. In honour of Paul's birthday, Hazel presented him with the moustache. Well, what more could a man ask for?

The hills of Devon were unrelenting, and we still had Cornwall to look forward to. We had so much invested in this ride now; it was too scary and frankly quite unhelpful to ponder too long on failure. Pip and I would just keep doing what we were doing and hope it somehow kept working. We would never consider ourselves to be proper cyclists, or perhaps we were? Did you have to go fast and furiously, head down in a peloton, never enjoying the scenery, to be a proper cyclist – perhaps we were the proper cyclists and those fast folks with broken wheels, and bent necks should be called something else?

It was the night of Day 14, and yet another Premier Inn. Every bedroom was the same, but most importantly every bedroom came with a very comfortable bed, just like the one before. Actually, I'm not sure the floor wouldn't have been comfortable about now?

We joked over our late dinner about those taster hills of Devon, and Adi confidently predicted that there would be more "pushing the pram" to follow – I think he was right.

****

January 2014

Sam organised the launch of the Rob George Foundation, for Saturday 4th January 2014. The event was to be held in London at a nightclub, Suriya. So Pip and I started as we meant to go on; this was going to be another first for us. "Night Club Virgins." Of course, generous to the core, we invited all our friends, who loyally pitched up with their coats and brollies. Pip and I arrived early and were pretty horrified. Had we really invited all our mature mates – here? "Don't worry," said Sam, "It'll look much better once we turn the lights off."

Sam had organised two bands to play, both of which were fabulous. One by one our friends crowded in, and were each in turn told there was nowhere to hang their coats; in fact people who frequented Suriya normally didn't wear coats! The music rocked out. Rob was tapping his feet in time to every beat. Sam performed his charity single "Broken", which he had recently launched in aid of Leukaemia and Lymphoma Research.

Young mixed with the young at heart, the old felt younger, or possibly older; it was difficult to tell. Photos of the evening captured everyone's desire to party, to get the RGF off to a rocking start. I stood up high, behind the band at one point, and looked down at the youngsters, (and some oldsters too) moshing. There right in the middle at the front was Katie.

Katie is now the wife of Mike, who was playing in one of the bands, and was an old friend of Sam's. Katie is a leukaemia survivor. Seeing her join in the powerful lyrics, pumping her fist into the air, I cried again. I cried with pride for Sam, and his moving performance, I cried for Rob who was no longer with us, and I cried for Katie, whose future would be formed by a disease she didn't deserve and nobody really understood.

The months ticked by and Abi was never far away. Thank goodness for that. Glen, James and Tuckers made regular trips around to visit. Their visits always involved a takeaway and Pip always paid. We wouldn't have had it any other way. Abi began her gruelling list of challenges, and we all joined in as best we could.

I turned my mind to Rob's cycle challenge, John O'Groats to Land's End. I made contact with Carl, who was distantly related to my family; well, he is the partner of my cousin's daughter! That was good enough for me. We began talking about a possible route, and I began putting a list together of possible cyclists.

A huge part of me wanted to go alone. After all it was the ride I was supposed to do with Rob. But Abi wouldn't hear of it, she'd made promises to Rob too. Pip was definitely coming along to look after me, and so the list grew. Let's make this a huge fundraiser for the RGF. The "holiday" of a lifetime was also mentioned, and so the planning began.

As time continued to march along, the lads from the Cricket Club had been true to their word, too. The plan, originally hatched on the evening of Rob's funeral, had taken shape, and a group of us were going to cycle from the Eiffel Tower in Paris, back to Colchester & East Essex CC, in aid of The Rob George Foundation. 400 miles in 6 days – they made it sound so simple. 21 of us were lined up, Pip went out and brought himself a "real" bike, Sam borrowed Nigel's spare, Abi had a bike for her birthday, Glen rode his Dad's, James rode a friends: and I don't know where Tuckers' bike came from! Some lads from the club got really into it and were pretty swankily kitted out, guided and inspired by Iain, the lad who all those months previously had stood on a land mine in Afghanistan, and Spesh, our club Chairman. Colchester was littered with unlikely moaning folks, trying to build up a few miles in the saddle.

As the Club gathered on Easter Sunday 2014, in Castle Park, Colchester, to enjoy the fun of a Cricket Festival in aid of the RGF, all we could all talk about was the "Big" ride. It seemed an impossible task, 400 miles. Now with the experience of JOGLE I'm not sure what I was worried about!

Along with many cricket teams, many of our friends gathered on that Easter Sunday, and it had been agreed that at 3.00pm the cricket would pause, the Rev. Rob would spring into action, and with all his friends around us, we would scatter Rob's earthly remains onto the outfield.

I know it was ridiculous, but I couldn't do it. I wasn't ready to part with him. Pip and I didn't row, or anything as dramatic as that, but he felt the time was right, and I didn't. It was irrational, unreasonable, upsetting, and I couldn't help any of it. We agreed that Rev. Rob would sprinkle a token portion; I needed more time.

As hundreds of friends and family gathered on the outfield, all the carnival of the cricket stilled, all the noise and banter paused; everyone took a few minutes and stood in total silence. It was every bit as horrendous as I had imagined. I could hardly bear to see the ashes flurry to the ground. Everything still felt totally raw.

Some months later Pip and I returned to Castle Park with Tom, Sam, Julie and Ella, and quietly scattered the rest of Rob's remains. It was something that needed to happen on my timetable, it is after all something that once done, can't be undone.

You are
stronger
than you
think!

Chapter 17

Saturday 16th May 2015
JOGLE Day 15
7.30am – and raring to go!
Barnstaple to Quintrell Downs
(84.3 miles +5419ft)

Both Pip and I greeted day 15 with a huge mixture of determination and trepidation. There had been much talk over the preceding months about how today's route would go. Nicola had been so concerned that she and Terry had even spent a few days on holiday in Barnstaple so that she could practise this particular section. I did think about doing the same, but decided that I'd prefer to surprise myself!

There were many levels of concern but they mostly focused around the hills (well we were in Devon), and the mileage – so nothing new then!! We were up bright and breezy, intent upon getting away sharply after a very early breakfast. It wasn't the chirpiest of gatherings. I think like a lot of things you can over-talk and over-think a situation. Pip and I had resolved to approach the day one mile at a time; well it had got us this far!

The first person I met that morning was Terry, who probably delivered his worst team morale-boosting sentence of all time. "Welcome to this impossible day!" I promptly burst into tears. When I recounted the story later Terry was mortified. A genuinely kind man, he wouldn't have wanted to upset me for the world. Well in these situations your choices are fairly simple. You can either give up, or keep going - a straightforward choice. I had the bonus of Rob's voice ringing in my ears. I know exactly what he would have said: "You're here, your healthy, suck it up and get on with it!" Harsh though it may sound; actually for me, they were very helpful words of advice.

Our little fivesome was busy packing our pockets with food, oiling our chains and checking our tyre pressure. We were ready to go. Nicola was in the middle of a massive faff and told us to head off without her – she'd been to Barnstaple before and so she knew the way. In no time at all she would catch us up. And so off we went, accompanied by Claire and Antonius.

We headed into the centre of Barnstaple. I absolutely love Barnstaple and on another kind of visit it would have been possible to pass many an hour filling the boot of Terry's car with local knick-knacks from the Pannier Market and Butchers Row. Historically, they actually used to make money in Barnstaple, when around the time Norman was busy conquesting they had their own mint – what a good idea! We efficiently located the bridge crossing the River Taw, which was adjacent to the railway station, where we picked up the end of the Tarka Trail. This is another disused steam railway route and so we had 17 miles of flat, tarmacked off-road to look forward to. The river ran alongside us and we had a blast. As a family, Pip and I had cycled and walked this route on many occasions with the boys – it's glorious Devon at its best. We were pretty early in the day, so well ahead of the bulk of the dog walkers on a Saturday morning. The sun was gleaming on the water; the sky was blue and the banter fun. Claire and Antonius soon pushed ahead, but we had enjoyed the first handful of miles in their company.

The old train track brings you around the estuary mouth to Instow. It is here that the Taw and Torridge meet, and if you walk out onto the sand at very low tide, to the very point where the rivers' currents converge, you will find the George Family Thinking Spot.

Pip and I cast our eyes out towards the beach where you will find the North Devon Cricket Club. Traditionally when we are here for the annual Sou'wester's CC fixture at Instow, a possie of George's visit the spot and think! It doesn't take long – the thinking that is - but it's further than it looks. Rob played Cricket at Instow, and Sam still does. David Shepherd (1895-1974) (International Test Match Umpire) came from Instow too. He played cricket at his home club and when he got to 111 runs – a Nelson – he insisted upon standing upon one leg and jumping up and down to negate the Nelson effect!! It worked for him!!!!

The boundary on two sides of the pitch is the sea. Sitting down on the far end of the ground to watch the cricket, I would normally be found slunk down in a low deckchair inside the sea wall, sheltering from the biting sea wind. The boys would remind me of a bunch of puppy dogs, chasing around after the hard red ball. I have a very special set of memories from this place. With the thatched pavilion as the backdrop and our smart club flag, in its Cambridge blue and gold livery, flapping madly from the flagpole, it's a highly recommended way to spend a summer's afternoon. Add to the memory a helping of arguably the best ice cream in the world from the van that is semi permanently parked by the sea wall, and we were all happy.

We sailed past the old signal box and carried onwards skirting the west walls of Tapeley Park. Our top-drawer cycle path continued on towards East-the-Water opposite Bideford.

Bideford isn't renowned for much, but it is reputed to be the place where the coal was mined and used to make Max Factor's jet-black mascara – now there's a random piece of information for you! That same very black coal had also more recently been exported to Australian Aborigines to be used to paint their bodies with for ceremonial events – it's difficult to believe that there isn't any coal suitable a bit closer, but I don't suppose the good folks of Bideford are complaining.

Both Pip and I have childhood memories of Bideford car park too. In my case, hours spent sulking in the back seat of the family car, whilst my folks broke open the thermos flask of tea.

The result was that all the windows would steam up and Dad would need to intermittently keep turning the demister and window wipers on and off so we could "enjoy" the view. We would be constantly looking out for a break in the rain clouds – but not so today - it was a stunner!

Elizabeth and I were keeping a sharp look out for a friend of ours. Emma lived in Taunton, and we'd met her on our Cuba cycle trip. She had messaged to say she would take her dogs and children for a walk hoping to meet us. She was going to walk towards us and, if the plan worked, we'd bump into each other. Everything went perfectly and just as the cycle route swings across the River Torridge, there her party was. It was smashing to receive such friendly support and enjoy our short reunion. We were so close to the end, and yet actually, in all honesty, still so far!

We reached the point where we had to branch off the track and re-join civilization. We were a little bemused not to have been caught up by Nicola, but bearing in mind her ability on a bike and her experience of the day's route, we didn't worry too much. We had another challenging steep climb for 3 miles, which certainly signified the end of the day's warm-up. The "B" road was good and we tackled it like a bunch of folks determinedly trying to look fitter and less knackered than they actually were. Langtree, Stibb Cross, Milton Damerel, Woolacott, and Holsworthy – we were flying this morning.

Holsworthy, still in Devon, appears in the Domesday book of 1086 and has been occupied since Saxon times. The Church of St Peter and St Paul might well have been worth a look - it would have given our bums a much needed rest. I would have liked to see the stained glass window depicting the Devil himself. History states that the church tower was built in 1450 atop a live human sacrifice to ensure a strong foundation!

We were 32 miles along the way, when Elizabeth answered a call from Nigel H. There was a large group of them; all having left together, and they were lost. They'd struggled to locate the beginning of the Tarka Trail, and then having done so, had left it too early. After cycling in a delightful circle, they'd ended up back in Barnstaple. Could we give them a landmark to head for - the circles were proving a little tiresome! Nicola was with them. I know it's mean to laugh, but Pip and I did. Ignoring Claire and Antonius, we were ahead of the pack – OK, maybe only due to a little bad luck on their parts, but hey we were going to take it – our hearts swelled with ...... well I suppose it wasn't really pride, as we'd not found ourselves out near the front by skill, but anyway – it cheered us up no end.

For the next few miles Elizabeth fended off calls from Nigel H. We honestly did try to help, but apart from head for Holsworthy, it was hard to know what else to say.

The lanes were quiet and bright. I know it probably sounds mad, but I'd been so looking forward to cycling along these lanes, lanes I had driven around for years. It was fabulous to finally be there. We found Carl and Terry in a layby near to North Tamerton; a break was most welcome. Nigel C's wife (Abi's step mum Tina) and Abi's sister Harri were also there and I think were probably a little alarmed by our total lack of sympathy for those folks who were some 25 miles behind us. I guess you needed to be in our shoes to share in our gloating! Terry was doing his "very stressed dance", which we didn't have the energy to join in with. Nicola had been lost, but just so long as she wasn't hurt and they were all together, everything would be fine. They'd be over-taking us again before we knew it – them all being behind us was totally temporary. We were going to milk our couple of hours leading the way – after all it was a very rare occurrence!

Tina and Harri were amazingly enthusiastic and encouraging and cheered us on our way, keen to capitalise on our advantage. My memory of the ride is simply of a continual string of loveliness. We rode a chicane of winding country lanes, bordered by hedgerows full of the finest wild flowers. We enjoyed sunshine on our backs, and miles under our wheels. The hills were relentless, but we were coping, we just needed to believe in ourselves and we might just pull this challenge off.

National Cycle Route 3 was a stunner – it comes highly recommended, absolutely no A39 for me, thank you very much!

We stopped every 5 miles for a bit of a stretch and a drink – with such a long day we needed to pace ourselves. We had an 8 mile section of serious climbing, but to be honest, Devon seemed to be one big hill. Beautiful hills, but hills none the less. We passed through pretty Hallworthy and finally reached the highest point of the day, near to Trevivian. Yet again the weather caught us out. Having thought we'd basically got the worst of the climbing cracked for the day, having reached the "top", the scenery unfolds before you, and then... the wind whistles around your ears!

The terrain changed to open moorland, and there was nothing to disperse the buffeting winds except us! Over to the right of us ran the disused WWII Davidstow Moor airstrip, and even further over to our right could be spotted Brown Willy, (or Born Wennii), Cornwall's highest point at 420m. All around was the buzz of folks out flying their battery operated model planes. The wind was punishing, which seemed hardly fair bearing in mind the magnitude of the day's undertaking. Still we all buried our chins in our chests and dug yet deeper. It seemed an unnecessary twist for my tired legs.

Having cycled for a mile and a half into a perfect head wind, we turned sharp left towards a pine forest and the Corwdy reservoir. It was wonderful; it was as if someone had turned the wind machine off. Our smiles returned and our little group celebrated by stopping for a handful of jelly babies each. Maybe Bodmin Moor wasn't so bad after all.

We were by now dab hands at the cattle grids placed to keep us awake, and the climbing had all added together to place us on, what felt like at that moment, the top of the world. The views surrounded us on all sides – it was stunning. We wove our way across the moor, dodging the friendly, if a little bemused sheep. Our reward for all that hard work - well basically an 8 mile descent. Of course don't forget this was Devon, so the downs were reliably linked by just enough of an up to make pedalling necessary, but it added to the variety of the day. We passed old derelict chimneys, marking forgotten mines – a stark reminder of life on the moors of years gone by.

10 miles of some of my favourite cycling of the entire trip followed. Elizabeth, Pip, Liz and myself pootled along on deserted lanes, with the spring flowers to keep us company; we found ourselves passing through St. Breward. We had crossed into Cornwall – our final county of the adventure. We had also cycled just over 1000 miles – it makes your eyes water just thinking about it!

This area is full of ancient remains, including the earthworks known as King Arthur's Hall; I plan to visit these sights on my next visit to Cornwall. There are also a number of stone circles close by. One of them, the Fernacre stone circle, has 76 standing stones – a stunning sight, apparently.

As we left the moor and headed down into Wenford Bridge, we picked up the path of the River Camel and were looking out for the Camel Trail. Yes, yet another disused steam train track! As we entered the car park, with a suitably inviting tearoom, we found Carl waiting for us. It was closing time but the owner of the tearoom, a keen cyclist himself, not only put the kettle on for us, but also, upon hearing about our charity ride, refused to charge us. I made my first visit to an Earth Toilet – which was actually pretty impressive – and we were updated on the progress of the rest of the cyclists. They were still behind us, although not very far. Carl was going to head off and get set up at the Hotel for the night, Terry had been and purchased fruit scones to dish out to them when they arrived. We still had 20 miles to cover, and it was 6.00pm. Curiously, we set off like a bunch of cats with the wind up our tails – we were having a very good day.

The trail entered the forested banks of the river and was a joyful 8 miles of nothing but nature to worry about. The surface was hard mud, and, I grant you, wouldn't have been much good in the rain, but today it was as dry as a bone, and we loved it. In the early evening it was deserted and peaceful, and even I managed to enjoy the bird song.

As we reached a junction in the line, we took a sharp right and went south of Dunmere, under the main A389 and past the Borough Arms. There, ahead of us, was Dunmere Halt, an old disused railway platform, complete with our nephew Peter sitting swinging his legs. I immediately heard his wife Kelly proclaiming as she came running back down towards the platform "I knew they'd come as soon as I decided to pop to the loo!" Bless the pair of them; they'd been waiting for hours to meet us. With the use of our tracker they had a rough idea of our progress and had timed a pint at the local hostelry to come and give us a hug. It was getting so late that we really couldn't stand around too long, but it was a very special and dear ten minutes. We'd see them again at Land's End.

As we turned off the trail at Boscarne it wasn't long before we heard the familiar heckling, but on this occasion approaching from behind. Here they came - Nigel H, Nigel C and Abi, Adi, Fossie and Nicola. You can imagine the banter that flew around about "taking their time", "learning how to use their Garmins", and generally "coming in late", Nicola also took a far bit of leg pulling on just how helpful had it been to come and rehearse the route earlier in the year, and so it went on and on and on... They'd cycled an extra 12 miles (although it had taken much longer than that mileage implies) and so were set for a 92-mile day – our little group all reckoned they should cycle round and round the car park when we found the hotel, and make it a nice round 100! Curiously, there weren't any takers for that particular idea! The truly wonderful thing was, though, that they had never seemed happier. The camaraderie within their group was splendid. No one was moaning, groaning or gave any display of annoyance. They had all enjoyed the adventure, had shared in the decisions that had led them off course, and had found the funny side of being lost and at the back. They'd stuck together and loved every minute and enjoyed every inch of the day's route.

We shared the remaining 10 miles, loving being part of their fun and games. I have to admit, though, it was fairly exhausting, or perhaps we were just fairly exhausted? Our usual little group had settled into a comfortable and fairly peaceful way of doing things. This lot of intruders were very noisy. Abi, of course, hardly pauses for breath at the best of times, and her

Dad Nigel along with Adi were adept at keeping the one-liners flying. Abi was also a master of the "Stop, Start" method of hills, which, whilst we had heard a lot about it, did take us a little by surprise. Whilst it did seem to work very well, there was never any notice given; Abi would just stop. Us unsuspecting slower coaches found the added responsibility of not crashing into her almost more than we were capable of at that stage!

By the time we arrived at St. Columb Major, the evening bell ringers were out practising, and the pub car parks were heaving. Sadly, we had missed the major sports event of the St Columb Major annual calendar. Twice a year the town plays host to hurling, a medieval game once common throughout Cornwall, but now only played in St Columb and St Ives. It is played on Shrove Tuesday and then again on the Saturday eleven days later. The game involves two teams of several hundred people who endeavour to carry a silver ball made of apple wood to goals two miles apart, making the parish, around 25 spare miles in area, the largest sports ground in the world.

Our final section of the day was a couple of miles on the A392. It's not a good idea to take up too much of an "A" road, so the speedier riders headed off, and we simply kept doing what had got us this far and finished the day not long after the rest of them.

What had been billed as our most challenging of days - possibly impossible - was done, and we had arrived in daylight too. We joined together for our last pre-cycle briefing and a hearty dinner with a real air of achievement pervading the gathering.

It was an emotionally charged evening; there was no getting away from that. 53 miles separated us from our finishing line, and the atmosphere was one of celebration. I tried not to be a bucket of cold water, but had to try and "sober" folks up. "Keep your eye on the prize", "Don't take your eye off the ball", I spouted them all. 16 X 53 miles meant we still had 848 miles to accomplish between us. The aim was still to get everyone of us to the champagne – there was more now at stake than ever. We needed to concentrate to the very end.

Our dinner included the presentation of the moustache by Paul; he passed it to Liz. It seemed a suitably fitting place for the black fluffy appendage to finish its ride. My oldest dancing friend had grafted her way with me at the very back almost to Land's End. It felt like the settling of some kind of trophy, and well deserved too.

****

August 2014

In the very early hours of Sunday 17th August we gathered at Colchester & East Essex CC. Lizzie, Iain's mum, and her sister were busy grilling bacon, and one by one our motley cycling crew arrived. Iain was the young lad badly injured whilst serving his country in Afghanistan, and his mum and I were good mates. We'd spent many a happy hour serving behind the bar of the cricket club together and she simply couldn't believe Pip and I were going to try and do this ride. She kept repeating, "Lorraine, you will be careful?" "I'll be fine" I repeatedly replied, I'm not sure I was as certain as I was trying to sound. Bikes were loaded onto one of our loaned vans and luggage was stacked up to the roof of the other. Our support drivers were flexing their muscles, and us "cyclists" bagzied our seats on the borrowed minibus.

Abi and Glen were meeting us in Paris, as was Sam who was flying in from Spain. We were picking up another straggler at the Tunnel, and Julian at the M25, but apart from that everyone was tucking into the tea and breakfast buns. There was nothing for it, "Come on chaps, all aboard, we've got a train to catch!" Off we set for the Channel Tunnel, bound for Paris.

We set off with a fist full of one-way Chunnel tickets, and our borrowed mini bus chugged its way towards Paris. We hadn't catered for the speed limiter and so it all took a little longer than we had calculated and some added patience too. We were setting off on a Sunday as my research had shown that on Sundays, you are permitted to park within ½ a mile of the Eiffel Tower, for free.

As we approached central Paris, Martin, our willing volunteer minibus driver, looked across at me and said, "Please tell me I am not about to drive this bus around the Arc de Triomphe?" Sadly for Martin, but with much excitement for the rest of us, I wasn't able to allay his fears! We have some fabulous footage taken on a Go Pro camera from the minibus of us entering that stream of seething traffic; it was a surreal experience.

We pulled up right outside the apartment that Abi, Glen and Sam had been staying in overnight, made use of the facilities, grabbed our bikes and walked to the starting point.

It was a memorable moment. 21 of us lined up, all in our special fluorescent tops, for that iconic photo under the Eiffel Tower. Japanese tourists appeared out of every bush and from every direction to take their photos too, some even insisting upon being in the photo themselves. "Wob? Wob? Hoo's Wob George?" they all chorused, it was hilarious.

My allergy to traffic isn't new, and on this trip, too, I had spent hours sorting out our route. We actually managed to navigate the first miles of our ride from the centre of Paris traffic free. Pip and I had taken a quick trip to Paris a month earlier to recce the route – it was a responsibility to get us all out of the enormous capital safely. It was time well spent and we navigated with confidence, heading firstly along the banks of the river Seine, past Notre Dame, then out of Paris, through Park de la Villette, and alongside the Canal Saint Martin.

Park de la Villette was beautiful on that August evening, swathed in sunshine, packed with families sprawling on the grass, reflected in the huge gleaming silver ball that stands beside the water. Locals sat around drinking wine and trying to forget that it was work in the morning, or rollerblading along the smooth cycle path. I was very proud of our route but had to smother a giggle as some of the lads expressed surprise that there was a route at all. They had thought we'd simply sort of head north, head for the Hoek van Holland, from where we'd catch the ferry back to Harwich and then home. Don't you just love the innocence of youth – who needs a plan, who needs a route?!!

Day 1 didn't exactly go to schedule. Those extra hours spent driving due to the speed limiter had left us a little short of time. We *only* had 33 miles to the first night's hotel, the idea being to miss the Monday morning rush hour traffic of Paris, and utilize the cheaper accommodation on the outskirts. The Canal St. Martin took us the first 22 miles, our only obstacle being the Parc Forestier de Sevran.

We entered the west gate with no problem, but didn't notice that it was nearing closing time, and so by the time we reached the exit on the eastern boundary, we had been locked in! Fortunately we were a fairly skinny bunch and so a good display of teamwork, readjusting the padlocked chain holding the gates together to maximize the slack available, we were able to prize the gates into a position which gave us just enough room to squeeze ourselves through and then wiggle the bikes through after us. It was our first major team building exercise of the trip.

As we turned north away from the canal we met our support team in Gressy. There was Tim and Nicki in one van, Ben in the other and Martin in the minibus. Already the best of the day's light was gone, so a quick gobble of jelly babies and we headed off.

We had another 12 miles to cover, and whilst the roads were deserted and smooth, it was quite difficult to steer our way simply by the headlights of the vans behind us. Cycling in the pitch dark had never been part of my plan, we didn't have a set of lights between us – oh well, another story to tell the grand children!

We stayed at the Lemon Hotel, Penchard – easily the worst hotel I have ever been to. It was rough, I mean really rough. The rooms were minute, and Pip and I were the lucky two. Each room slept three people, and we had to store our bikes in our rooms overnight too. The youngsters were amazing; they just got on with it. The bathrooms, all shared, were dirty, smelly and disgusting. Paddling in pee is vile, and if I had had the energy I really should have posted a suitable Trip Advisor report warning any unsuspecting tourist off. However I suppose it was extraordinarily cheap!

Day 2 was pretty hilly and we quickly split into two groups; the zooming ahead group and the chilled group. No prizes for where you would have found Pip, Abi, Sam and me. 80 miles of hills, in the glorious August sunshine, and the team spirit was memorable as we headed for St. Quentin. Cycling due north across open countryside, you would have been dazzled by our smiles. We'd set off fairly early, having sent Tim and Nicki to purchase breakfast and meet us along the route. We certainly weren't going to linger around Penchard and our Lemon Hotel any longer than we needed to.

We were flagged down in the village of Acy-en-Multien, and ushered into a local Tabac. Our host was serving fresh coffee, and our fabulous supporters had laid out a small banquet; the local Frenchmen looked on in some confusion. It was a wonderful breakfast complete with warm fresh croissants and crusty French bread with delicious local jam, but we learnt that it was not the best way to start the day. We were starving after cycling for 10 miles, and we spent the rest of the day trying to top up our calorie intake to match those being expended. So much of these trips depend upon getting your nutrition right. We would eat first thing in future.

Vic-sur-Aisne saw us nearly half way through the day's mileage, and neatly parked in a small town square was our chirpy entourage, now on first name terms with the proprietor of Le Welcome Cottage. Beers were circulated, a picnic was spread on our collapsible camping table, and we all enjoyed a delicious lunch - perhaps rather too much!

A stupid thing to say, I know, but France is unmistakably French. With its powder-blue painted shuttered windows, and its summer sleepiness, it actually felt like a holiday. There was just the matter of a few days of cycling to contend with. Spurred on by the amazing amount of sponsorship accumulating on our fundraising page, spirits soared. Every village proudly nurtured its little square, either adorned by a sculpture, ancient or very modern, or perhaps a lush oasis of greenery for everyone to enjoy, and of course the local church was always prominent. We loved it all.

Searching for the Hotel Campanile in St Quentin wasn't without its stresses, but we got there in the end, and a hearty supper soon followed.

Day 3 was another 80 miler, but if we made it to Vimy Ridge at about the 30-mile mark, we only had the cobbles left to worry about. Getting out of St Quentin was rather easier than getting in, and before we knew it we were making a fairly good speed across the French hedge-less countryside. Everywhere is huge, and open – it was truly beautiful and the weather was set fair to match. I don't know where the French were, but it was August, and I suppose they had heard we were coming and decided it was safer to head for the beach – it felt like we had the place to ourselves.

Iain and Spesh were "in charge" and I was there to try to not annoy them both too much by commenting on the details. It was obvious that it was simply not feasible for us to cycle as one group - there was such a disparity in our abilities, and patience levels. Some of the lads, high on testosterone, headed off in a well-honed peloton. The rest of us were happy to rattle along and enjoy the view. So, off our little group of frustrated Tour de France participants headed, and the rest of us continued to please ourselves.

Tim and Nicki scouted the French countryside for exquisite morsels to grace our picnic table and Ben followed us at the rear with the music blaring and the windows wound down, criticising our cycling technique – well we gave him lots to critique! North we continued sticking to the French "D" roads, perfect for cycling. Everywhere we turned we would pass a small, pristine cemetery or war memorial. In this the 100th Anniversary year of WW1 it all felt particularly poignant. We went right through the middle of Roubaix, making good use of a wonderful network of cycle paths. At no point was traffic a worry, and when we did meet a car, it patiently waited for us – oh joy!

Julian felt very strongly that we needed to experience sections of the infamous Paris to Roubaix route. Well, all I would add is, that if you are so inclined, give me a ring first! I'm sure I can tell you enough about it to make the need for you to suffer those huge, bulbous, man-eating cobbles an unnecessary experience. Mark actually threw his bike into a ditch after one section. We spent that night in Lille.

Day 4, yet another 80-mile day from Lille to Antwerp, lay ahead of us. We completed the first 4½ miles before we reached the river Leie and the Belgium border. Iain had a couple of his army mates with us on the ride and they had spotted that we joined the river very close to the town of Menen. Would we mind if they took a quick detour to visit the famous Menen Gate Memorial? In this anniversary year it was an opportunity to go and spend a few moments honouring their fallen friends, certainly not to be missed.

I always hate to think I've potentially missed anything so most of us decided to make the detour with them. "Did they know where we were going?" I asked. "Oh yes!" I suppose how difficult did it sound, to find the Menen Gate in Menen? Off we went, whilst Pip, Rob's cousin Rich, Sam, Spesh and Mark continued along the planned route, on the stunning cycle route alongside the river.

Into Menen we headed, and around the town we cycled. At the point when we hit the start of our circular ride of the town we decided to ask a local for directions. Ahhh, we meant the Menin Gate, near Ypres, and that was some 25 kms up the road! Who would have thought that little letter "i" could make so much difference? Well they never lived that little debacle down – never trust the Army, especially if they are operating without a map!! We retraced our steps and Pip tried not to look too smug when we recounted our misadventure later.

I'd fiddled with a variety of approaches to Ghent, but when I realized how stunningly beautiful it was, I took the decision that we would simply go right through the middle. If you decide to go around the outside of most large towns all you see is the industrial areas. In the heart is where you find all the history.

As we approached through the suburbs we all shared a giggle at the shop windows. To begin with I had thought they were dummies, and we were passing dress shop after dress shop. Then we realized that actually the windows were full of young ladies, selling themselves! I bet our speeding peloton had missed that!!

The centre of Ghent is gorgeous. Pip and I have been back there subsequently, too, and enjoyed a wonderful wander around. The cobbles were a bit unnecessary, but after yesterday's joggling we now considered ourselves experts. Of course, the addition of tramlines too, made for a dangerous mix and both Rich and Pip came unstuck. We took a team shot on the bridge of Sint Michielsplein, with the river Leie flowing beneath us. The amazingly well preserved medieval architecture spread all around us, and we didn't know what to photograph first.

We wobbled our way past the churches of Sint Niklaaskert and then Sint Baafspein. We rattled our way past the Sint Baafskathedraal. We dodged the road works and made good use of the builders' portaloos and our lack of Flemish. We went back over the river Leie as it loops its way around the historic centre and over the Portus Ganda before we picked up the banks of the River Scheldt and another fine traffic-free cycle path. We were half way through our fourth day, and all in fine form.

Continuing on our north-easterly course and heading for Antwerp, we followed the main railway track. There was nothing unused about this track and as we enjoyed our dedicated bike route, the trains roared beside us. 13 miles of nattering and painless progress – perfect. We chatted away, crossing the rails from side to side at intervals. Level Crossings are particularly dodgy on a bike, and at one particular intersection I think 5 of our group fell. One of them was Pip, who had been bouncing on and off his bike since Paris – all I could think to yell was "For goodness sake, stop falling off your bike!" The lads agreed that I wasn't very sympathetic!

At one small countryside station, Heide Kalmthout, we paused at a very moving memorial. We were homing in on the Belgium

and Holland border and these two young men were eyeballing each other. This area has seen terrible conflict and bloodshed over the past 100 years. It took our breath away; two young men, not so long ago standing for real, ready to shoot each other. War is hideous. I suppose we had all been thinking about death a lot recently, and this ride seemed to be literally surrounded by it at every corner. Actually it is true to say that as soon as you take a walk, or ride your bike, you begin to notice memorials almost everywhere you turn. Nobody wants to forget their dead.

Our path finished at Beveren but was replaced by an equally desirous segregated route. They know how to look after us two wheelers on the continent. We sailed down into Antwerp ready to cross the river Scheldt.

There are famously no bridges across the river Scheldt at Antwerp - only tunnels - and they are all effectively motorways. We needed to find the Sint Anna pedestrian tunnel, which also allows bikes. As we entered the lift to take us down the required 30 meters, we were like a bunch of children. We managed to miss the famous Art Deco escalators, but you have to leave something for your return trip! We cycled the 527 meters to the other side and the large lift transported us back up to the road.

Our final 4 miles of the day took us alongside the river and then hopped from island to island deep in the industrial waterways. Huge berths lay all around us, and every bridge was busy opening and closing to allow the enormous container ships to pass through. It was unlike anything I had ever seen before.

Day 5, Thursday was a mere 68 miles to the Hoek van Holland. Again we were very well looked after with a network of dedicated cycle paths that made cycling a sheer pleasure. The whole day was a fabulous mix of cycle paths linked by massive bridges spanning from island to island as we moved from Belgium quickly into Holland. The wind was a complete killer with not a hill in sight to dilute its force, but the lads looked after us oldies, huddling around us to take the wind for us. The only real problem with us spending so many miles off road, was that it added to the challenge our support crew faced, trying to meet up with us. Of course we managed, and for us on two wheels it was a price worth paying.

On this particular day the lunch rendezvous proved a particular struggle. Spesh and Iain on their bikes, and then Tim and Nicki in their van, exchanged many phone calls, and there was much examining of the paper maps. It all got very heated. Tim knew exactly where he was, but I'm not sure we exactly knew were we were, and the young men were hungry and bad tempered. Anyway, eventually we found them, and with full stomachs folks started nattering away and normal humour was resumed. In the corner of this particular farmers lay-by was another very handily located portaloo. One of the lads went over to make use of it, and as he placed his hand on the door handle a loud "horn" went off. We all leapt out of our skins. As if he had received an electric shock, he sprang back. We all cast our eyes around; there was no one but us for miles. So, it was decided that he should try again. As the door was opened, yet again this ear piercing sound filled the countryside – and over a nearby wall popped the head of an extremely vocal donkey! A suitable fuss was made of our noisy neighbour, and he seemed very pleased to share our picnic.

As we got nearer to Rotterdam, the bridges got more and more impressive. The views as we swung across the vast expanses of water, with all the working barges chugging past beneath us, some complete with washing hanging out to dry, bicycles, and in some cases even a small car on the deck, was truly memorable. Sadly, the lads still committed to their speedy peloton saw nothing but the wheel 6 inches in front of them. I'm guessing, but I reckon they missed the stunning fields of begonias too, vibrantly coloured and complete with their own windmills – another precious photo opportunity.

One such water way crossing was made by ferry rather than bridge. We all gathered, and waited for the approaching boat. Nicki and Tim were parked up waiting too, and I think Tim had gone into the shop to see about buying tickets. The boat arrived and we all cycled on, giddy with silly excitement. The boat departed and as the water divided us from the quayside our wonderful friends could be seen steaming towards the ever increasing gap. We paid on board and Tim and Nicki caught the next ferry. Tim's language can be "colourful" at the best of times; I reckon poor Nicki needed earplugs at that moment!

We finished the day on board our ferry, departing from the Hook van Holland bound for Harwich, and that's when the party really got started. Tour fines were issued, the local Penguin (a bin that apparently needed to be liberated) was taken on a tour of the boat, and some folks didn't even make it to their cabins until it was nearly time to dis-embark.

The final 20 miles from Harwich back into Colchester in the morning were pretty steady, needing to take into account the number of fragile heads about the place! A few friends joined us for the last morning, from Pip's firm, Birkett Long. One gentleman expressed surprise that we were so slow. I'm afraid I did give him a bit of an earful!

For those final 20 miles between the finishing post, and us, everyone's spirits were high. There was a slight possibility that we may have started our celebrations a little prematurely, but we managed. As we approached our cricket club, we could see a crowd gathered to cheer us in, it was a very special moment. We'd raised £56,000 for the RGF, Rob's friends had truly honoured their lost teammate, and none of us would be quite the same again.

Upon the wall of the clubhouse, Rob's old clubhouse, you will now find two framed "pictures". One is of his 20/20 team top, mounted proudly displaying:

GEORGE
21
"Be Happy!"

Alongside that emotion-stirring frame proudly hangs a framed "Ride for Rob '14" cycle jersey. It comes complete with a photograph of the 21 riders and our four support crew (including our mini bus driver Martin who helped transport us all to Paris to begin with) standing proudly in front of the Eiffel Tower, and then the finale photo of us on the steps of Rob's wonderful Colchester and East Essex Cricket Club, complete with champagne, flowers and £56,000 in the bank account of The Rob George Foundation.

Rob's amazing young friends had achieved all that they had set themselves as a target and more besides. They had set the RGF on its way.

Sunday 17th August, 2014
Eiffel Tower, Paris.

Friday 22nd August, 2014
Colchester & East Essex Cricket Club.

“Pushing the Pram”
- the only time Fossie got off his bike on a hill, and Adi was there to record it!!

Chapter 18

Sunday 17th May 2015
JOGLE Day 16
Quintrell Downs to Land's End (53.0 miles)

Although it possibly sounds strange, this is, as I am writing this book, the final chapter to be written. I have already written the whole of Rob's story; all about the other rides I've recently participated in, and have saved the last 53 miles of my JOGLE to the end. I am weirdly reluctant to write it. After everything that has happened, Rob's illness, Rob's death, my various cycle rides culminating in JOGLE – well, writing the final instalment means it is finally all over. That thought actually leaves my eyes welling up with tears, but as Pip comforted me, "It'll never be over." He is, as is so often the case, (but not always!) right.

We had all psyched ourselves up so heavily for the previous day's ride, that our final day was approached with a rather dangerous air of having "already finished." Well the fat lady most definitely hadn't sung yet, so we all needed to get pedalling and keep a very sharp sense of focus on the roads ahead. Our devoted group of 5 left bright and breezily at 8.00am, waved off by Abi's step mum Tina and her sister Harri. The plan was that we would all rendezvous in a little car park just shy of Land's End. We had started together, and it was everyone's wish that we should finish together.

Cornwall is geographically in a class of its own. Having cycled Scotland, Cumbria and Devon (to name but a few), I think we all thought that there wasn't much that could possibly remain to surprise us in terms of undulations. Cornwall, however, immediately managed to establish itself as A* in the hill department, and took everyone's breath away. Hills reached a new level all together. Hill, after hill, after hill, after ... We picked up NCR 32 and thrashed our way to the north coastal village of Perranporth. We then followed the coast road taking in the wonderful panorama out to sea. We passed the old Perranporth Airfield nestling between us and the ocean. The geography that made it perfect for potentially landing small planes on conspired, however, to leave the wind trying to take our heads off! The high verges did nothing to protect us and whilst we were all bundled up against the freezing temperature, at least the sky was a vivid blue and the sun was beating down.

The rest of the group went steaming past us, offering suitable words of encouragement, and disappeared into the distance. Not too much further along we enjoyed a fabulous "weeee" down into Portreath. The bay was eye catching and a perfect teashop winked at us all on the harbour side. There indeed was the predicable line up of bicycles, and as we wobbled past, Hazel came out to invite us all in.

I think if we had stopped there, our legs would have turned to jelly and that would have been that. In fact, Pip and I agreed that if we had started this ride from Land's End, and had to tackle Cornwall first, we wouldn't have got very far. We could see the humungous hill pulling out the other side of Portreath and agreed that we needed to crack on. Somehow or another we got up it, but it wasn't beautiful cycling.

It seemed that every other vehicle to overtake us in Cornwall was a Volkswagen Camper Van. I had no idea that they came in so many different colours, although almost identical in every other way, with a very distinctive engine sound as it approaches you from behind. Unless you had your wetsuit on board and your surfboard strapped to the roof you were indeed, a nobody. We also saw more tussled sun bleached hair do's per square mile than anywhere else I've ever visited in the world – surfer's paradise. It all added to the entertainment.

Liz and I did pause to catch our breath at Hell's Mouth, peering down to the churning ocean way below the cliff top. It was my favourite kind of scenery, but incredibly hard work on a bike. As we cast our eyes about us, ignoring the modern tarmac road carving its way across the cliff tops, we could imagine ourselves stepping back in time. We laughed that nearly two weeks ago I had mistakenly looked for my heart throb Ross Poldark up on the north coast of Scotland, but here I was more likely to bump into him. The coastline was glorious, dotted with old mine shafts and derelict chimneys – it was wild and wonderful.

The 30 mile marker signalled our arrival at Hayle, and more significantly the flattest section of our final day. From Hayle on the north coast, we would be crossing the county to the south. It probably doesn't sound very logical, but if you look at a map, and want to avoid the main 'A' roads, it's a perfect route.

It was total bliss to be able to pick up a little more steam, and as we left Hayle on NCR 3, everyone from the teashop caught us up. We cycled together for a few miles enjoying a real party atmosphere. As we negotiated St Erth, the narrow street struggling to accommodate a large group of heady amateurs on bikes, there was a commotion behind us. Horns were tooting and folks were yelling. We all sort of spread out, and eased as closely as we could to the curb to let the irate driver squeeze past. As it did so Liz announced, "I think that was my husband and two of my children." I had known they were planning on being at Land's End, but it was to be a surprise, it gave Liz such a boost to see them all.

Not long after that, we stopped for lunch. Carl had laid out the usual spread, which we enjoyed as always. Everyone agreed that today was one of the hardest we had faced. Perhaps we had peeked or relaxed too soon, allowing the sense of achievement from yesterday's epic mileage to lull us into a false sense of security. Suddenly 53 miles hadn't sounded so far – but when all is said and done, 53 miles is still a real bike ride!

We attacked the climb of New Dairy Lane with gusto, ready for the big reveal ahead of us. As the road fell away before us, there was the wonderful view down to Marazion, Penzance and Mount's Bay, looking out to the famous St. Michael's Mount. Back in 1755 there was reportedly the only British Tsunami ever recorded, here in this very bay. Well on this particular sunny Sunday in May 2015, the sea was like a millpond. The cycle path along the front was a bit tricky, having been partially covered by the beach, but it was wonderful to be by the sea. Just as we approached Penzance Harbour there was our nephew and his wife again. Peter and Kelly, last seen in the depths of the forest surrounding the Camel Trail, were enjoying their weekend in Cornwall supporting their aged Uncle and Aunt; we absolutely adored having them there with us.

Penzance merges into Newlyn, the main distinguishing factor being the stench of fish. The eye-watering whiff oozes from the busy sheds lining the waters' edge. Hugging the coastal route we wound our way to Mousehole. "Moouzall", as it is pronounced, was home to the original Penlee Lifeboat. In the hurricane of 1981 the entire 8-man crew had lost their lives. The new Penlee lifeboat is based at Newlyn; we'd spotted it on our way through. I had warned everyone about "*the*" hill, but this one needed to be seen to be believed. I had no intention of even trying to cycle up it, but there were those amongst us who weren't going to give up on their personal challenges, certainly not without a fight. A couple of expletives escaped from Elizabeth before she turned her bike around and freewheeled back to the bottom. Apparently a run up was required – well good luck with that, my dear friend! Of course, true to form she soon came steaming past us pedestrians. At least she had the decency to turn a nice pink colour and puff loudly as she passed.

We were down to our last 10 miles. Our little group gained a few mates as Nigel H, Nigel C, Abi, Fossie and Adi all joined us. I felt like a champagne bottle with the wire cage already unwound. I was having a few annoying technical issues with my bike, if I applied the rear brakes, they then became stuck in the on position! Nigel C had a go at sorting them out, but in the end I decided the easiest thing was to simply try not to use them at all – not ideal! Adi had fixed a puncture and desperately needed to find a pump to blow his back tyre up properly, but we limped along chirpily.

It was the strangest of 10 miles, in one sense endless, in another speeding past way too quickly. Nigel H and I shared a moment, agreeing that we would both happily simply keep cycling. I knew I didn't want our ride to be over – yup! I know; mad as a box of frogs!

Our final clusters of houses were found at Lamorna and Boleigh. We sped past the stone circle known as the Merry Maidens and on to St. Buryan. Everywhere you looked you'd see a Celtic stone cross, ancient standing stone or some other reminder of Cornwall's rich history. You could easily believe that a little old smuggler was lurking behind any of those windswept stonewalls or deep inside the pockets of trees. It was easy to let your mind wander.

True to our trusty National Cycle Route 3, we approached our final pit stop, Sennen Cove. There, in the car park, 1½ miles shy of our finishing line, everyone had gathered. Claire and Antonius had enjoyed forty winks in the long grass, and I guess everyone else had paced up and down trying to keep warm. There is a designated cycle path especially for folks like us. I am guessing that at peak times there can be a lot of challenge rides coming and going, mingling with all the coach parties and day trippers. Everything I had read about arriving at Land's End had warned me to avoid the main A30 as an approach. Of course it was 4.15pm on a chilly Sunday in May, and most other people had gone home for the day. That was of no consequence for us - our friends and families would be waiting for us - and that was all that mattered. Anyway, we peeled off our warm outer layers to display our special Rob's Ride '15 cycle tops, and we stuck to the plan and our precious route and battled up the rough NCR 3. It beggars belief that no one has thought to put a proper surface on it, but nothing was going to spoil our final mile.

Pip and I were invited to lead everyone in; Abi saved her best "joke" for last:

"Did we hear about the idiot who won the Tour de France?
He did a lap of honour!"

Then amidst our final groan the most westerly tip of England came into sharp focus. Claire and Antonius were alongside us, when I suddenly realized, that Antonius was running, not riding, with his bike. With Land's End in sight he'd had a puncture! And so we all stopped. It was the fastest puncture repair of all time, and probably the most photographed. We'd set off to cycle JOGLE and Antonius was certainly not going to finish on foot!

Thinking back, the last mile seemed to happen in slow motion. Unsure of the exact way in from our rough cycle path and seeing no signposts to help, I managed to lead everyone up one final garden path and entered a blocked car park. Carl was stood high on a grassy bank way over near the road with his very smart posh camera poised to record our big finish, he was frantically waving to us that we'd gone the wrong way! I led our party back on itself passing Fossie at the rear, yelling at him that we'd decided to head straight back to John O'Groats.

We'd cycled 1114 miles. As a group of 16 cyclists we'd covered some 17,500 miles. We'd dealt with a grand total of only 7 punctures, Antonius 2, Nicola 2, Adi 2 and Paul 1. We'd broken 2 chains, (Adi and Liz,) used a shop full of brake pads, 1 gear cable, 2 packets of steri-strips and a lot of sticky bandage; which most of us had used to hold some part of our anatomy together for most of the trip. And here we all were, every one of us about to cross the finish line. It was a truly emotional moment. It was an astonishing achievement.

As we approached the Land's End Visitors Centre and that famous well photographed signpost, all I could focus on was the amazing group of our supporters gathered to cheer us in, and Rob's smile swimming in my tears. I was thrilled and, of course, relieved to have finished, but actually I was also just a little bit sad. It wasn't a huge crowd, but those there meant the world to us. I punched the air and wiped my eyes, I had kept my promise. I'd cycled from John O'Groats to Land's End for my precious Rob. I'd done it as we had planned to do it together. I had ridden it for us both.

As you can imagine there was a lot of hugging going on. Pip was in tears in the arms of our nephew Peter, and Abi and I found each other. We'd done it and Rob would be proud of us, we were proud of ourselves. The photo taken of us under that famous sign sits proudly upon my desk. I think it will stay there for a long time to come. The official photographer asked me what he should write on the spare arm of the signpost. That was easy, I wanted to see Rob's name up in lights, and as Claire handed me a glass of perfectly chilled champagne (thank you Terry) she draped her arm around my shoulders and we watched together as "The Rob George Foundation, 17th May 2015" filled the slots. We agreed it looked pretty good.

I glanced down to the cross bar of my bike. There was my inspirational photo of Rob; he'd been with me every inch of the ride. Alongside Rob was my RGF sticker - there was one on my helmet too – "You're Stronger than you think!" Well that's certainly true.

"In every champagne bubble," and in "every beautiful place" Rob had promised me. Well at 4.30pm, on that chilly, cloudy, windy, but wonderful afternoon of Sunday 17th May 2015, he was at Land's End, a fully paid up member of Rob's Ride'15 – and he was in my heart.

"Forever, Together."

****

Of course the day was far from over, we were miles from anywhere, exhausted yet jubilant. Abi didn't throw her bike into the sea as threatened, but her bike along with all the others was loaded onto Carl's van along with some of us riders. Others travelled with their families to Trethorne Golf Club, Launceston, for our final night's rest and a jolly good party.

As we whizzed along in the van the sensation of speed was startling. 16 days on a bike and the world had indeed settled to a very steady pace. The van was full of quietness; of course we were tired, but also deep in our own thoughts. Soon we arrived at our Hotel and couldn't wait to meet up in the bar.

A delicious carvery was about to be followed by a few words from yours truly. Nigel C swiftly leapt to his feet and asked if he might go first? No problem – go for it! Nigel C owns his own firework company, Dynamic Fireworks. He asked if we would all follow him outside and what followed was the icing on the cake, it was a firework display to end all displays. Nigel had commissioned special frames to show the RGF logo and also to ask the question "Day 2?" – all in fabulous fireworks. The Day 2 question was of course referring to the fact that Nigel C had been missing for the first three days and so had dodged the biblical weather we experienced on our second day in the saddle. Then there was the final burst and the words "Rob, forever in our hearts" blazing brightly for everyone to see. It was an extraordinary display and an extraordinary gift, made with such generosity, care and love.

I can't remember exactly what I rambled on about that night, but I am sure I said a thank you from the depths of my heart to each and every one who had shared the challenge. I certainly mentioned the hills, and the fact that we had climbed the equivalent of cycling up Mount Snowdon 17½ times! Pip proudly shared that we had raised a staggering £57,000 and Nigel H made a speech from his heart; that reduced us all to tears. Nigel C's wife presented all the men with specially engraved cuff links, and all the ladies with an inscribed compact mirror, a keepsake to treasure. She had also had a very special picture made for Pip and me. It is of two little interlocking maps, the first of the tip of Scotland showing John O'Groats and the second of Cornwall, depicting Land's End. Wow, that will be treasured forever.

A friend of Nigel H said at the end of the ride that "Pain and discomfort are temporary, but achievement and glory lasts forever" – I think I would have to agree with that. I was left feeling weary, weary to my bones. It didn't help that many of us were plagued with exhausting dreams for many weeks after we had finished. Dreams about cycling, about friends from the ride, weird (really weird) dreams about such strange happenings whilst cycling – it just seemed too hard to forget about the bikes. Pip and I would laugh each morning as he begged to be allowed to stop pedalling.

But I also felt proud, honoured, satisfied, grateful, content and relieved. We all have many shared memories, but of course mostly our heads are full of our own private memories and thoughts.

Rob's Ride '15 only happened because Rob couldn't do it – that fact remains unaltered.

****

October 2014

Finally, because things do have a habit of coming full circle, Elizabeth and I headed off to Cuba. All this started with talk of Cycling Cuba, and here I was packing to fulfil that challenge too. I'd spoken to Elizabeth back in June/July 2013, when Rob had relapsed, and asked her to cancel my place. I hadn't really given it much thought after that. The trip was off, and that was that. At the time, of course, I'd been at full stretch with Rob.

I think it may have been at Nigel and Elizabeth's New Year's party 2013/14, when I finally had the chance to chat away to Elizabeth, and I asked how the process of pulling out of the Cuba trip had gone. Well, as it turned out, she hadn't exactly cancelled our places! The Charity we were due to be travelling with had been extremely kind and helpful, and had urged Elizabeth not to cancel entirely, but to postpone to the October 2014 trip. We could always cancel further down the line, but you never know, we might both have still wanted to go? Elizabeth had not been even slightly tempted to travel alone on an earlier trip, despite me urging her. We had signed up together, and we'd either go together, or not go at all.

Both Elizabeth and I knew that Rob would have wanted me to go. It was, after all the trip that had kicked off all this cycling malarkey in the first place. So we packed our cases, made sure we had extra strong sun cream and headed for the Caribbean. It was an incredible trip. 51 amazing women cycling, amazing locals cheering us through every town and village, amazing scenery and weather, and then an amazing lie down on a sun-bed for a few days at the end. We had a terrific trip. What a totally good idea it had been all those years before!

Cuba is a complicated place and I'm still trying to work out what I think about it. The wonderful thing about our trip was that whilst we were staying in "holiday" destinations each evening, during the day we criss-crossed the island and saw bits that most visitors don't get even close to.

As soon as you venture off the main roads everything deteriorates. The vintage American cars, held together by chewing gum and will power, spewing out noxious fumes, dwindle in numbers and you feel more like you are on the set of a wild west movie, with the preferred method of transport being either horse back, or horse drawn cart. I think my overwhelming memory of Cuba will be the pong of horse dung; it's everywhere and the odour lingers.

The heat was incredible, and probably our biggest challenge. On the first day, we paused to take on fluid, and Elizabeth looked at me, full of concern. "Are you alright? Have you hurt yourself?" I didn't fully understand; I was fine? Then as I looked down towards my arms and legs I could see why she was concerned. I was covered in a fine film of dust from the local deep red fields. Sweating so much, the rivulets of perspiration were running down through the dust, it looked like I was bleeding from every pore.

The Cubans are so poor. Still living under a Socialist government, (they are keen that you don't mistakenly think they are Communists), they continue to survive under a system of rationing. Their jobs, homes, income, food... everything is dealt with by the State. However they are all so content and happy. Everywhere you go, and I mean everywhere, is pulsating to the sound of live music and people dancing; and every corner of Cuba, is filled by someone selling amazing original artwork. In the towns and villages it's vibrant and buzzing. In the villages it is sleepy, steaming hot but with a totally chilled vibe. Every building looks like it should be condemned, and many still display bullet holes! Some main roads are good, but once you turn off these, everything deteriorates to linked potholes at best, and stones and earth after that.

It's a very confusing place. I'm glad I went, and I'm especially glad to have shared the trip with Elizabeth, but I won't be rushing back. The women raising funds for women's cancer charities were a diverse and outstanding group of ladies, and a handful of them have remained in touch. One of the ladies, Gev, even followed our JOGLE ride with her class of school children!

Thank you "Women Vs. Cancer" for starting off this whole adventure on a bike. Cycling has given me an outlet for my grief, for my fury, for my anger. The energy that accompanied Rob's death needed channelling, and now, two years, a couple of thousand miles of cycling, and writing a book later has left me with a kind of emptiness. What I do feel though, is that my memories are safe. Perhaps now I will find some way of relaxing – ohh and a good night's sleep would be nice too!

I'm going to go and poor myself a glass of wine now, and toast the future. Beware though - I'm on the look out for another challenge!

****

November 2014

Returning home after all that sunshine came as an unwelcome shock. As November took a hold, Pip and I were invited back to Loughborough University. It was a freezing damp day. We had been invited to attend the dedication of a plaque in the University Garden of Remembrance. It was a total exhibition in how to do something badly.

Fortunately, guided by my efficient husband we arrived early. We therefore had time to go and find the Garden of Remembrance, and to find the new plaque, hung as a permanent reminder that Rob had been a student there, and had died. It was shocking, to see such a cold and stark statement of the truth. At least, though, I had the chance to catch my breath, get my head around it; do all those things in private, before the proceedings got under way.

The whole thing was shamefully conducted. The two folks officiating were as bad as each other. No preparation had been made with regards to the three individuals we had all gathered there to honour. No details were mentioned of their lives or their deaths. It was clear that the other two gentlemen had died in old age, but that was about it.

We were totally unprepared for the point when we were invited up, to the front, to place a red rose next to Rob's name, and when I burst into tears the Chaplain paused, turned to Pip and asked, "Is your wife OK? She seems rather emotional." For pity's sake man, I wanted to yell, this is my 21-year-old son we are talking about here. He has been dead for 11 months, and you haven't done him or us the courtesy of finding out anything about him.

The Vice Chancellor graced us with his presence too, and made it clear he would rather be watching the University's Rubgy match. I shook with rage as he proudly announced, "We did another one of these little services last week, for Remembrance Day, that went pretty well too." It was a hideous experience of something that could have been so very meaningful.

Almost exactly a month later we returned to Loughborough. In all honesty neither Pip nor I were looking forward to going back. The very fact that we were to be surrounded yet again by all those wonderful, vibrant, young people and that it was the place where Rob had been so happy made it very hard for us. On this occasion we were to attend the winter graduation ceremony, and had been asked to attend in Rob's place, to receive his degree.

Having completed two years of his studies, Rob had actually achieved a Diploma level of his course. However, his Geography course tutor championed his corner with the University Senate. She shared with us, the view that Rob was an exemplary student. Despite everything, he had done so well in his second year summer examinations, but also within the world of cricket – as he had been due to take up his role of Chairman. A full degree seemed appropriate.

The University took the decision to award Rob his full Bachelor of Science. As we sat in the front row of the packed awards ceremony, and then in our turn queued up with all those wonderful young people - they all dressed proudly in their graduation robes - I have never felt prouder in my life. As someone who never went to university herself, I did have to smile. I could imagine what Rob would have thought – probably something alone the lines of "it was the closest I was going to get to a degree!" - but he would have wanted us there to represent him.

Now the record seems straight. Robert Joseph Philip George was awarded the Bachelor of Science – Aegrotat (basically meaning "he was ill") – in Geography and Management. Forever, Rob's name will appear on the Roll of Honour at Loughborough University alongside his friends; and quite right too. The alternative was that his name might just have disappeared. He didn't give up on his degree, and the records may have been interpreted as Rob had dropped out. Now, history is clear; Rob is recorded as a Graduate of Loughborough University – that would have meant the world to him, as it does to Pip and me.

Life is full of surprising coincidences. Some months later we received an application from a student at Loughborough. Emily Deason had qualified to represent Team GB at the World Duathlon Games in Adelaide, Australia, in October 2015. She needed help with the finances. Emily had graduated at that same ceremony in December 2014 and had watched Pip and me collect Rob's certificate. Emily had been a contemporary of Rob's at Loughborough, and now we were going to help her fulfil her place, and enable her to represent her country. The RGF bought her a fabulous racing bike.

Months later, Emily's dad ran the London Marathon in aid of the RGF, and he, you may remember, also popped up late on the 9th day of JOGLE and nursed me into Preston – in the dark!

Elle and Elizabeth – "Teamwork"

Chapter 19

The idea of writing this book had been taking shape in my head for months before I actually started tapping away at the computer. Before I ever even set off for JOGLE, I'd been thinking about it. Rob's story deserved to be recorded. There was so much that Tom and Sam hadn't shared, and I wanted there to be a record of all that Rob had endured, if ever they wished to know. Equally I simply couldn't continue to live trying to remember it all. I couldn't go on waking up in a cold sweat in the middle of the night, because some detail had returned to my head, and having to reach for my stack of Post-it notes so that I could release that memory by writing it down.

All through Rob's Ride, I talked about "The Book". I suppose, whilst I do feel I have a story to tell, it is actually a kind of madness that has driven me to write it all down. Perhaps grief sends you a bit mad? Replaying the events of Rob's illness had become a sort of addiction. Rather than pitch up at some expensive rehab' clinic in order to kick the habit of constantly remembering, I've written it all down here – it's not an original self help tool.

Every time I sat down to start committing my memories to a page, I was struck by the enormous gulf left in my life. The space, the void that Rob's death has left behind him. All the hours spent transporting him around. Before cancer it was back and forth to University, but latterly of course, to and fro to hospital. Now I have all this empty time. Now our home has become so incredibly quiet. All his friends that used to regularly litter the place; drape themselves over the furniture, drink our beer – that has pretty much stopped. There is always Abi of course, and Glen, James and Tuckers – so I shouldn't complain too much - but it will never be the same again. The cooking, the laundry, it's all drastically reduced. Of course this would all have happened anyway, in due course, but it all stopped within the blink of an eye. But the thing I miss the most, is the touch of him. I had spent hours and hours gently massaging his feet, or with his head in my lap, rubbing his temples. He had always been a tactile child, freely throwing his arms around me, and I miss being able to touch him the most of all.

On one particular day, I had pushed Rob in his wheelchair, into the dining room at the Hospice. As we had paused to look into the glass-fronted fridge, to choose a can of drink, I had wrapped my arms around him and nestled my chin into his short stubbly hair. It had only so recently started to sprout after the last chemotherapy. The reflection had caught Rob's eye too, and he had lifted both hands and took mine in his. Our eyes locked and I had breathed in the scent of him, tried to commit it to memory. I can, just about, remember that wonderful familiar smell. I had looked at our reflection in the glass door and taken a photo in my head. Often, if I catch a sight of myself in a shop window or glass door, I see Rob sitting in his wheelchair with me too. It is a picture that catches me unawares. I can remember the warmth that came from his body. If I close my eyes I can remember how connected we felt during those hours and hours of gently rubbing his feet, how he never tired of it, and how when I would moan that my fingers were tired, he would wink and say, "Just 5 more minutes?" I am glad I never refused him.

And so, back to my book...the combination of Rob's story alongside our epic cycle challenge seemed a comfortable fit. It is just possible that it might ultimately make a reasonable read. It's not a new or original idea, but most of the best ideas have already been had! The act of writing, like the training to try to cycle a long way, would at least fill some of the hours without Rob. I hope it will also allow me to sleep easier, close my eyes and lose the haunting memories of everything Rob suffered. I don't want to forget, but equally I can't live, remembering all the time - or worse still scared of forgetting. I want to relax again. I would like to find a little of my previously enjoyed inner peace. I know my life will never be the same as it was before, but I can work to make life now, the best I can. I want anyone that might be interested to be able to read all about our extraordinary young man, who left the world too soon, but left a legacy of enormous love and courage behind him - my youngest son Rob.

I began the writing process with a few days away in Brighton. I love the seaside. I love being on the edge. Once I had begun, the words simply poured out of me. My greatest sadness of all of this is that it has served to remind me of what a lamentably poor education I received. My Comprehensive Education has not equipped me to write a book, of the calibre I would like. I am scared it will read like the words of a child, but in any case I can only write it as me, so this will have to do. If I started splattering the text with a whole host of long words, folks that knew me would just have a good laugh, and say that Pip had helped!

Anyway, back to Brighton. The pattern was to write after breakfast, go for a long walk along the seafront in the early afternoon, and then write before and after dinner. I made a lot of progress. On my third day, as I walked towards town I noticed a string of coaches pulling up, crowds of people dressed soberly were alighting and heading for the beach. Well it's rude to stare, so I walked on.

On my return I was drawn, by some kind of irresistible pull - probably just plain nosiness - to the crowd on the beach. They were all pretty chilled, standing around swigging beer from cans, chatting. The crowd was called to order and everyone sat down. I couldn't leave then, it would have been too obvious and I didn't want to spoil the moment or make a spectacle of myself. Everyone around me was so young. There were lots of dreadlocks and a good supply of fairly intimidating tattoos and piercings. Someone had obviously died. It wasn't clear how, or exactly who, but they had definitely been young, too young to die. A small casket was passed from person to person, friend to friend, brother to sister, each one sharing their special memories. Then the young persons ashes were sprinkled into the surf. All you could hear on that gloriously sunny afternoon in July 2015, were the waves breaking on the pebbles, the squawking of the gulls, and the quiet sobbing of the young mourners. Dying is all around us; it is part of our living. I felt truly privileged to share in their sorrow. I don't think it mattered that I didn't know their young lost soul, I remembered Rob, I cried for him. I put my hand to my heart, and saw Rob flash me a cheeky wink. He'd be with me, forever.

Just before I'd left for my journey of words, I heard that Katie and Mike had safely delivered their first child. Katie had been at the RGF launch back in January 2014, jumping to the music and punching the sky, sticking two fingers up to her entanglement with leukaemia. She was now a young mum, she had beaten the odds; there was a little boy to nurse into the future.

And so what about my future, who knows? Sam is about to take a Spanish bride, Estrella. She met Rob once, although he was already terminally ill, but thank goodness she met him! She supported Sam through the darkest of days and I will never be able to thank her enough for that! Pip and I, will endeavour to be, grand parents of extraordinary proportions. I hope we will find time and find a way to enjoy being together once again. We have spent so much time together in total misery; it's now so hard to laugh and find fun. We will spend precious time with Tom, Julie, Ella and Holly visiting Dubai, or wherever our family takes us. We will most especially learn to once again enjoy the very simple things. Our home, our family, our friends; the air we breathe. Life won't ever be the same again, but we will make sure we truly live and we will never regret any part of our lives that included Rob.

I look at Pip and I see a true reflection of what I know I am feeling. How are we supposed to help each other? Being together sometimes feels like we are simply doubling up the pain. But then leukaemia has taken enough. It won't take my future too. We'll make it work, in truth Pip's patience and love will make it work, I'm just lucky I married him! We'll grab every opportunity that comes our way. I also hope to carve out more time to just "sit on the edge".

The RGF will exist for as long as it lasts. If it's forever, great, if it's not, that's great too. We will continue to support young people, one individual at a time, as Rob hoped. Whatever the future holds for the RGF, all the young people we manage to support will always have received help in Rob's name. Nothing will ever take that away.

Maybe this book will be a "Best Seller." Ha Ha! If it is, I reserve the right to take Pip back to our route for a few weeks and retrace those special miles (with the help of an engine), through the eyes of Rob. Most importantly though, in the unlikely event of there being any proceeds to worry about, it will, of course, go to the RGF. After all, without Rob, there would be nothing for me to write about. A dancing teacher on a bike isn't really much of a basis for an entertaining read! Nothing would seem a more fitting consequence than for this book to help provide support to some of the flood of young applicants the RGF has identified. Daily, applications arrive requesting help with rent, utility bills, new bedding, food… and that is just aim 1!

Of course after the book has become a best seller, I'll start work on the screenplay – I am still laughing here! All the riders have already selected who will play them; Julie Walters gets to play me! Pip chose Colin Firth – yeh right, in his dreams!

Maybe there will be another challenge; who knows? For now my bike is for fun only. It is programmed only to head for teashops or pubs, oh and it's only allowed out when the sun is shining. I've cycled far enough in the rain to last me a lifetime!

I've always been a nosey bugger, but I am now, fascinated by other people. Whilst trying to write this book of memories and thoughts I have spent some time travelling alone.

It's undoubtedly been a therapy of sorts, simple solitude; a friend dared to call it retreating. However, I've been quite careful to make sure that whilst I was alone, there were usually, although not always, people around. You've heard what people say, it's easiest to feel lonely in a crowd.

I loved my life before leukaemia. I loved my life as a busy mum, as a busy dance teacher, Granny, busy active listening Samaritan, a happy contented wife. But the trouble is - and try as I might - leukaemia has taken the essence of that away. Somehow I need to find a way to thaw that core of ice that has taken root inside me, that feeling of loneliness, of deep sadness. Of course you will all be chirruping – but you still have Pip, you still have all your fab' friends and family, you still have your beautiful two sons and you now have two gorgeous little grand daughters too. But you see, it's not enough, I want Rob too – yup, I'm a greedy moo.

I am absolutely certain that there may well be people reading this book who are saying: "I too have lost a child, you're nothing special". I know that is true too. If, however, you too have suffered such pain, you will understand that feeling of the natural order of things being disturbed. No child should die before its parent, it's not the way nature intended things. I look back in history and can see that not so very long ago lots of children died young. You only have to take a wander around an average graveyard and read a few head stones to see how many folks never made old bones. Or think of what it must have been, or indeed is like, to live through a War; not knowing what your loved ones were or are going through, hoping the postman isn't about to knock at your door. None of us lives forever; death is the one certainty in life, well, apart from taxes! As I said at the beginning of this book, I suppose whenever you die, it's nearly always too soon.

I also asked at the beginning of this book for a new word for mothers like me. Simply being bereaved didn't seem adequate. Well I've changed my mind on that one. I am happy to simply remain Pip's wife, and Tom, Sam and Rob's Mum. That'll do nicely.

However, having said all that, I still don't understand why we can put men on the Moon, and not cure a vibrant, clever, witty, charming, handsome young man of cancer. I don't understand why we would build skyscrapers in the desert, or dredge islands out of the sea to build marinas or luxurious holiday destinations and not be able to cure young Rob, who had so much to contribute to the world. I don't understand how foul-mouthed folks, with no intention of contributing to this world, manage to live to a ripe old age on a diet of fast food, cigarettes, fizz and booze. I don't understand why people who abuse others and seem incapable of loving one another are spared. I don't understand why some people can go around destroying life and society, whilst young people who might make the world a better place are robbed of the chance to try.

In one way I consider myself lucky. I am not filled or haunted by regrets. I don't believe that the doctors and nurses, or indeed Pip and I, could have done anything more to try and save Rob. He had every treatment his consultant could possibly think of, and he had every care we could all lavish upon him. One of my remaining questions is, though, that during the years leukaemia lived with us, I wanted my old life back. I hope that doesn't mean I was wishing Rob dead? I don't understand how my youngest son might now become a plaque on a wall or a rose bush in a memorial garden. I will use all my energy to make sure Rob's life lives through me – I bet Rob's chuckling at that, I bet he's wondering what we might do next!

Of course what I do understand, is that cancer is a very intelligent disease. Leukaemia is up there in the top of its class. In the case of "the Forgotten Tribe", or should I say "young adults", leukaemia is still making the medics run to stand still. It is constantly reinventing the rules, you see. Every time Rob's leukaemia came back it had mutated itself, just a little bit; each time with a memory of the medicines that had already been tried to erase it. How clever is that? We simply ran out of poisons or chemo to try. Of course, I haven't forgotten that for younger patients the scientists have made much progress, and the survival rate for the little ones is much better, improving all the time. That is a million miles from the situation that faces young adults. I shudder to think how many other parents have found themselves hearing the haunting announcement, "Doors Closing, Lift Going Up!" My heart goes out to them, each and every one of them.

And then of course I don't understand, or feel the presence of a God anymore. I miss that almost as much as I miss Rob. At best, if God exists, I don't much feel like worshipping him – where exactly was He when he was needed to step up? Why wouldn't He choose to save Rob, or any other child? If you created this world, then you would want to love and cherish the good bits – surely? I feel I did reach out, and I heard nothing. Of course, right now, I am almost deafened by the chorus of folks yelling – "well you obviously didn't look hard enough", or "you should never give up on God", or thinking of that bookmark we've all seen, with the two sets of foot prints in the golden sand, that become one set – as God carries you when times get tough. Well I don't feel carried. I, at no point throughout all of this, have felt carried. Ultimately, of course, I have very few options; I just have to get on with it, what other choice do I really have? I need to let all the fury and confusion go, it's exhausting. At least the writing of this book has left me with the feeling and knowledge that Rob's story and my memories are safe. Safely recorded, to be visited as and when I wish.

As I stood with Pip, Sam, Tom, Julie and little Ella, and let the remains of Rob's ashes trickle onto the grass of Colchester & East Essex Cricket Club all I could think was "Ashes to Ashes, Dust to Dust." We start off as a miracle of nature, and sometimes that miracle cocks up. It was our privilege to have known Rob and share his short life; he gave so many people so much. A good life must not mean a long life. A life that makes a little difference for the better is a good life. A life that radiated love – was a good life. Rob's life was a good life. His legacy is making a difference, maybe not for ever, but then none of us lives for ever, but the young people the Rob

George Foundation is currently managing to help, in his name, will never be taken away from him.

Pip and I have been invited, on occasions to talk to people about The Rob George Foundation. I usually finish our presentation by asking people this question:

"If you had two words left in this world, what would you choose to say?"

Rob's were...

"Be Happy!"

I'm still working on mine!

Lorraine George, an Essex girl, born in 1962. Married to Philip (Pip), proud mum of three smashing boys, Tom, Sam and Rob. Trained as a ballet teacher, she has for the past 21 years run her own performing arts school in Colchester, Essex.

www.therobgeorgefoundation.org
www.facebook.com/therobgeorgefoundation
Twitter @RGFCharity

14085728R00193

Printed in Great Britain
by Amazon.co.uk, Ltd.,
Marston Gate.